Writing

High-Performance

.NET Code

Ben Watson

Writing High-Performance .NET Code

Version 1.1

ISBN-13: 978-0-9905834-3-1

ISBN-10: 990583430

Copyright © 2014 Ben Watson

Trademarks

Any trademarked names, logos, or images used in this book are assumed valid trademarks of their respective owners. There is no intention to infringe on the trademark.

Disclaimer

While care has been taking to ensure the information contained in this book is accurate, the author takes no responsibility for your use of the information presented.

Contact

For more information about this book, please visit www.writinghighperf.net or email feedback@writinghighperf.net.

Cover Design

Cover design by Claire Watson, http://www.bluekittycreations.co.uk.

Table of Contents

About the Author

Ben Watson has been a software engineer at Microsoft since 2008. On the Bing platform team, he has built one of the world's leading .NET-based, high-performance server applications, handling high-volume, low-latency requests across thousands of machines for millions of customers. In his spare time, he enjoys geocaching, books of all kinds, classical music, and spending time with his wife Leticia and daughter Emma. He is also the author of the book C# 4.0 How-To, published by Sams.

About the Technical Editor

Mike Magruder has been a software engineer since the early 90's. He worked on the .Net Runtime team from v1 thru v4, and he worked on the Bing platform team where he architected one of the world's leading .NET-based, high-performance server applications. In his spare time, he enjoys snowboarding, building snowboards, and spending time with his wife Helen.

Acknowledgements

Thank you to my friend and technical editor Mike Magruder for his invaluable feedback on this book, and more importantly, for his three years of mentorship at Microsoft that changed my career. This has made me a hundred times the engineer I was.

I also owe a big thank you to Maoni Stephens for her in-depth guidance and feedback about the garbage collector. Thank you as well to Abhinaba Basu for information about the CLR on Windows Phone, and Brian Rasmussen for feedback on a number of topics.

I would not have started this book without a random conversation with my brother-in-law James Adams that got me thinking about actually writing a book like this. Thanks to my editors, my dad Michael Watson and my wife Leticia for their many hours of reading and rereading of the drafts.

Very special thanks to Leticia and our daughter Emma who supported many hours of absence while I worked on this book. I could not have done this without your support and encouragement.

Introduction

Purpose of this Book

.NET is an amazing system for building software. It allows us to build functional, connected apps in a fraction of the time it would have taken us a decade ago. So much of it *just works*, and that is a great thing. It offers applications memory and type safety, a robust framework library, services like automatic memory management, and so much more.

Programs written with .NET are called *managed* applications because they depend on a runtime and framework that manages many of their vital tasks and ensures a basic safe operating environment. Unlike unmanaged, or native, software written directly to the operating system's APIs, managed applications do not have free reign of their process.

This layer of management between your program and the computer's processor can be a source of anxiety for developers who assume that it must add some significant overhead. This book will set you at ease, demonstrate that the overhead is worth it, and that the supposed performance degradation is almost always exaggerated. Often, the performance problems developers blame on .NET are actually due to poor coding patterns and a lack of knowledge of how to optimize their programs on this framework. Skills gained from years of optimizing software written in C++, Java, or VB may not always apply to managed code, and some advice is actually detrimental. Sometimes the rapid development nature of .NET can encourage people to build bloated, slow, poorly optimized code faster than ever before. Certainly, there are other reasons why code can be of poor quality: lack of skill generally, time pressure, poor design, lack of developer resources, laziness, and so on. This book will explicitly remove lack of knowledge about the framework as an excuse and attempt to deal with some of the others as well. With the principles explained in this book, you will learn how to build lean, fast, efficient applications that avoid these missteps. In all types of code, in all platforms, the same thing is true: if you want performant code, you have to work for it.

This is not a language reference or tutorial. It is not even a detailed discussion of the CLR. For those topics, there are other resources (see Appendix C—Bibliography for a list of useful books, blogs, and people to pay attention to). To get the most out of this book you should already have in-depth experience with .NET.

There are many code samples, especially of underlying implementation details in IL or assembly code. I caution you not to gloss over these sections. You should try to replicate my results as you work through this book so that you understand exactly what is going on.

This book will teach you how to get maximum performance out of managed code, while sacrificing none or as little of the benefits of .NET as possible. You will learn good coding techniques, specific things to avoid, and perhaps most importantly, how to use freely available tools to easily measure your performance. This book will teach you those things with minimum fluff. This book is what you need to know, relevant and concise, with no padding of the content. Most chapters begin with general knowledge and background, followed by specific tips, and finally ending with a section on step-by-step measurement and debugging for many different scenarios.

Along the way you will deep-dive into specific portions of .NET, particularly the underlying Common Language Runtime (CLR) and how it manages your memory, generates your code, handles concurrency, and more. You will see how .NET's architecture both constrains and enables your software, and how your programming choices can drastically affect the overall performance of your application. As a bonus, I will share relevant anecdotes from the last six years of building very large, complex, high-performance .NET systems at Microsoft. You will likely notice that my bias throughout this book is for server applications, but nearly everything discussed in this book is applicable to desktop and mobile applications as well. Where appropriate, I will share advice for those specific platforms.

You will gain a sufficient understanding of .NET and the principles of well-performing code so that when you run into circumstances not specifically covered in this book, you can apply your newfound knowledge and solve unanticipated problems.

Programming under .NET is not a completely different experience from all the programming you have ever done. You will still need your knowledge of algorithms and most standard programing constructs are pretty much the same, but we are talking about performance optimizations, and if you are coming from an unmanaged programming mindset, there are very different things you need to observe. You may not have to call delete explicitly any more (hurray!), but if you want to get the absolute best performance, you better believe you need to understand how the garbage collector is going to affect your application.

If high availability is your goal, then you are going to need to be concerned about JIT compilation to some degree. Do you have an extensive type system? Interface dispatch might be a concern. What about the APIs in the .NET Framework Class Library itself? Can any of those negatively influence performance? Are some thread synchronization mechanisms better than others?

Beyond pure coding, I will discuss techniques and processes to measure your performance over time and build a culture of performance in yourself and in your team. Good performance is not something you do once and then move on. It needs constant nourishment and care so that it does not degrade over time. Investing in a good performance infrastructure will pay massive dividends over time, allowing you to automate most of the grunt work in maintaining good performance.

The bottom line is that the amount of performance optimization you get out of your application is directly proportional to the amount of understanding you have not only of your own code, but also your understanding of the framework, the operating system, and the hardware you run on. This is true of *any* platform you build upon.

All of the code samples in this book are in C#, the underlying IL, or occasionally x86 assembly code, but all of the principles here apply to any .NET language. Throughout this book, I assume that you are using .NET 4 or higher. If this is not the case, strongly consider moving to the latest version so that you can take advantage of the latest technologies, features, bug fixes, and performance improvements.

I do not talk about specific sub-frameworks of .NET, such as WPF, WCF, ASP.NET, Windows Forms, MVC, ADO.NET, or countless others. While each of those frameworks has its own issues and performance techniques, this book is about the fundamental knowledge and techniques that you must master to develop code under all scenarios in .NET. Once you acquire these fundamentals, you can apply this knowledge to every project you work on, adding domain-specific knowledge as you gain experience.

Why Should You Choose Managed Code?

There are many reasons to choose managed code over unmanaged code:

- Safety—The compiler and runtime can enforce type safety (objects can only be used as what they really are), boundary checking, numeric overflow detection, security guarantees, and more. There is no more heap corruption from access violations or invalid pointers.
- Automatic memory management—No more `delete` or reference counting.
- Higher level of abstraction—Higher productivity with fewer bugs.

- Advanced language features—Delegates, anonymous methods, and dynamic typing.
- Huge existing code base—Framework Class Library, Entity Framework, Windows Communication Framework, Windows Presentation Foundation, Task Parallel Library, and so much more.
- Easier extensibility—With reflection capabilities, it is much easier to dynamically consume late-bound modules, such as in an extension architecture.
- Phenomenal debugging—Exceptions have a lot of information associated with them. All objects have metadata associated with them to allow thorough heap and stack analysis in a debugger, often without the need for PDBs (symbol files).

All of this is to say that you can write more code quickly, with fewer bugs. You can diagnose what bugs you do have far more easily. With all of these benefits, managed code should be your default pick.

.NET also encourages use of a standard framework. In the native world, it is very easy to have fragmented development environments with multiple frameworks in use (STL, Boost, or COM, for example) or multiple flavors of smart pointers. In .NET, many of the reasons for having such varied frameworks disappear.

While the ultimate promise of true "write once, run everywhere" code is likely always a pipe dream, it is becoming more of a reality. .NET now supports Portable Class Libraries, which allow you to target platforms such as Windows, Windows Phone, and Windows Store with a single class library. For more information about cross-platform development, see http://www.writinghighperf.net/go/1/. With each release of .NET, the various platforms share more of the same set of APIs.

Given the enormous benefits of managed code, if native code is an option for your project, consider it to have the burden of proof. Will you actually get the performance improvement you think you will? Is the generated code really the limiting factor? Can you write a quick prototype and prove it? Can you do without all of the features of .NET? In a complex native application, you may find yourself implementing some of these features yourself. You do not want to be in awkward position of duplicating someone else's work.

One reason for considering native code over managed code is access to the full processor instruction set, particularly for advanced data processing applications using SIMD instructions. However, this is changing. See Chapter 3 for a discussion of the abilities of future versions of the JIT compiler.

Another reason is a large existing native code base. In this case, you can consider the interface between new code and the old. If you can easily manage it with a clear API, consider making all new code managed with a simple interop layer between it and the native code. You can then transition the native code to managed code over time.

Is Managed Code Slower Than Native Code?

There are many unfortunate stereotypes in this world. One of them, sadly, is that managed code cannot be fast. This is not true.

What is closer to the truth is that the .NET platform makes it very easy to write slow code if you are sloppy and uncritical.

When you build your C#, VB.NET, or other managed language code, the compiler translates the high-level language to Intermediate Language (IL) and metadata about your types. When you run the code, it is just-in-time compiled ("JITted"). That is, the first time a method is executed, the CLR will invoke the compiler on your IL to convert it to assembly code (e.g., x86, x64, ARM). Most code optimization happens at this stage. There is a definite performance hit on this first run, but after that you will always get the compiled version. As we will see later, there are ways around this first-time hit when it is necessary.

The steady-state performance of your managed application is thus determined by two factors:

1. The quality of the JIT compiler
2. The amount of overhead from .NET services

The quality of generated code is generally very good, with a few exceptions, and it is getting better all the time, especially quite recently.

The cost of the services .NET provides is not free, but it is also lower than you may expect. You do not have to reduce this cost to zero (which is impossible); just reduce it to a low enough threshold that other factors in your application's performance profile are more significant.

In fact, there are some cases where you may see a significant benefit from managed code:

- Memory allocations—There is no contention for memory allocations on the heap, unlike in native applications. Some of the saved time is transferred to garbage collection, but even this can be mostly erased depending on how you configure your application. See Chapter 2 for a thorough discussion of garbage collection behavior and configuration.
- Fragmentation—Memory fragmentation that steadily gets worse over time is a common problem in large, long-running native applications. This is less of an issue in .NET applications because garbage collection will compact the heap.

- JITted code—Because code is JITted as it is executed, its location in memory can be more optimal than that of native code. Related code will often be collocated and more likely to fit in a single memory page. This leads to fewer page faults.

The answer to the question "Is managed code slower than native code?" is an emphatic "No" in most cases. Of course, there are bound to be some areas where managed code just cannot overcome some of the safety constraints under which it operates. They are far fewer than you imagine and most applications will not benefit significantly. In most cases, the difference in performance is exaggerated. See Chapter 3 (JIT Compilation) for a discussion of these areas.

It is much more common to run across code, managed or native, that is in reality just poorly written code; e.g., it does not manage its memory well, it uses bad patterns, it defies CPU caching strategies or is otherwise unsuitable for good performance.

Am I Giving Up Control?

One common objection to using managed code is that it can feel like you are giving up too much control over how your program executes. This is a particular fear over garbage collection, which occurs at what feels like random and inconvenient times. For all practical purposes, however, this is not actually true. Garbage collection is deterministic, and you can significantly affect how often it runs by controlling your memory allocation patterns, object scope, and GC configuration settings. What you control is different from native code, but the ability is certainly there.

Work With the CLR, Not Against It

People new to managed code often view things like the garbage collector or the JIT compiler as something they have to "deal with" or "tolerate" or "work around." This is the wrong way to look at it. Getting great performance out of any system requires dedicated performance work, regardless of the specific frameworks you use. For this and other reasons, do not make the mistake of viewing the GC and JIT as "problems" that you have to fight.

As you come to appreciate how the CLR works to manage your program's execution, you will realize that you can make many performance improvements just by choosing to work with the CLR rather than against it. All frameworks have expectations about how they are used and .NET is no exception. Unfortunately, many of these assumptions are implicit and the API does not, nor cannot, prohibit you from making bad choices.

I dedicate a large portion of this book to explaining how the CLR works so that your own choices may more finely mesh with what it expects. This is especially true of garbage collection, for example, which has very clearly delineated guidelines for optimal performance. Choosing to ignore these guidelines is a recipe for disaster. You are far more likely to achieve success by optimizing for the framework rather than trying to force it to conform to your own notions, or worse, throwing it out altogether.

Some of the advantages of the CLR can be a double-edged sword in some sense. The ease of profiling, the extensive documentation, the rich metadata, and the ETW event instrumentation allow you to find the source of problems quickly, but this visibility also makes it easier to place blame. A native program might have all sorts of similar or worse problems with heap allocations or inefficient use of threads, but since it is not as easy to see that data, the native platform will escape blame. In both the managed and native cases, often the program itself is at fault and needs to be fixed to work better with the underlying platform. Do not mistake easy visibility of the problems for a suggestion that the entire platform is the problem.

All of this is not to say that the CLR is *never* the problem, but the default choice should always be the application, never the framework, operating system, or hardware.

Layers of Optimization

Performance optimization can mean many things, depending on which part of the software you are talking about. In the context of .NET applications, think of performance in four layers:

Figure 0-1. Layers of abstraction—and performance priority.

At the top, you have your own software, the algorithms you are using to process data. This is where all performance optimization starts because it has the greatest potential impact to overall performance. Changing your own code causes all the layers below it to change drastically, so make sure you have that right first. Only then should you move down the layers. This rule of thumb is related to a similar rule with debugging: An experienced programmer will always assume their own code is buggy rather than blaming the compiler, platform, operating system, or hardware. That definitely applies to performance optimization as well.

Below your own code is the .NET Framework—the set of classes provided by Microsoft or 3rd parties that provide standard functionality for things like strings, collections, parallelism, or even full-blown sub-frameworks like Windows Communication Framework, Windows Presentation Foundation, and more. You cannot avoid using at least some portion of the framework, but most individual parts are optional. The vast majority of the framework is implemented using managed code exactly like your own application's code (you can even read the framework code online at http://www.writinghighperf.net/go/2 or from within Visual Studio).

Below the Framework classes lies the true workhorse of .NET, the Common Language Runtime (CLR). This is a combination of managed and unmanaged components that provide services like garbage collection, type loading, JITting, and all the other myriad implementation details of .NET.

Below that is where the code hits the metal, so to speak. Once the CLR has JITted the code, you are actually running processor assembly code. If you break into a managed process with a native debugger, you will find assembly code executing. That is all managed code is—regular machine assembly instructions executing in the context of a particularly robust framework.

To reiterate, when doing performance design or investigation, you should always start at the top layer and move down. Make sure your program's structure and algorithms make sense before digging into the details of the underlying code. Macro-optimizations are almost always more beneficial than micro-optimizations.

This book is primarily concerned with those middle layers: the .NET Framework and the CLR. These consist of the "glue" that hold your program together and are often the most invisible to programmers. However, many of the tools we discuss are applicable to all layers. At the end of the book I will briefly touch on some practical and procedural things you can do to encourage performance at all layers of the system.

Note that, while all the information in this book is publically available, it does discuss some aspects of the internal details of the CLR's implementation. These are all subject to change.

Sample Source Code

This book makes frequent references to some sample projects. These are all quite small, encapsulated projects meant to demonstrate a particular principle. As simple examples, they will not adequately represent the scope or scale of performance issues you will discover in your own investigations. Consider them a starting point of techniques or investigation skills, rather than as serious examples of representative code.

You can download all of the sample code from the book's web site at http://www.writinghighperf.net. They were developed in Visual Studio Ultimate 2012, but should open and build with minimal fuss in other versions as well.

Why Gears?

Finally, I would like to say a brief note about the cover. The image of gears has been in my mind since well before I decided to write this book. I often think of effective performance in terms of clockwork, rather than pure speed, though that is an important aspect too. You must not only write your program to do its own job efficiently, but it has to mesh well with .NET, its own internal parts, the operating system, and the hardware. Often, the right approach is just to make sure your application is not doing anything that interferes with the gear works of the whole system, but encourages it to keep running smoothly, with minimal interruptions. This is clearly the case with things like garbage collection and asynchronous thread patterns, but this metaphor also extends to things like JIT, logging, and much more.

As you read this book, keep this metaphor in mind to guide your understanding of the various topics.

1 Performance Measurement and Tools

Choosing What to Measure

Before collecting numbers, you need to know what you intend to measure. This sounds obvious, but it is actually a lot more involved than you may think. Consider memory. You *obviously* want to measure memory usage and minimize it. But which kind of memory? Private working set? Commit size? Paged pool? Peak working set? .NET heap size? Large object heap? Individual processor heaps to ensure they're balanced? Some other variant? For tracking memory usage over time, do you want the average for an hour, the peak? Does memory usage correlate with processing load size? As you can see, there are easily a dozen or more metrics just for the concept of memory alone. And we haven't even touched the concept of private heaps or profiling the application to see what kind of objects are using memory!

Be as specific as possible when describing what you want to measure.

> **Story** In one large server application I was responsible for, we tracked its private bytes as a critical metric and used this number to decide when we needed to do things like restart the process before beginning a large, memory-intensive operation. It turned out that quite a large amount of those "private bytes" were actually paged out over time and not contributing to the memory load on the system, which is what we were really concerned with. We changed our system to measure the working set instead. This had the benefit of "reducing" our memory usage by a few gigabytes. (As I said, this was a rather large application.)

Once you have decided what you are going to measure, come up with goals for each of those metrics. Early in development, these goals may be quite malleable, even unrealistic. The point at the beginning is not necessarily to meet the goals, but to force you to build a system that automatically measures you against those goals.

Your goals should be quantifiable. A high-level goal for your program might state that it should be "fast." Of course it should. That is not a very good metric because "fast" is subjective and there is no well-defined way to know you are meeting that goal. You must be able to assign a number to this goal and be able to measure it.

Bad: "The user interface should be responsive."

Good: "No operation may block the UI thread for more than 20 milliseconds."

However, just being quantifiable is not good enough either. You need to be very specific, as we saw in the memory example earlier.

Bad: "Memory should be less than 1 GB."

Good: "Working set memory usage should never exceed 1 GB during peak load of 100 queries per second."

The second version of that goal gives a very specific circumstance that determines whether you are meeting your goal. In fact, it suggests a good test case.

Another major determining factor in what your goals should be is the kind of application you are writing. A user interface program must at all costs remain responsive on the UI thread, whatever else it does. A server program handling dozens, hundreds, or even thousands of requests per second must be incredibly efficient in handling I/O and synchronization to ensure maximum throughput and keep the CPU utilization high. You design a server of this type in a *completely* different way than other programs. It is very difficult to fix a poorly written application retroactively if it has a fundamentally flawed architecture from an efficiency perspective.

A potentially useful exercise while designing your system and planning performance measurement is to consider what the optimal theoretical performance of your system is. If you could eliminate all overhead like garbage collection, JIT, thread interrupts, or whatever you deem is overhead in your application, then what is left to process the actual work? What are the theoretical limits that you can think of, in terms of workload, memory usage, CPU usage, and internal synchronization? This often depends on the hardware and OS you are running on. For example, if you have a 16-processor server with 64 GB of RAM with two 10 GB network links, then you have an idea of your parallelism threshold, how much data you can store in memory, and how much you can push over the wire every second. It will help you plan how many machines of this type you will need if one is not enough. All of this information should strongly inform your goals.

You have likely heard the phrase, coined by Donald Knuth, "Premature optimization is the root of all evil." This applies only to micro-optimizations at the code level. You need to understand your architecture and its constraints as you design or you will miss something crucial and severely hamstring your application. You must bake performance goals into the design up front. Performance, like security and many other aspects of software design, cannot be an afterthought, but needs to be included as an explicit goal from the start. It is not impossible to redesign an existing application from the ground up, but it is far more expensive than doing it right in the first place.

The performance analysis you will do at the beginning of a project is different from that which occurs once it is been written and is being tested. At the beginning, you must make sure the design is scalable, that the technology can theoretically handle what you want to do, and that you are not making huge architectural blunders that will forever haunt you. Once a project reaches testing, deployment, and maintenance phases, you will instead spend more time on micro-optimizations, analyzing specific code patterns, trying to reduce memory usage, etc.

Finally, you need to understand Ahmdals's Law (See http://www.writinghighperf.net/go/3 [PDF]), in particular how it applies to sequential programs and picking which parts of a program to optimize. Micro-optimizing code that does not significantly contribute to overall inefficiency is largely a waste of time. You always want to optimize the most inefficient portions of a program first to get the largest benefit. You will never have time to optimize everything, so start intelligently. This is why having goals and an excellent measurement system in place is critical—otherwise, you don't even know where to start.

Average vs. Percentiles

When considering the numbers you are measuring, consider what the most appropriate statistics are. Most people default to average, which is certainly important in most circumstances, but you should also consider percentiles. If you have availability requirements, you will almost certainly need to have goals stated in terms of percentiles. For example:

"Average latency for database requests must be less than 10ms. The 95th percentile latency for database requests must be less than 100ms."

If you are not familiar with this concept, it is actually quite simple. If you take 100 measurements of something and sort them, then the 95th entry in that list is the 95th percentile value of that data set. The 95th percentile says, "95% of all samples have this value or less." Alternatively, "5% of requests have a value higher than this."

The general formula for calculating the index of the Pth percentile of a sorted list is

$$(P/100) \times N$$

where P is the percentile and N is the length of the list.

Consider a series of measurements for generation 0 garbage collection pause time (see Chapter 2) in milliseconds with these values (pre-sorted for convenience):

$$1, 2, 2, 4, 5, 5, 8, 10, 10, 11, 11, 11, 15, 23, 24, 25, 50, 87$$

For these 18 samples, we have an average of 17ms, but the 95th percentile is much higher at 50ms. If you just saw the average number, you may not be concerned with your GC latencies, but knowing the percentiles, you have a better idea of the full picture and that there are some occasional GCs happening that are far worse.

This series also demonstrates that the median value (50th percentile) can be quite different from the average. The average value of a series of measurements is often prone to strong influence by values in the higher percentiles.

Percentiles values are usually far more important for high-availability services. The higher availability you require, the higher percentile you will want to track. Usually, the 99th percentile is as high as you need to care about, but if you deal in a truly enormous volume of requests, 99.99^{th}, 99.999^{th}, or even higher percentiles will be important. Often, the value you need to be concerned about is determined by business needs, not technical reasons.

Percentiles are valuable because they give you an idea of how your metrics degrade across your entire execution context. Even if the average user or request experience in your application is good, perhaps the 90th percentile metric shows some room for improvement. That is telling you that 10% of your execution is being impacted more negatively than the rest. Tracking multiple percentiles will tell you how fast this degradation occurs. How important this percentage of users or requests is must ultimately be a business decision, and there is definitely a law of diminishing returns at play here. Getting that last 1% may be extremely difficult and costly.

I stated that the 95th percentile for the above data set was 50ms. While technically true, it is not useful information in this case—there is not actually enough data to make that call with any statistical significance, and it could be just a fluke. To determine how many samples you need, just use a rule of thumb: You need one "order of magnitude" more samples than the target percentile. For percentiles from 0-99, you need 100 samples minimum. You need 1,000 samples for 99.9^{th} percentile, 10,000 samples for 99.99^{th} percentile, and so on. This mostly works, but if you are interested in determining the actual number of samples you need from a mathematical perspective, http://www.writinghighperf.net/go/4 is a good place to start.

Measurement Tools

If there is one single rule that is the most important in this entire book, it is this:

Measure, Measure, Measure!

You do NOT know where your performance problems are if you have not measured accurately. You will definitely gain experience and that can give you some strong hints about where performance problems are, just from code inspection or gut feel. You may even be right, but resist the urge to skip the measurement for anything but the most trivial of problems. The reasons for this are two-fold:

First, suppose you are right, and you have accurately found a performance problem. You probably want to know how much you improved the program, right? Bragging rights are *much* more secure with hard data to back them up.

Second, I cannot tell you how often I have been wrong. Case in point: While analyzing the amount of native memory in a process compared to managed memory, we assumed for while that it was coming from one particular area that loaded an enormous data set. Rather than putting a developer on the task of reducing that memory usage, we did some experiments to disable loading that component. We also used the debugger to dump information about all the heaps in the process. To our surprise, most of the mystery memory was coming from assembly loading overhead, not this dataset. We saved a lot of wasted effort.

Optimizing performance is meaningless if you do not have effective tools for measuring it. Performance measurement is a continual process that you should bake into your development toolset, testing processes, and monitoring tools. If your application requires continual monitoring for functionality purposes, then it likely also requires performance monitoring.

The remainder of this chapter covers various tools that you can use to profile, monitor, and debug performance issues. I give emphasis to software that is freely available, but know there are many commercial offerings that can in some cases simplify the tasks. If you have the budget for these tools, go for it. However, there is a lot of value in using some of the leaner tools I describe (or others like them). For one, they may be easier to run on customer machines or production environments. More importantly, by being a little "closer to the metal," they will encourage you to gain knowledge and understanding at a very deep level that will help you interpret data, regardless of the tool you are using.

For each of the tools, I describe basic usage and general knowledge to get started. Sections throughout the book will give you detailed steps for very specific scenarios, but will often rely on you already being familiar with the UI and the basics of operation.

Tip Before digging into specific tools, a general tip for how to use them is in order. If you try to use an unfamiliar tool on a large, complicated project, it can be very easy to get overwhelmed, frustrated, or even get erroneous results. When learning how to measure performance with a new tool, create a test program with well-known behavior, and use the tool to prove its performance characteristics to you. By doing this, you will be more comfortable using the tool in a more complicated situation and less prone to making technical or judgmental mistakes.

Visual Studio

While it is not the only IDE, most .NET programmers use Visual Studio, and if you do, chances are this is where you will start to analyze performance. Different versions of Visual Studio come with different tools. This book will assume you have at least the Professional version installed. If you do not have the right version, then skip ahead to the other tools mentioned.

Assuming you installed Visual Studio Professional or higher, you can access the performance tools via the Performance Wizard in the Analyze menu. In Visual Studio 2013, you must first launch the Performance and Diagnostics view from the Analyze menu, which will then allow you to use the Performance Wizard.

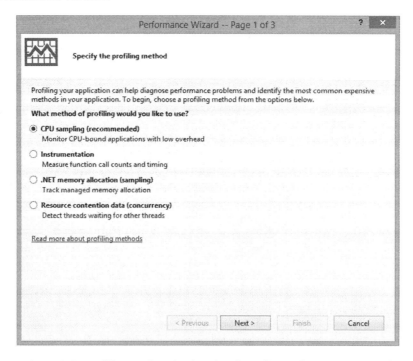

Figure 1-1. Profiling options in the Visual Studio Performance Wizard.

Visual Studio can analyze CPU usage, memory allocations, and resource contentions. This is perfect for use during development or when running comprehensive tests that accurately exercise the product.

However, it is very rare for a test to accurately capture the performance characteristics of a large application running on real data. If you need to capture performance data on non-development machines, say a customer's machine or in the datacenter, you need a tool that can run outside of Visual Studio. For that, there is the Visual Studio Standalone Profiler, which comes with the Professional or higher versions of Visual Studio. You will need to install it from your installation media separately from Visual Studio. On my ISO images for both 2012 and 2013 Professional version, it is in the Standalone Profiler directory. See http://www.writinghighperf.net/go/5 for specific instructions on where to find it and how to install it.

To collect data from the command line with this tool:

1. Navigate to the installation folder (or add the folder to your path)
2. Run: VsPerfCmd.exe /Start:Sample /Output:outputfile.vsp
3. Run the program you want to profile
4. Run: VsPerfCmd.exe /Shutdown

This will produce a file called outputfile.vsp, which you can open in Visual Studio.

VsPerfCmd.exe has a number of other options, including all of the profiling types that the full Visual Studio experience offers. Aside from the most common option of Sample, you can choose:

- Coverage—Collects code coverage data
- Concurrency—Collects resource contention data
- Trace—Instruments the code to collect method call timing and counts

Trace vs. Sample mode is an important choice. Which to use depends on what you want to measure. Sample mode should be your default. It interrupts the process every few milliseconds and gets the stacks of all threads. This is the best way to get a good picture of CPU usage in your process. However, it does not work well for I/O calls, which will not have much CPU usage, but may still contribute to your overall run time.

Trace mode requires modification of every function call in the process to record time stamps. It is much more intrusive and causes your program to run much slower. However, it records actual time spent in each method, so may be more accurate, especially for I/O scenarios.

Coverage mode is not for performance analysis, but is useful for seeing which lines of your code were executed. This is a nice feature to have when running tests to see how much of your product the tests cover. There are commercial products that do this for you, but you can do it yourself without much more work.

Concurrency mode records events that occur when there is contention for a resource via a lock or some other synchronization object. This mode can tell you if your threads are being blocked due to contention. See Chapter 4 for more information about asynchronous programming and measuring the amount of lock contention in your application.

The Visual Studio tools are among the easiest to use, but if you do not already have the right version of Visual Studio, they are quite expensive. I provide plenty of free alternatives below if you cannot use Visual Studio. Nearly all performance measurement tools use the same underlying mechanism (at least in Windows 8/Server 2012 and above kernels): ETW events. ETW stands for Event Tracing for Windows and this is the operating system's way of logging all interesting events in an extremely fast, efficient manner. All applications generate these events and profilers can capture them to do extensive analysis. Chapter 8 describes how to take advantage of ETW events in your own program, whether that is capturing existing events or defining your own.

This leads to another reason I often like to use other tools, especially when monitoring production systems: The Visual Studio tools are very specialized—they collect and display one type of data at a time, while a tool like PerfView can collect arbitrary ETW events all at once and you can analyze all of them separately from one collection run. It is a minor point, but one worth pointing out. Sometimes I think of Visual Studio performance analysis as "development-time" while the other tools are for the real system. Your experience may differ and you should use the tools that give you the most bang for the buck.

Performance Counters

These are some of the simplest ways to monitor your application's and the system's performance. Windows has hundreds of counters in dozens of categories, including many for .NET. The easiest way to access these is via the built-in utility PerformanceMonitor (PerfMon.exe).

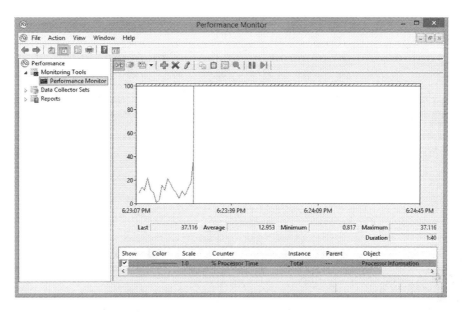

Figure 1-2. PerfMon's main window showing a processor counter for a small window of time. The vertical line represents the current instance and the graph will wrap around after 100 seconds by default.

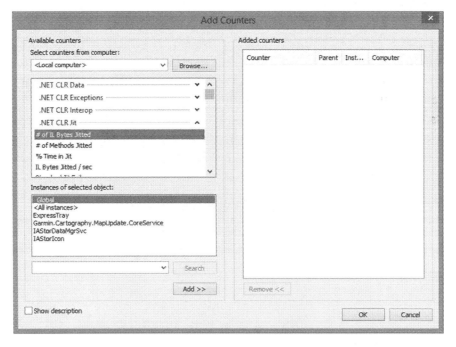

Figure 1-3. One of the hundreds of counters in many categories, showing all of the applicable instances (processes, in this case).

Each counter has a category and a name. Many counters also have instances of the selected counter as well. For example, for the % Processor Time counter in the Process category, the instances are the various processes for which there are values. Some counters also have meta-instances, such as _Total or <Global>, which aggregate the values over all instances.

Many of the chapters ahead will detail the relevant counters for that topic, but there are general-purpose counters that are not .NET-specific that you should know. There are performance counters for nearly every Windows subsystem, but these are generally applicable to every program.

However, before continuing, you should familiarize yourself with some basic operating system terminology:

- **Physical Memory**—The actual physical memory chips in a computer. Only the operating system manages physical memory directly.
- **Virtual Memory**—A logical organization of memory in a given process. Virtual memory size can be larger than physical memory. For example, 32-bit programs have a 4 GB address space, even if the computer itself only has 2 GB of RAM. Windows allows the program to access only 2 GB of that by default, but all 4 GB is possible if the executable is large-address aware. (On 32-bit versions of Windows, large-address aware programs are limited to 3 GB.) As of Windows 8.1 and Server 2012, 64-bit processes have a 128 TB process space, far larger than the 4 TB physical memory limit. Some of the virtual memory may be in RAM while other parts are stored on disk in a paging file. Contiguous blocks of virtual memory may not be contiguous in physical memory. All memory addresses in a process are for the virtual memory.
- **Reserved Memory**—A region of virtual memory address space that has been reserved for the process and thus will not be allocated to a future requester. Reserved memory cannot be used for memory allocation requests because there is nothing backing it—it is just a description of a range of memory addresses.
- **Committed Memory**—A region of memory that has a physical backing store. This can be RAM or disk.
- **Page**—An organizational unit of memory. Blocks of memory are allocated in a page, which is usually a few KB in size.
- **Paging**—The process of transferring pages between regions of virtual memory. The page can move to or from another process (soft paging) or the disk (hard paging). Soft paging can be accomplished very quickly by mapping the existing memory into the current process's virtual address space. Hard paging involves a relatively slow transfer of data to or from disk. Your program must avoid this at all costs to maintain good performance.
- **Page In**—Transfer a page from another location to the current process.

- **Page Out**—Transfer a page from the current process to another location, such as disk.
- **Context Switch**—The process of saving and restoring the state of a thread or process. Because there are usually more running threads than available processors, there are often many context switches per second.
- **Kernel Mode**—A mode that allows the OS to modify low-level aspects of the hardware's state, such as modifying certain registers or enabling/disabling interrupts. Transitioning to Kernel Mode requires an operating system call, and can be quite expensive.
- **User Mode**—An unprivileged mode of executing instructions. There is no ability to modify low-level aspects of the system.

I will use some of those terms throughout the book, especially in Chapter 2 when I discuss garbage collection. For more information on these topics, look at a dedicated operating system book such as *Windows Internals*. (See the bibliography in Appendix C.)

The Process category of counters surfaces much of this critical information via counters with instances for each process, including:

- **% Privileged Time**—Amount of time spent in executing privileged (kernel mode) code.
- **% Processor Time**—Percentage of a single processor the application is using. If your application is using two logical processor cores at 100% each, then this counter will read 200.
- **% User Time**—Amount of time spent in executing unprivileged (user mode) code.
- **IO Data Bytes/sec**—How much I/O your process is doing.
- **Page Faults/sec**—Total number of page faults in your process. A page fault occurs when a page of memory is missing from the current working set. It is important to realize that this number includes both soft and hard page faults. Soft page faults are innocuous and can be caused by the page being in memory, but outside the current process (such as for shared DLLs). Hard page faults are more serious, indicating data that is on disk but not currently in memory. Unfortunately, you cannot track hard page faults per process with performance counters, but you can see it for the entire system with the Memory\Page Reads/sec counter. You can do some correlation with a process's total page faults plus the system's overall page reads (hard faults). You can definitively track a process's hard faults with ETW tracing with the Windows Kernel/Memory/Hard Fault event.
- **Pool Nonpaged Bytes**—Typically operating system and driver allocated memory for data structures that cannot be paged out such as operating system objects like threads and mutexes, but also custom data structures.
- **Pool Paged Bytes**—Also for operating system data structures, but these are allowed to be paged out.

- **Private Bytes**—Committed virtual memory private to the specific process (not shared with any other processes).
- **Virtual Bytes**—Allocated memory in the process's address space, some of which may be backed by the page file, shared with other processes, and memory private to the process.
- **Working Set**—The amount of virtual memory currently resident in physical memory (usually RAM).
- **Working Set-Private**—The amount of private bytes currently resident in physical memory.
- **Thread Count**—The number of threads in the process. This may or may not be equal to the number of .NET threads. See Chapter 4 (Asynchronous Programming) for a discussion of .NET thread-related counters.

There are a few other generally useful categories, depending on your application. You can use PerfMon to explore the specific counters found in these categories.

- **IPv4/IPv6**—Internet Protocol-related counters for datagrams and fragments.
- **Memory**—System-wide memory counters such as overall paging, available bytes, committed bytes, and much more.
- **Objects**—Data about kernel-owned objects such as events, mutexes, processes, threads, semaphores, and sections.
- **Processor**—Counters for each logical processor in the system.
- **System**—Context switches, alignment fixes, file operations, process count, threads, and more.
- **TCPv4/TCPv6**—Data for TCP connections and segment transfers.

It is surprisingly difficult to find detailed information on performance counters on the Internet, but thankfully, they are self-documenting! In the Add Counter dialog box in PerfMon, you can check the "Show description" box at the bottom to display details on the highlighted counter.

PerfMon also has the ability to collect specified performance counters at scheduled times and store them in logs for later viewing, or even perform a custom action when a performance counter passes a threshold. You do this with Data Collector Sets and they are not limited just to performance counter data, but can also collect system configuration data and ETW events.

To setup a Data Collector Set, in the main PerfView window:

1. Expand the Data Collector Sets tree.
2. Right-click on User Defined.
3. Select New.

4. Select Data Collector Set.

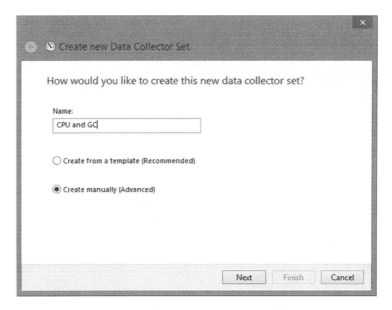

Figure 1-4. Data Collector Set configuration dialog box for setting up regular counter collections.

5. Give it a name, check "Create manually (Advanced)", and click Next
6. Check the Performance counter box under "Create data logs for" and click Next

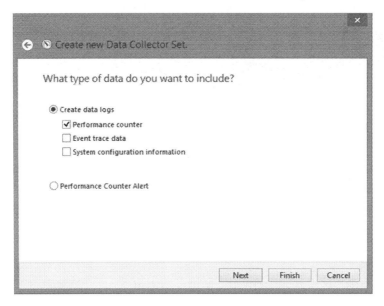

Figure 1-5. Specify the type of data you want to store.

7.   Click Add to select the counters you want to include

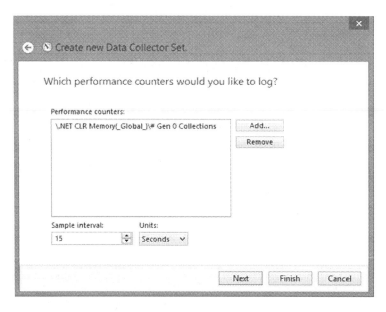

Figure 1-6. Select the counters to collect.

8.   Click Next to set the path where you want to store the logs and Next again to select
     security information.

Once done, you can open the properties for the collection set and set a schedule for collection.
You can also run them manually by right clicking on the job node and selecting Start. This will
create a report, which you can view by double-clicking its node under Reports in the main tree
view.

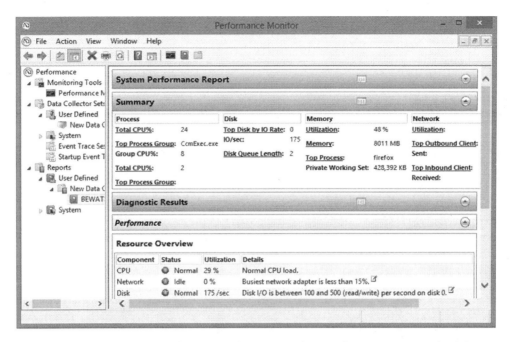

Figure 1-7. A Saved report file. Use the toolbar buttons to change the view to a graph of the captured counter data.

To create an alert, follow the same process but select the "Performance Counter Alert" option in the Wizard.

It is likely that everything you will need to do with performance counters can be done using the functionality described here, but if you want to take programmatic control or create your own counters, see Chapter 7 (Performance Counters) for details. You should consider performance counter analysis a baseline for all performance work on your application.

ETW Events

Event Tracing for Windows (ETW) is one of the fundamental building blocks for all diagnostic logging in Windows, not just for performance. This section will give you an overview of ETW and Chapter 8 will teach you how to create and monitor your own events.

Events are produced by providers. For example, the CLR contains the Runtime provider that produces most of the events we are interested in for this book. There are providers for nearly every subsystem in Windows, such as the CPU, disk, network, firewall, memory, and many, many more. The ETW subsystem is extremely efficient and can handle the enormous volume of events generated, with minimal overhead.

Each event has some standard fields associated with it, like event level (informational, warning, error, verbose, and critical) and keywords. Each provider can define its own keywords. The CLR's Runtime provider has keywords for things like GC, JIT, Security, Interop, Contention, and more. Keywords allow you to filter the events you would like to monitor.

Each event also has a custom data structure defined by its provider that describes the state of some behavior. For example, the Runtime's GC events will mention things like the generation of the current collection, whether it was background, and so on.

What makes ETW so powerful is that, since most components in Windows produce an enormous number of events describing nearly every aspect of an application's operation, at every layer, you can do the bulk of performance analysis only with ETW events.

Many tools can process ETW events and give specialized views. In fact, starting in Windows 8, all CPU profiling is done using ETW events.

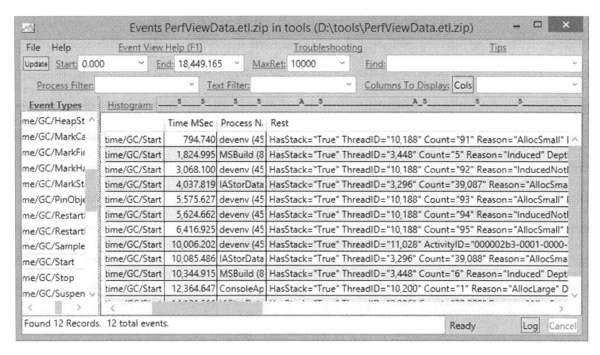

Figure 1-8. A list of all GC Start events taken in a 60-second trace. Notice various pieces of data associated with the event, such as the Reason and Depth.

To see a list of all the ETW providers registered on your system, open a command prompt and type:

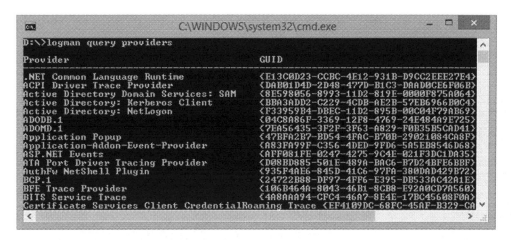

You can also get details on the keywords for a specific provider:

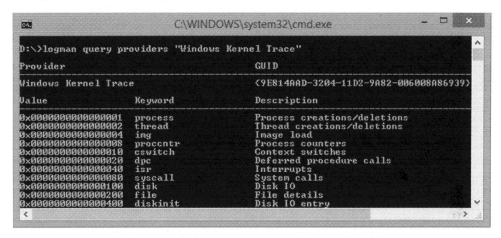

See http://www.writinghighperf.net/go/6 for more information about ETW. Unfortunately, there is no good online resource to explain what events exist in, say, the Windows Kernel Trace provider. Some common ETW events for all Windows processes include those in the Windows Kernel Trace category:

- Memory/Hard Fault
- DiskIO/Read
- DiskIO/Write
- Process/Start
- Process/Stop
- Tcplp/Connect
- Tcplp/Disconnect
- Thread/Start

- Thread/Stop

To see other events from this provider or others, you can collect ETW events and examine them yourself.

Throughout the book, I will mention the important events you should pay attention to in an ETW trace, particularly from the CLR Runtime provider. For a list of all CLR Keywords, see http://www.writinghighperf.net/go/7. To see what events the CLR makes available, see http://www.writinghighperf.net/go/8.

PerfView

Many tools can collect and analyze ETW events, but PerfView, written by Microsoft .NET performance architect Vance Morrison, is my favorite. You can download it from http://www.writinghighperf.net/go/9. The previous screenshot of ETW events is from this tool. PerfView's utility lies in its extremely powerful stack grouping and folding mechanism that lets you drill into events at multiple layers of abstraction.

While other ETW analysis tools can be useful, I often prefer PerfView for a few reasons:

1. It requires no installation so it is easy to run on any computer.
2. It is extremely configurable.
3. It is easily scriptable.
4. You can pick which events to capture at a very granular level, which allows you, for example, to take hours-long traces of just a few categories of events.
5. It generally causes very little impact to the machine or processes it monitors.
6. Its stack grouping and folding capability is unparalleled.
7. You can customize PerfView with extensions that take advantage of the built-in stack grouping and folding functionality.

Here are some common questions that I routinely answer using PerfView:

- Where is my CPU usage going?
- Who is allocating the most memory?
- What types are being allocated the most?
- What is causing my Gen 2 garbage collections?
- How long is the average Gen 0 collection?
- How much JITting is my code doing?
- Which locks are most contentious?
- What does my managed heap look like?

To collect and analyze events using PerfView follow these basic steps:

1. From the Collect menu, select the Collect menu item.
2. From the resulting dialog, specify the options you need.
   a. Expand Advanced Options to narrow down the type of events you want to capture.
   b. Check the "No V3.X NGEN Symbols" if you are not using .NET 3.5.
   c. Optionally specify "Max Collect Sec" to automatically stop collection after the given time.
3. Click the Start Collection button.
4. If not using a "Max Collect Sec" value, click the Stop Collection button when done.
5. Wait for the events to be processed.
6. Select the view to use from the resulting tree.

During event collection, PerfView captures ETW events for all processes. You can filter events per-process after the collection is complete.

Collecting events is not free. Certain categories of events are more expensive to collect than others are and you will need to learn which events result in unusably enormous trace files, or which events adversely affect the operation of the application. For example, a CPU profile generates a huge number of events, so you should keep the profile time very limited (around a minute or two) or you could end up with multi-gigabyte files that you cannot analyze.

PerfView Interface and Views

Most views in PerfView are variations of a single type, so it is worth understanding how it works.

PerfView is mostly a stack aggregator and viewer. When you record ETW events, the stack for each event is recorded. PerfView analyzes these stacks and shows them to you in a grid that is common to CPU, memory allocation, lock contention, exceptions thrown, and most other types of events. The principles you learn while doing one type of investigation will apply to other types, since the stack analysis is the same.

You also need to understand the concepts of grouping and folding. Grouping turns multiple sources into a single entity. For example, there are multiple .NET Framework DLLs and which DLL a particular function is in is not usually interesting for profiling. Using grouping, you can define a grouping pattern, such as "System.*!=>LIB", which coalesces all System.*.dll assemblies into a single group called LIB. This is one of the default grouping patterns that PerfView applies.

Folding allows you to hide some of the irrelevant complexity of the lower layers of code by counting its cost in the nodes that call it. As a simple example, consider where memory allocations occur—always via some internal CLR method invoked by the new operator. What you really want to know is which types are most responsible for those allocations. Folding allows you to attribute those underlying costs to their parents, code which you can actually control. For example, in most cases you do not care about which internal operations are taking up time in String.Format; you really care about what areas of your code are calling String.Format in the first place. PerfView can fold those operations into the caller to give you a better picture of your code's performance.

Folding patterns can use the groups you defined for grouping. So, for example, you can just specify a folding pattern of "LIB" which will ensure that all methods in System.* are attributed to their caller outside of System.*.

The user interface of the stack viewer needs some brief explanation as well.

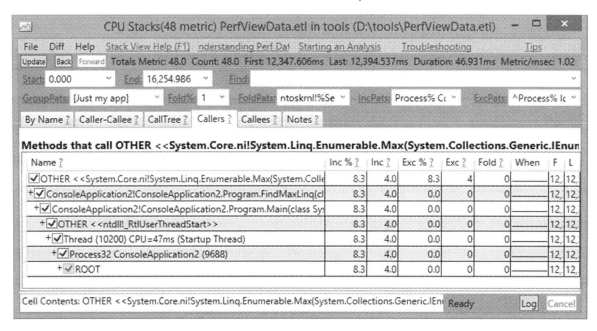

Figure 1-10. A typical stack view in PerfView. The UI contains many options for filtering, sorting, and searching.

Controls at the top allow you to organize the stack view in multiple ways. Here is a summary of their usage, but you can click on them in the program to bring up a help field that gives you more details.

- **Start**—Start time (in microseconds) which you want to examine.
- **End**—End time (in microseconds) which you want to examine.
- **Find**—Text to search for.
- **GroupPats**—A semi-colon-delimited list of grouping patterns.
- **Fold%**—Any stack that takes less than this percentage will be folded into its parent.
- **FoldPats**—A semi-colon-delimited list of folding patterns.

- **IncPats**—Stacks must have this pattern to be included in the analysis. This usually contains the process name.
- **ExcPats**—Exclude anything with this pattern from analysis. By default, this includes just the Idle process.

There are a few different view types:

- **By Name**—Shows every node, whether type, method, or group. This is good for bottom-up analysis.
- **Caller-Callee**—Focuses on a single node, showing you callers and callees of that node.
- **CallTree**—Shows a tree of all nodes in the profile, starting at ROOT. This works well for doing top-down analysis.
- **Callers**—Shows you all callers of a particular node.
- **Callees**—Shows you all called methods of a particular node.
- **Notes**—Allows you to save notes on your investigation in the ETL files themselves.

In the grid view, there are a number of columns. Click on the column names to bring up more information. Here is a summary of the most important columns:

- **Name**—The type, method, or customized group name.
- **Exc %**—Percentage of exclusive cost. For memory traces, it is the amount of memory attributed to this type/method only. For CPU traces, it is the amount of CPU time attributed to this method.
- **Exc**—The number of samples in just this node, excluding children nodes. For memory traces, the number of bytes attributed to this node exclusively. For CPU traces, the amount of time (in milliseconds) spent here.
- **Exc Ct**—Number of samples exclusively on this node.
- **Inc %**—Percentage of cost for this type/method and all its children, recursively. This is always at least as big as Exc %.
- **Inc**—Cost of this node, including all children recursively. For CPU usage, this is the amount of CPU time spent in this node plus all of its children.
- **Inc Ct**—Number of samples on this node and all its children.

In the chapters that follow, I will give instructions for solving specific problems with various types of performance investigations. A complete overview of PerfView would be worth a book on its own, or at least a very detailed help file—which just so happens to come with PerfView. I strongly encourage you to read this manual once you have gone through a few simple analyses.

It may seem like PerfView is mostly analyzing memory or CPU, but do not forget that it is really just a generic stack aggregation program, and those stacks can come from any ETW event. It can analyze your sources of lock contention, disk I/O, or any arbitrary application event with the same grouping and folding power.

CLR Profiler

CLR Profiler is a good alternative to PerfView's memory analysis capabilities if you want a graphical representation of the heap and relationships between objects. CLR Profiler can show you a wealth of detail. For example:

- Visual graph of what the program allocates and the chain of methods that led to the allocation.
- Histograms of allocated, relocated, and finalized objects by size and type.
- Histogram of objects by lifetime.
- Timeline of object allocations and garbage collections, showing the change in the heap over time.
- Graphs of objects by their virtual memory address, which can show fragmentation quite easily.

I rarely use CLR Profiler because of some of its limitations, but it is still occasionally useful, despite its age. It has unique visualizations that no other free tool currently matches. You can download it from http://www.writinghighperf.net/go/10. It comes with 32-bit and 64-bit binaries as well as documentation and the source code.

The basic steps to get a trace are:

1. Pick the correct version to run: 32-bit or 64-bit, depending on your target program. You cannot profile a 32-bit program with the 64-bit profiler or vice-versa.
2. Check the Profiling active box.
3. Optionally check the Allocations and Calls boxes.
4. If necessary, go to the File | Set Parameters... menu option to set options like command line parameters, working directory, and log file directory.
5. Click the Start Application button
6. Browse to the application you want to profile and click the Open button.

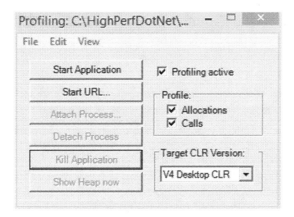

Figure 1-11. CLR Profiler's main window.

This will start the application with profiling active. When you are done profiling, exit the program, or select Kill Application in CLR Profiler. This will terminate the profiled application and start processing the capture log. This processing can take quite a while, depending on the profile duration (I have seen it take over an hour before).

While profiling is going on, you can click the "Show Heap now" button in CLR Profiler. This will cause it to take a heap dump and open the results in a visual graph of object relationships. Profiling will continue uninterrupted, and you can take multiple heap dumps at different points.

When it is done, you will see the main results screen.

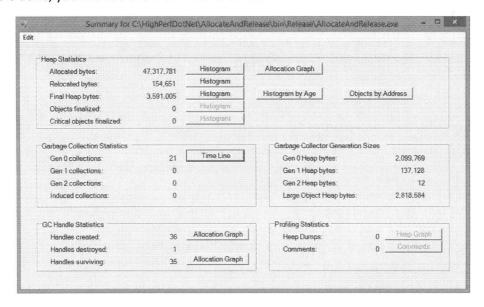

Figure 1-12. CLR Profiler's Results Summary view, showing you the data it collected during the trace.

From this screen, you can access different visualizations of heap data. Start with the Allocation Graph and the Time Line to see some of the essential capabilities. As you become comfortable analyzing managed code, the histogram views will also become an invaluable resource.

> **Note** While CLR Profiler is generally great, I have had a few major problems with it. First, it is a bit finicky. If you do not set it up correctly before starting to profile, it can throw exceptions or die unexpectedly. For example, I always have to check the Allocations or Calls boxes before I start profiling if I want to get any data at all. You should completely disregard the Attach to Process button, as it does not seem to work reliably. CLR Profiler does not seem to work well for truly huge applications with enormous heaps or a large number of assemblies. If you find yourself having trouble, PerfView may be a better solution because of its polish and extreme customizability through very detailed command-line parameters that allow you to control nearly all aspects of its behavior. Your mileage may vary. On the other hand, CLR Profiler comes with its own source code so you can fix it!

Windbg

Windbg is a general purpose Windows Debugger distributed for free by Microsoft. If you are used to using Visual Studio as your main debugger, using this barebones, text-only debugger may seem daunting. Don't let it be. Once you learn a few commands, you will feel comfortable and after a while, you will rarely use Visual Studio for debugging except during active development.

Windbg is far more powerful than Visual Studio and will let you examine your process in many ways you could not otherwise. It is also lightweight and more easily deployable to production servers or customer machines. In these situations, it is in your best interest to become familiar with Windbg.

With Windbg, you can quickly answer questions such as these:

- How many of each object type are on the heap, and how big are they?
- How big are each of my heaps and how much of them is free space (fragmentation)?
- What objects stick around through a GC?
- Which objects are pinned?
- Which threads are taking the most CPU time? Is one of them stuck in an infinite loop?

Windbg is not usually my first tool (that is often PerfView), but it is often my second or third, allowing me to see things that other tools will not easily show. For this reason, I will use Windbg extensively throughout this book to show you how to examine your program's operation, even when other tools do a quicker or better job. (Don't worry; I will also cover those tools.)

Do not be daunted by the text interface of Windbg. Once you use a few commands to look into your process, you will quickly become comfortable and appreciative of the speed with which you can analyze a program. The chapters in this book will add to your knowledge little by little with specific scenarios.

To get Windbg, go to http://www.writinghighperf.net/go/11 and follow the instructions to install the SDK. (You can choose to install only the debuggers if you wish.)

To work with managed code, you will need to use .NET's SOS extensions, which ship with each version of the .NET Framework. A very handy SOS reference cheat sheet is located at http://www.writinghighperf.net/go/12.

To get started with Windbg, let's do a simple tutorial with a sample program. The program will be basic enough—a straightforward, easy-to-debug memory leak. You can find it in the accompanying source code in the MemoryLeak project.

```
using System;
using System.Collections.Generic;
using System.Threading;

namespace MemoryLeak
{
  class Program
  {
    static List<string> times = new List<string>();

    static void Main(string[] args)
    {
      Console.WriteLine("Press any key to exit");
      while (!Console.KeyAvailable)
      {
        times.Add(DateTime.Now.ToString());
        Console.Write('.');
        Thread.Sleep(1000);
      }
    }
  }
}
```

Startup this program and let it run for a few minutes.

Run Windbg from where you installed it. It should be in the Start Menu if you installed it via the Windows SDK. Take care to run the correct version, either x86 (for 32-bit processes) or x64 (for 64-bit processes). Go to File | Attach to Process (or hit F6) to bring up the Attach to Process dialog.

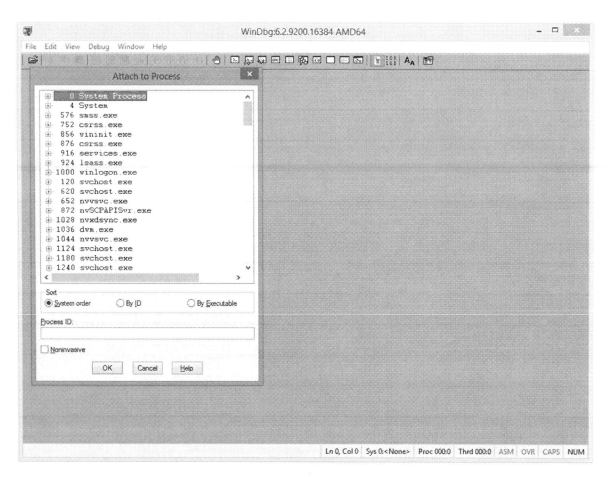

Figure 1-13. WinDbg's Attach to Process screen.

From here, find the MemoryLeak process. (It may be easier to check the By Executable sort option.) Click OK.

Windbg will suspend the process (This is important to know if you are debugging a live production process!) and display any loaded modules. At this point, it will be waiting for your command. The first thing you usually want to do is load the CLR debugging extensions. Enter this command:

```
.loadby sos clr
```

If it succeeds, there will be no output.

If you get an error message that says "Unable to find module 'clr'" it most likely means the CLR has not yet been loaded. This can happen if you launch a program from Windbg and break into it immediately. In this case, first set a breakpoint on the CLR module load:

```
sxe ld clr
g
```

The first command sets a breakpoint on the load of the CLR module. The g command tells the debugger to continue execution. Once you break again, the CLR module should be loaded and you can now load SOS with the .loadby sos clr command, as described previously.

At this point, you can do any number of things. Here are some commands to try:

```
g
```

This continues execution. You cannot enter any commands while the program is running.

```
<Ctrl-Break>
```

This pauses a running program. Do this after you Go to get back control.

```
.dump /ma d:\memorydump.dmp
```

This creates a full process dump to the selected file. This will allow you to debug the process's state later, though since it is a snapshot, of course you will not be able to debug any further execution.

```
!DumpHeap -stat
```

DumpHeap shows a summary of all managed objects on the object heap, including their size (just for this object, not any referenced objects), count, and other information. If you want to see every object on the heap of type System.String, type !DumpHeap -type System.String. You will see more about this command when investigating garbage collection.

```
~*kb
```

This is a regular Windbg command, not from SOS. It prints the current stack for all threads in the process.

To switch the current thread to a different one, use the command:

```
~32s
```

This will change the current thread to thread # 32. Note that thread numbers in Windbg are not the same as thread IDs. Windbg numbers all the threads in your process for easy reference, regardless of the Windows or .NET thread ID.

```
!DumpStackObjects
```

You can also use the abbreviated version: !dso. This dumps out the address and type of each object from all stack frames for the current thread.

Note that all commands located in the SOS debugging extension for managed code are prefixed with a ! character.

The other thing you need to do to be effective with the debugger is set your symbol path to download the public symbols for Microsoft DLLs so you can see what is going on in the system layer. Set your _NT_SYMBOL_PATH environment variable to this string:

```
symsrv*symsrv.dll*c:\symbols*http://msdl.microsoft.com/download/symbols
```

Replace c:\symbols with your preferred local symbol cache path (and make sure you create the directory). With the environment variable set, both Windbg and Visual Studio will use this path to automatically download and cache the public symbols for system DLLs. During the initial download, symbol resolution may be quite slow, but once cached, it should speed up significantly. You can also use the .symfix command to automatically set the symbol path to the Microsoft symbol server and local cache directly:

```
.symfix c:\symbols
```

.NET IL Analyzers

There are many free and paid products out there that can take a compiled assembly and decompile it into IL, C#, VB.NET, or any other .NET language. Some of the most popular include Reflector, ILSpy, and dotPeek, but there are others.

These tools are valuable for showing you the inner details of other people's code, something critical for good performance analysis. I use them most often to examine the .NET Framework itself when I want to see the potential performance implications of various APIs.

Converting your own code to readable IL is also valuable because it can show you many operations, such as boxing, that are not visible in the higher-level languages.

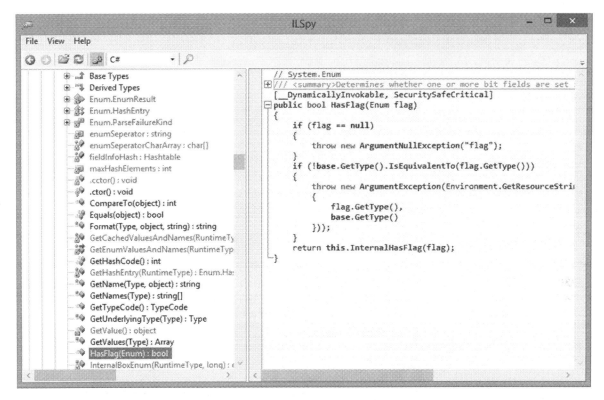

Figure 1-14. ILSpy with a decompilation of Enum.HasFLag in C#. ILSpy is a powerful tool for learning how 3rd-party code works and performs.

Chapter 6 discusses the .NET Framework code and encourages you to train a critical eye on every API you use. Tools like ILSpy and Reflector are vital for that purpose and you will use them daily as you become more familiar with existing code. You will often be surprised at how much work goes into seemingly simple methods.

MeasureIt

MeasureIt is a handy micro-benchmark tool Vance Morrison (the same author of PerfView). It shows the relative costs of various .NET APIs in many categories including method calls, arrays, delegates, iteration, reflection P/Invoke, and many more. It compares all the costs to calling an empty static function as a benchmark.

MeasureIt is primarily useful to show you how design choices will affect performance at an API level. For example, in the locks category, it shows you that using `ReaderWriteLock` is about four times slower than just using a regular `lock` statement.

You can download MeasureIt from http://www.writinghighperf.net/go/13.

It is easy to add your own benchmarks to the MeasureIt's code. It ships with its own code packed inside itself—just run `MeasureIt /edit` to extract it. Studying this code will give you a good idea of how to write accurate benchmarks. There is a lengthy explanation in the code comments about how to do high-quality analysis, which you should pay special attention to, especially if you want to do some simple benchmarking yourself.

For example, it prevents the compiler from inlining function calls:

```
[MethodImpl(MethodImplOptions.NoInlining)]
public void AnyEmptyFunction()
{
}
```

There are other tricks it uses such as working around processor caches and doing enough iterations to produce statistically significant results.

Code Instrumentation

The old standby of brute-force debugging via console output is still a valid scenario and should not be ignored. Rather than console output, however, I encourage you to use ETW events, as detailed in Chapter 8, instead, which allows much more sophisticated analysis.

Performing accurate code timing is also a useful feature at times. Never use `DateTime.Now` for tracking performance data. It is just too slow for this purpose. Instead, use the `System.Diagnostics.Stopwatch` class to track the time span of small or large events in your program with extreme accuracy, precision, and low overhead.

```
var stopwatch = Stopwatch.StartNew();
...do work...
stopwatch.Stop();
TimeSpan elapsed = stopwatch.Elapsed;
long elapsedTicks = stopwatch.ElapsedTicks;
```

See Chapter 6 for more information about using times and timing in .NET.

If you want to ensure that your own benchmarks are accurate and reproducible, study the source code and documentation to MeasureIt, which highlights the best practices on this topic. It is often harder than you would expect and performing benchmarks incorrectly can be worse than doing no benchmarks at all because it will cause you to waste time on the wrong thing.

SysInternals Utilities

No developer, system administrator, or even hobbyist should be without this great set of tools. Originally developed by Mark Russinovich and Bryce Cogswell and now owned by Microsoft, these are tools for computer management, process inspection, network analysis, and a lot more. Here are some of my favorites:

- **ClockRes**—Shows the resolution of the system's clock (which is also the maximum timer resolution). See Chapter 4.
- **Diskmon**—Monitors all disk activity.
- **Handle**—Monitors which files are opened by which processes.
- **ProcDump**—A highly configurable process dump creator.
- **Process Explorer** —A much better Task Manager, with a wealth of detail about every process.
- **Process Monitor**—Monitor file, registry, and process activity in real-time.
- **VMMap**—Analyze a process's address space.

There are dozens more. You can download this suite of utilities (individually or as a whole) from http://www.writinghighperf.net/go/14.

Database

The final performance tool is a rather generic one: a simple database—something to track your performance over time. The metrics you track are whatever is relevant to your project, and the format does not have to be a full-blown SQL Server relational database (though there are certainly advantages to such a system). It can be a collection of reports stored over time in an easily readable format, or just CSV files with labels and values. The point is that you should record it, store it, and build the ability to report from it.

When someone asks you if your application is performing better, which is the better answer?

1. Yes

Or

2. In the last 6 months, we've reduced CPU usage by 50%, memory consumption by 25%, and request latency by 15%. Our GC rate is down to one in every 10 seconds (it used to be every second!), and our startup time is now dominated entirely by configuration loading (35 seconds).

As mentioned earlier, bragging about performance gains is so much better with solid data to back it up!

Other Tools

You can find many other tools. There are plenty of static code analyzers, ETW event collectors and analyzers, assembly decompilers, performance profilers, and much more.

You can consider the list presented in this chapter as a starting point, but understand that you can do significant work with just these tools. Sometimes an intelligent visualization of a performance problem can help, but you will not always need it.

You will also discover that as you become more familiar with technologies like Performance Counters or ETW events, it is easy to write your own tools to do custom reporting or intelligent analysis. Many of the tools discussed in this book are automatable to some degree.

Measurement Overhead

No matter what you do, there is going to be some overhead from measuring your performance. CPU profiling slows your program done somewhat, performance counters will require memory and/or disk space. ETW events, as fast as they are, are not free.

You will have to monitor and optimize this overhead in your code just like all other aspects of your program. Then decide whether the cost of measurement in some scenarios is worth the performance hit you will pay.

If you cannot afford to measure all the time, then you will have to settle for some kind of profiling. As long as it is often enough to catch issues, then it is likely fine.

You could also have "special builds" of your software, but this can be a little dangerous. You do not want these special builds to morph into something that is unrepresentative of the actual product.

As with many things in software, there is a balance you will have to find between having all the data you want and having optimal performance.

Summary

The most important rule of performance is **Measure, Measure, Measure!**

Know what metrics are important for your application. Develop precise, quantifiable goals for each metric. Average values are good, but pay attention to percentiles as well, especially for high-availability services. Ensure that you include good performance goals in the design upfront and understand the performance implications of your architecture. Optimize the parts of your program that have the biggest impact first. Focus on macro-optimizations at the algorithmic or systemic level before moving on to micro-optimizations.

Have a good foundation of performance counters and ETW events for your program. For analysis and debugging, use the right tools for the job. Learn how to use the most powerful tools like Windbg and PerfView to solve problems quickly.

2 Garbage Collection

Garbage collection will be the first and last thing you work on. It is the apparent source of the most obvious performance problems, those that are quickest to fix, and will be something that you need to constantly monitor to keep in check. I say "apparent source" because as we will see, many problems are actually due to an incorrect understanding of the garbage collector's behavior and expectations. In .NET, you need to think of memory performance at least as much as CPU performance. It is so fundamental to smooth .NET operation, that the most significant chunk of this book's content is dedicated to just this topic.

Many people get very nervous when they think of the overhead a garbage collection can cause. Once you understand it, though, it becomes straightforward to optimize your program for its operation. In the Introduction, you saw that the garbage collector can actually give you better overall heap performance in many cases because it deals with allocation and fragmentation better. Garbage collection is definitely a benefit to your application.

The native heap in Windows maintains free lists to know where to put new allocations. Despite the use of low fragmentation heaps, many long-running native code applications struggle with fragmentation. Time spent in memory allocation gradually increases as the allocator spends more and more time traversing the free lists looking for an open spot. Memory use continues to grow and, inevitably, the process will need to be restarted to begin the cycle anew. Some native programs deal with this by replacing the default implementation of `malloc` with custom allocation schemes that work hard to reduce this fragmentation.

In .NET, memory allocation is trivial because it usually happens at the end of a memory segment and is not much more than a few additions, decrements, and a comparison in the normal case. In these simple cases, there are no free lists to traverse and little possibility of fragmentation. GC heaps can actually be more efficient because objects allocated together in time tend to be near one another on the heap, improving locality.

In the default allocation path, a small code stub will check the desired object's size against the space remaining in a small allocation buffer. As long as the allocation fits, it is extremely fast and has no contention. Once the allocation buffer is exhausted, the GC allocator will take over and find a spot for the object. Then a new allocation buffer will be reserved for future allocation requests.

The assembly code for this process is only a handful of instructions and useful to examine.

The C# to demonstrate this is just a simple allocation:

```
class MyObject {
   int x;
   int y;
   int z;
}

static void Main(string[] args)
{
   var x = new MyObject();
}
```

First, here is the breakdown of the calling code for the allocation:

```
; Copy method table pointer for the class into
; ecx as argument to new()
; You can use !dumpmt to examine this value.
mov    ecx,3F3838h

; Call new
call   003e2100

; Copy return value (address of object) into a register
mov    edi,eax
```

Here is the actual allocation:

```
; NOTE: Most code addresses removed for formatting reasons.
;
; Set eax to value 0x14, the size of the object to
; allocate, which comes from the method table
mov    eax,dword ptr [ecx+4] ds:002b:003f383c=00000014

; Put allocation buffer information into edx
mov    edx,dword ptr fs:[0E30h]
```

```
; edx+40 contains the address of the next available byte
; for allocation. Add that value to the desired size.
add    eax,dword ptr [edx+40h]

; Compare the intended allocation against the
; end of the allocation buffer.
cmp    eax,dword ptr [edx+44h]

; If we spill over the allocation buffer,
; jump to the slow path
ja     003e211b

; update the pointer to the next free
; byte (0x14 bytes past old value)
mov    dword ptr [edx+40h],eax

; Subtract the object size from the pointer to
; get to the start of the new obj
sub    eax,dword ptr [ecx+4]

; Put the method table pointer into the
; first 4 bytes of the object.
; eax now points to new object
mov    dword ptr [eax],ecx

; Return to caller
ret

; Slow Path - call into CLR method
003e211b  jmp clr!JIT_New (71763534)
```

In summary, this involves one direct method call and only nine instructions in the helper stub. That's hard to beat.

If you are using some configuration options such as server GC, then there is not even contention for the fast or the slow allocation path because there is a heap for every processor. .NET trades the simplicity in the allocation path for more complexity during de-allocation, but you do not have to deal with this complexity directly. You just need to learn how to optimize for it, which is what you will learn how to do in this chapter.

I am covering garbage collection at the beginning of the book because so much of the stuff that comes later will relate back to this chapter. Understanding the effect your program has on the garbage collector is so fundamental to achieving good performance, that it affects nearly everything else.

Basic Operation

The details of how the garbage collector makes decisions are continually being refined, especially as .NET becomes more prevalent in high-performance systems. The following explanation may contain details that will change in upcoming .NET versions, but the overall picture is unlikely to change drastically in the near future.

In a managed process there are two types of heaps—native and managed. Native heaps are allocated with the VirtualAlloc Windows API and used by the operating system and CLR for unmanaged memory such as that for the Windows API, OS data structures, and even much of the CLR. The CLR allocates all managed .NET objects on the managed heap, also called the GC heap, because the objects on it are subject to garbage collection.

The managed heap is further divided into two types of heaps: the small object heap and the large object heap (LOH). Each one is assigned its own segments, which are blocks of memory belonging to that heap. The size of each segment can vary depending on your configuration and hardware platform, but can be on the order of a few hundred megabytes or more for a large application. Both the small object heap and the large object heap can have multiple segments assigned to them.

The small object heap segments are further divided into generations. There are three generations, referenced casually as gen 0, gen 1, and gen 2. Gen 0 and gen 1 are always in the same segment, but gen 2 can span multiple segments, as can the large object heap. The segment that contains gen 0 and gen 1 is called the ephemeral segment.

Graphically, the heap looks like this to start out with, with the two segments labeled A and B. Higher addresses are on the right side:

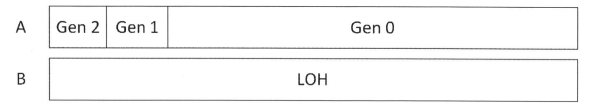

The small object heap is made up of segment A and the large object heap has segment B. Gen 2 and gen 1 start off at only a few bytes in size because they are empty so far.

Objects allocated on the small object heap pass through a lifetime process that needs some explanation. The CLR allocates all objects that are less than 85,000 bytes in size on the small object heap. They are always allocated in gen 0, usually at the end of the current used space. This is why allocations in .NET are extremely fast, as seen at the beginning of this chapter. If the fast allocation path fails, then the objects may be placed anywhere they can fit inside gen 0's boundaries. If it will not fit in an existing spot, then the allocator will expand the current boundaries of gen 0 to accommodate the new object. If this pushes past the end of the segment, it may trigger a garbage collection.

Objects always begin their life in gen 0. As long as they are still alive, the GC will promote them to subsequent generations each time a collection happens. Collections of gen 0 and gen 1 are sometimes called ephemeral collections.

When a garbage collection occurs, a compaction may occur, in which case the GC physically moves the objects to a new location to free space in the segment. If no compaction occurs, the boundaries are merely redrawn. After a few garbage collections with no compaction, the heap diagram could look like this:

A	Gen 2	Gen 1	Gen 0	

B	LOH

The individual objects have not moved, but the boundary lines have.

Compaction may occur in the collection of any generation and this is a relatively expensive process because the GC must fix up all of the references to those objects so they point to the new location, which may require pausing all managed threads. Because of this expense, the garbage collector will only do compaction when it is productive to do so, based on some internal metrics.

Once an object reaches gen 2, it remains there for the remainder of its lifetime. This does not mean that gen 2 grows forever—if the objects in gen 2 finally die off and an entire segment has no live objects, then the garbage collector can return the segment to the operating system or reclaim it for other generations as part of additional segments in the heap. This can happen during a full garbage collection.

So what does alive mean? If the GC can reach the object via any of the known GC *roots*, following the graph of object references, then it is alive. A root can be the static variables in your program, the threads which have the stacks (which will point to local variables) from all running methods, strong GC handles (such as pinned handles), and the finalizer queue. Note that you may have objects that no longer have roots to them, but if the objects are in gen 2, then a gen 0 collection will not clean them up. They will have to wait for a full collection.

If gen 0 ever starts to fill up a segment and a collection cannot compact it enough, then the GC will allocate a new segment. The new segment will house a new gen 1 and gen 0 while the old segment is converted to gen 2. Everything from the old generation 0 becomes part of the new generation 1 and the old generation 1 is likewise promoted to generation 2 (which conveniently does not have to be copied). The segments now look like this:

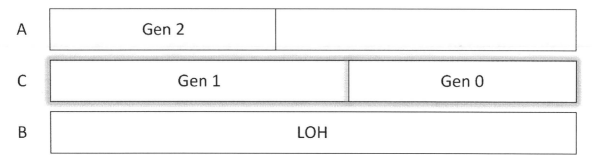

If gen 2 continues to grow, then it can span multiple segments. The LOH heap can also span multiple segments. Regardless of how many segments there are, generations 0 and 1 will always exist on the same segment. This knowledge of segments will come in handy later when we are trying to figure out which objects live where on the heap.

The large object heap obeys different rules. Any object that is at least 85,000 bytes in size is allocated on the LOH automatically and does not pass through the generational model. The only types of objects that normally exceed this size are arrays and strings. For performance reasons, the LOH is *not* automatically compacted during collection, but starting in .NET 4.5.1, you can compact it on-demand. Like gen 2, if memory in the LOH is no longer needed, then it can be reclaimed for other portions of the heap, but we will see later that ideally you do not want memory on the large object heap to be garbage collected at all.

In the LOH, the garbage collector always uses a free list to determine where to best place allocated objects. We will explore some techniques in this chapter to reduce fragmentation on this heap.

> **Note** If you go poking around at the objects in the LOH in a debugger, you will notice that not only can the entire heap be smaller than 85,000 bytes in size, but that it can also have objects that are smaller than that size allocated on that heap. These objects are usually allocated by the CLR and you can ignore them.

A garbage collection runs for a specific generation and all generations below it. If it collects gen 1, it will also collect gen 0. If it collects gen 2, then all generations are collected, and the large object heap is collected as well. When a gen 0 or gen 1 collection occurs, the program is paused for the duration of the collection. For a gen 2 collection, portions of the collection can occur on a background thread, depending on the configuration options.

There are four phases to a garbage collection:

1. Suspension—All managed threads in the application are forced to pause before a collection can occur.
2. Mark—Starting from each root, the garbage collector follows every object reference and marks those objects as seen.
3. Compact—Reduce memory fragmentation by relocating objects to be next to each other and update all references to point to the new locations. This happens on the small object heap when needed and there is no way to control it. On the large object heap, compaction does not happen automatically at all, but you can instruct the garbage collector to compact it on-demand.
4. Resume—The managed threads are allowed to resume.

The mark phase does not actually need to touch every single object on the heap. It will only go through the collected portion of the heap. For example, a gen 0 collection considers objects only from gen 0, a gen 1 collection will mark objects in both gen 0 and gen 1, and a gen 2, or full, collection, will need to traverse every live object in the heap, making it potentially very expensive. An additional wrinkle here is that an object in a higher generation may be a root for an object in a lower generation. This will cause the garbage collector to traverse a subset of objects in the higher generation, but it is not as expensive as a full collection for that generation.

There are a couple of important consequences to the behavior described above.

First, the time it takes to do a garbage collection is almost entirely dependent on the number of live objects in the collected generation, not the number of objects you allocated. This means that if you allocate a tree of a million objects, as long as you cut off that root reference before the next GC, those million objects contribute nothing to the amount of time the GC takes.

Second, the frequency of a garbage collection is determined by how much memory is allocated in a specific generation. Once that amount passes an internal threshold, a GC will happen for that generation. The threshold continually changes and the GC adapts to your process's behavior. If doing a collection on a particular generation is productive (it promotes many objects), then it will happen more frequently, and the converse is true. Another trigger for GCs is the total available memory on a machine, independent of your application. If available memory drops below a certain threshold, garbage collection may happen more frequently in an attempt to reduce the overall heap size.

From this description, it may feel like that garbage collections are out of your control. This could not be farther from the truth. Manipulating your GC statistics by controlling your memory allocation patterns is one of the easiest optimizations to make. It requires understanding of how the GC works, what configuration options are available to you, your allocation rate, and how well you control object lifetimes.

Configuration Options

The .NET Framework does not give you very many ways to configure the garbage collector out the box. It is best to think of this as "less rope to hang yourself with." For the most part, the garbage collector configures and tunes itself based on your hardware configuration, available resources, and application behavior. What few options are provided are for very high-level behaviors, and are mainly determined by the type of program you are developing.

Workstation vs. Server GC

The most important choice you have is whether to use workstation or server garbage collection.

Workstation GC is the default. In this mode, all GCs happen on the same thread that triggered the collection and run at the same priority. For simple apps, especially those that run on interactive workstations where many managed processes run, this makes the most sense. For computers with a single processor, this is the only option and trying to configure anything else will not have any effect.

Server GC creates a dedicated thread for each logical processor or core. These threads run at highest priority (THREAD_PRIORITY_HIGHEST), but are always kept in a suspended state until a GC is required. After the GC, they sleep again.

In addition, the CLR creates a separate heap for each processor. Within each processor heap, there is a small object heap and a large object heap. From your application's perspective, this is all logically the same heap—your code does not know which heap that objects belong to and object references exist between all the heaps (they all share the same virtual address space).

Having multiple heaps gives a couple of advantages:

1. Garbage collection happens in parallel. Each GC thread collects one of the heaps. This can make garbage collection significantly faster than in workstation GC.
2. In some cases, allocations can happen faster, especially on the large object heap, where allocations are spread across all the heaps.

There are other internal differences as well such as larger segment sizes, which can mean a longer time between garbage collections.

You configure server GC in the app.config file inside the `<runtime>` element:

```
<configuration>
    <runtime>
     <gcServer enabled="true"/>
    </runtime>
</configuration>
```

Should you use workstation or server GC? If your app is running on a multi-processor machine dedicated to just your application, then the choice is clear: server GC. It will provide the lowest latency collection in most situations.

On the other hand, if you need to share the machine with multiple managed processes, the choice is not so clear. Server GC creates many high-priority threads and if multiple apps do that, they can all negatively affect one other with conflicting thread scheduling. In this case, it might be better to use workstation GC.

If you really want to use server GC in multiple applications on the same machine, another option if is to affinitize the competing applications to specific processors. The CLR will create heaps only for the processors which are enabled for that application.

Whichever one you pick, most of the tips in this book apply to both types of collection.

Background GC

Background GC changes how the garbage collector performs gen 2 collections. Gen 0 and gen 1 collections remain foreground GCs that block all application threads from executing.

Background GC works by having a dedicated thread for garbage collecting generation 2. For server GC there will be an additional thread per logical processor. Yes, this means if you use server GC and background GC, you will have two threads per processor dedicated to GC, but this is not particularly concerning. It is not a big deal for processes to have many threads, especially when most of them are doing nothing most of the time.

The garbage collection happens concurrently with your application's threads. It is still possible, however, that a blocking collection will be requested. In this case, the background GC thread is paused with the rest of the app's threads while the GC happens.

If you are using workstation GC, then background GC is always enabled. Starting with .NET 4.5, it is enabled on server GC by default, but you do have the ability to turn it off.

This configuration will turn off the background GC:

```
<configuration>
   <runtime>
      <gcConcurrent enabled="false"/>
   </runtime>
</configuration>
```

In practice, there should rarely ever be a reason to disable background GC. If you want to prevent these background GC threads from ever taking CPU time from your application, but do not mind a potential increase in full, blocking GC latency or frequency, then you can turn this off.

Low Latency Mode

If you have periods of time that require critical performance, you can tell the GC not to perform expensive gen 2 collections. Depending on your other settings, assign the GCSettings.LatencyMode property one of the following values:

- LowLatency—For workstation GC only, it will suppress gen 2 collections.
- SustainedLowLatency—For workstation and server GC, it will suppress full gen 2 collections, but it will allow background gen 2 collections. You must enable background GC for this option to take effect.

Both modes will greatly increase the size of the managed heap because compaction will not occur. If your process uses a lot of memory, you should avoid this feature.

Right before entering this mode, it is a good idea to force a last full GC by calling GC.Collect(2, GCCollectionMode.Forced). Once your code leaves this mode, do another one.

You should never use this feature by default. It is designed for applications that must run without serious interruptions for a long time, but not 100% of the time. A good example is stock trading: during market hours, you do not want full garbage collections happening. When the market closes, you turn this mode off and perform full GCs until the market reopens.

Only turn it on if all of the following criteria apply:

- The latency of a full garbage collection is never acceptable during normal operation.
- The application's memory usage is far lower than available memory.
- Your program can survive long enough to either turn off low latency mode, restart itself, or manually perform a full collection.

This is a rarely used setting and you should think twice about using it because of the potential unintended consequences. If you think this is useful, perform careful measurement to make sure. Turning this feature on may cause other performance problems because a side effect will be having more ephemeral collections (gen 0 and 1) in an attempt to deal with the lack of full collections. You may just trade one set of problems for another.

Finally, note that low latency mode is not a guarantee. If the garbage collector has the choice between doing a full collection or throwing an `OutOfMemoryException`, it may choose the full collection regardless of your mode setting.

Reduce Allocation Rate

This almost goes without saying, but if you reduce the amount of memory you are allocating, you reduce the pressure on the garbage collector to operate. You can also reduce memory fragmentation and CPU usage as well. It can take some creativity to achieve this goal and it might conflict with other design goals.

Critically examine each object and ask yourself:

- Do I really need this object at all?
- Does it have fields that I can get rid of?
- Can I reduce the size of arrays?
- Can I reduce the size of primitives (Int64 to Int32, for example)?
- Are some objects used only in rare circumstances and can be initialized only when needed?
- Can I convert some classes to structs so they live on the stack, or as part of another object?
- Am I allocating a lot of memory, to use only a small portion of it?
- Can I get this information in some other way?

Story In a server that handled user requests, we found out that one type of common request caused more memory to be allocated than the size of a heap segment. Since the CLR caps the maximum size of segments and gen 0 must exist in a single segment, we were guaranteed a GC on every single request. This is not a good spot to be in because there are few options besides reducing memory allocations.

The Most Important Rule

There is one fundamental rule for high-performance programming with regard to the garbage collector. In fact, the garbage collector was explicitly designed with this idea in mind:

Collect objects in gen 0 or not at all.

Put differently, you want objects to have an extremely short lifetime so that the garbage collector will never touch them at all, or, if you cannot do that, they should go to gen 2 as fast as possible and stay there forever, never to be collected. This means that you maintain a reference to long-lived objects forever. Often, this also means pooling reusable objects, especially anything on the large object heap.

Garbage collections get more expensive in each generation. You want to ensure there are many gen 0/1 collections and very few gen 2 collections. Even with background GC for gen 2, there is still a CPU cost that you would rather not pay—that is a processor the rest of your program should be using.

> **Note** You may have heard the myth that you should have 10 gen 0 collections for each gen 1 collection and 10 gen 1 collections for each gen 2 collection. This is not true—just understand that you want to have lots of fast gen 0 collections and very few of the expensive gen 2 collections.

You want to avoid gen 1 collections mostly because an object that is promoted from gen 0 to gen 1 will tend to be promoted to gen 2 in due course. Gen 1 is a sort of buffer before you get to gen 2.

Ideally, every object you allocate goes out of scope by the time the next gen 0 comes around. You can measure how long that interval is and compare it to the duration that data is alive in your application. See the end of the chapter for how to use the tools to retrieve this information.

Obeying this rule requires a fundamental shift in your mindset if you are not used to it. It will inform nearly every aspect of your application, so get used to it early and think about it often.

Reduce Object Lifetime

The shorter an object's scope, the less chance it has of being promoted to the next generation when a GC comes along. In general, you should not allocate objects until right before you need them. The exception would be when the cost of object creation is so high it makes sense to create them at an earlier point when it will not interfere with other processing.

On the other side of the object use, you want to make sure that objects go out of scope as soon as possible. For local variables, this can be after the last local usage, even before the end of the method. You can lexically scope it narrower by using the { } bracket, but this will probably not make a practical difference because the compiler will generally recognize when an object is no longer used anyway. If your code spreads out operations on an object, try to reduce the time between the first and last uses so that the GC can collect the object as early as possible.

Sometimes you will need to explicitly null out a reference to an object if it is a field on a long-lived object. This may make the code slightly more complicated because you will have more checks for nulls scattered around. This can also create a tension between efficiency and always having full state available, particularly for debugging.

One option is to convert the object you want to null out to another form, such as a log message, that can more efficiently record the state for debugging later.

Another way to manage this balance is to have variable behavior: run your program (or a specific portion of your program, say for a specific request) in a mode that does not null out references but keeps them around as long as possible for easier debugging.

Reduce Depth of Trees

As described at the beginning of this chapter, the GC works by following object references. In server GC, it does this on multiple threads at once. You want to exploit parallelism as much as possible, and if one thread hits a very long chain of nested objects, the entire collection process will not finish until that long-running thread is complete. In later versions of the CLR, this is less of a concern as the GC threads now use work-stealing algorithms to balance this load better. If you suspect you have very deep trees of objects, this may be something worth looking at.

Reduce References between Objects

This is related to the depth of trees in the previous section, but there are a few other considerations.

Objects that have many references to other objects will take more time for the garbage collector to traverse. A long GC pause time is often an indication of a large, complex object graph.

Another danger is that it becomes much harder to predict object lifetimes if you cannot easily determine all of the possible references to them. Reducing this complexity is a worthy goal just for sane code practices, but it also makes debugging and fixing performance problems easier.

Also, be aware that references between objects of different generations can cause inefficiencies in the garbage collector, specifically references from older objects to newer objects. For example, if an object in generation 2 has a reference to an object in generation 0, then every time a gen 0 GC occurs, a portion of gen 2 objects will also have to be scanned to see if they are still holding onto this reference to a generation 0 object. It is not as expensive as a full GC, but it is still unnecessary work if you can avoid it.

Avoid Pinning

Pinning exists so that you can safely pass managed memory references to native code. It is most common to pass arrays or strings. If you are not doing interop with native code, you should not have the need to pin at all.

Pinning an object fixes it in place so that the garbage collector cannot move it. While the pinning operation itself is inexpensive, it throws a bit of a wrench into the GC's operation by increasing the likelihood of fragmentation. The garbage collector tracks those pinned objects so that it can use the free spaces between them, but if you have excessive pinning, it can still cause fragmentation and heap growth.

Pinning can be either explicit or implicit. Explicit pinning is performed with use of a GCHandle of type GCHandleType.Pinned or the fixed keyword and must be inside code marked as unsafe. The difference between using fixed or a handle is analogous to the difference between using and explicitly calling Dispose. fixed/using is more convenient, but cannot be used in asynchronous situations, whereas you can pass around a handle and dispose of it in the callback.

Implicit pinning is more common, but can be harder to see and more difficult to remove. The most obvious source of pinning will be any objects passed to unmanaged code via Platform Invoke (P/Invoke). This is not just your own code—managed APIs that you call can, and often do, call native code, which will require pinning.

The CLR will also have pinned objects in its own data structures, but these should normally not be a concern.

Ideally, you should eliminate as much pinning as you can. If you cannot quite do that, follow the same rules for short-lived managed objects: keep lifetime as short as possible. If objects are only pinned briefly then there is less chance for them to affect the next garbage collection. You also want to avoid having very many pinned objects at the same time. Pinning objects located in gen 2 or the LOH is generally fine because these objects are unlikely to move anyway. This can lead to a strategy of either allocating large buffers on the large object heap and giving out portions of them as needed, or allocating small buffers on the small object heap, but before pinning, ensure they are promoted to gen 2. This takes a bit of management on your part, but it can completely avoid the issue of having pinned buffers during a gen 0 GC.

Avoid Finalizers

Never implement a finalizer unless it is required. Finalizers are code, triggered by the garbage collector to cleanup unmanaged resources. They are called from a single thread, one after the other, and only after the garbage collector declares the object dead after a collection. This means that if your class implements a finalizer, you are guaranteeing that it will stay in memory even after the collection that should have killed it. This decreases overall GC efficiency and ensures that your program will dedicate CPU resources to cleaning up your object.

If you do implement a finalizer, you must also implement the IDisposable interface to enable explicit cleanup, and call GC.SuppressFinalize(this) in the Dispose method to remove the object from the finalization queue. As long as you call Dispose before the next collection, then it will clean up the object properly without the need for the finalizer to run. The following example correctly demonstrates this pattern.

```
class Foo : IDisposable
{
  ~Foo()
  {
    Dispose(false);
  }

  public void Dispose()
  {
    Dispose(true);
    GC.SuppressFinalize(this);
  }

  protected virtual void Dispose(bool disposing)
  {
    if (disposing)
    {
      this.managedResource.Dispose();
    }
```

```
    // Cleanup unmanaged resourced
    UnsafeClose(this.handle);
    // If the base class is IDisposable object
    // make sure you call:
    //base.Dispose(disposing);
  }
}
```

See http://www.writinghighperf.net/go/15 for more information about the Dispose Pattern and finalization.

> **Note** Some people think that finalizers are guaranteed to run. This is generally true, but not absolutely so. If a program is force-terminated then no more code runs and the process dies immediately. There is also a time limit to how long all of the finalizers are given on process shutdown. If your finalizer is at the end of the list, it may be skipped. Moreover, because finalizers execute sequentially, if another finalizer has an infinite loop bug in it, then no finalizers after it will ever run. While finalizers are not run on a GC thread, they are triggered by a GC so if you have no collections, the finalizers will not run. Therefore, you should not rely on finalizers to clean up state external to your process.

Avoid Large Object Allocations

The boundary for large object allocations was set at 85,000 bytes by doing a statistical analysis of programs of the day. Any object of that size or greater was judged to be "large" and go on a separate heap.

You want to avoid allocations on the large object heap as much as possible. Not only is collecting garbage from this heap more expensive, it is more likely to fragment, causing unbounded memory increases over time.

To avoid these problems, you need to strictly control what your program allocates on the large object heap. What does go there should last for the lifetime of your program and be reused as necessary in a pooling scheme.

The LOH does not automatically compact, but you may tell it to do so programmatically starting with .NET 4.5.1. However, you should use this only as a last resort, as it will cause a very long pause. Before explaining how to do that, I will explain how to avoid getting into that situation in the first place.

Avoid Copying Buffers

You should always avoid copying data whenever you can. For example, suppose you have read file data into a `MemoryStream` (preferably a pooled one if you need large buffers). Once you have that memory allocated, treat it as read-only and every component that needs to access it will read from the same copy of the data.

If you need to represent a sub-range of the entire buffer, use the `ArraySegment<T>` class to represent just a portion of the underlying `byte[]` buffer. This `ArraySegment` can be passed around to APIs independent of the original stream, and you can even attach a new `MemoryStream` to just that segment. Throughout all of this, no copy of the data has been made.

```
var memoryStream = new MemoryStream();
var segment = new ArraySegment<byte>(memoryStream.GetBuffer(), 100, 1024);
...
var blockStream = new MemoryStream(segment.Array,
                  segment.Offset,
                  segment.Count);
```

The biggest problem with copying memory is not the CPU necessarily, but the GC. If you find yourself needing to copy a buffer, then try to copy it into another pooled or existing buffer to avoid any new memory allocations.

Pool Long-Lived and Large Objects

Remember the cardinal rule from earlier: Objects live very briefly or forever. They either go away in gen 0 collections or last forever in gen 2. Some objects are essentially static—they are created and last the lifetime of the program naturally. Other objects do not obviously need to last forever, but their natural lifetime in the context of your program ensures they will live longer than the period of a gen 0 (and maybe gen 1) garbage collection. These types of objects are candidates for pooling. While effectively a manual memory strategy, this does actually work well in this situation. Another strong candidate for pooling is any object that you allocate on the LOH heap, typically collections.

There is no single way to pool and there is no standard pooling API you can rely on. It really is up to you to develop a way that works for your application and the specific objects you need to pool.

One way to think about poolable objects is that you are turning a normally managed resource (memory) into something that you have to manage explicitly. .NET already has a pattern for dealing with finite managed resources: the IDisposable pattern. See earlier in this chapter for the proper implementation of this pattern. A reasonable design is to derive a new type and have it implement IDisposable, where the Dispose method puts the pooled object back in the pool. This will be a strong clue to users of that type that they need to treat this resource specially.

Implementing a good pooling strategy is not trivial and can depend entirely on how your program needs to use it, and what types of objects need to be pooled. Here is some code that shows one example of a simple pooling class to give you some idea of what is involved. This code is from the PooledObjects sample program.

```csharp
interface IPoolableObject : IDisposable
{
  int Size { get; }
  void Reset();
  void SetPoolManager(PoolManager poolManager);
}

class PoolManager
{
  private class Pool
  {
    public int PooledSize { get; set; }
    public int Count { get { return this.Stack.Count; } }
    public Stack<IPoolableObject> Stack { get; private set; }
    public Pool()
    {
      this.Stack = new Stack<IPoolableObject>();
    }

  }
  const int MaxSizePerType = 10 * (1 << 10); // 10 MB

  Dictionary<Type, Pool> pools =
    new Dictionary<Type, Pool>();

  public int TotalCount
  {
    get
    {
      int sum = 0;
      foreach (var pool in this.pools.Values)
      {
        sum += pool.Count;
```

```
      }
      return sum;
   }
}

public T GetObject<T>()
   where T : class, IPoolableObject, new()
{
   Pool pool;
   T valueToReturn = null;
   if (pools.TryGetValue(typeof(T), out pool))
   {
      if (pool.Stack.Count > 0)
      {
         valueToReturn = pool.Stack.Pop() as T;
      }
   }
   if (valueToReturn == null)
   {
      valueToReturn = new T();
   }
   valueToReturn.SetPoolManager(this);
   return valueToReturn;
}

public void ReturnObject<T>(T value)
   where T : class, IPoolableObject, new()
{
   Pool pool;
   if (!pools.TryGetValue(typeof(T), out pool))
   {
      pool = new Pool();
      pools[typeof(T)] = pool;
   }

   if (value.Size + pool.PooledSize < MaxSizePerType)
   {
      pool.PooledSize += value.Size;
      value.Reset();
      pool.Stack.Push(value);
   }
}
}
```

```
class MyObject : IPoolableObject
{
  private PoolManager poolManager;
  public byte[] Data { get; set; }
  public int UsableLength { get; set; }

  public int Size
  {
    get { return Data != null ? Data.Length : 0; }
  }

  void IPoolableObject.Reset()
  {
    UsableLength = 0;
  }

  void IPoolableObject.SetPoolManager(
    PoolManager poolManager)
  {
    this.poolManager = poolManager;
  }

  public void Dispose()
  {
    this.poolManager.ReturnObject(this);
  }
}
```

It may seem a burden to force pooled objects to implement a custom interface, but apart from convenience, this highlights a very important fact: In order to use pooling and reuse objects, you must be able to fully understand and control them. Your code must reset them to a known, safe state every time they go back into the pool. This means you should not naively pool 3rd-party objects directly. By implementing your own objects with a custom interface, you are providing a very strong signal that the objects are special. You should especially be wary of pooling objects from the .NET Framework.

It is particularly tricky pooling collections because of their nature—you do not want to destroy the actual data storage (that is the whole point of pooling, after all), but you must be able to signify an empty collection with available space. Thankfully, most collection types implement both Length and Capacity parameters that make this distinction. Given the dangers of pooling the existing .NET collection types, it is better if you implement your own collection types using the standard collection interfaces such as IList<T>, ICollection<T>, and others. See Chapter 6 for general guidance on creating your own collection types.

An additional strategy is to have your poolable types implement a finalizer as a safety mechanism. If the finalizer runs, it means that `Dispose` was never called, which is a bug. You can choose to write something to the log, crash, or otherwise signal the problem.

Remember that a pool that never dumps objects is indistinguishable from a memory leak. Your pool should have a bounded size (in either bytes or number of objects) and once that has been exceeded, it should drop objects for the GC to clean up. Ideally, your pool is large enough to handle normal operations without dropping anything and the GC is only needed for brief spikes of activity. Depending on the size and number of objects contained in your pool, dropping them may lead to long, full GCs. It is important to make sure your pool is tunable for your situation.

Story I do not usually run to pooling as a default solution. As a general-purpose mechanism, it is clunky and error-prone. However, you may find that your application will benefit from pooling of just a few types. In one application that suffered from too many LOH allocations, we discovered that if we pooled a single type of object, we could eliminate 99% of all problems with the LOH. This was `MemoryStream`, which we used for serialization and transmitting bits over the network. The actual implementation is more complex than just keeping a queue of `MemoryStream` objects because of the need to avoid fragmentation, but conceptually, that is exactly what it is. Every time a `MemoryStream` object was disposed, it was put back in the pool for reuse.

Reduce Large Object Heap Fragmentation

If you cannot completely avoid large object heap allocations, then you want to do your best to avoid fragmentation.

The LOH can grow indefinitely if you are not careful, but it is mitigated by the free list. To take advantage of this free list, you want to increase the likelihood that memory allocations can be satisfied from holes in the heap.

One way to do this is to ensure that all allocations on the LOH are of uniform size, or at least multiples of some standard size. For example, a common need for LOH allocations is for buffer pools. Rather than have a hodge-podge of buffer sizes, ensure that they are all the same size, or in multiples of some well-known number such as one megabyte. This way, if one of the buffers does need to get garbage collected, there is a high likelihood that the next buffer allocation can fill its spot rather than going to the end of the heap.

Story To continue the previous story about pooled `MemoryStreams`, the first implementation of `PooledMemoryStream` pooled the streams as a whole and allowed the buffers to grow to

---

whatever size they needed. This used the underlying `MemoryStream`'s buffer growth algorithm, which doubles the buffer when capacity is exceeded. This solved many of the LOH woes, but left us with a horrible fragmentation problem. The second iteration threw that away in favor of pooling individual `byte[]` buffers, each of 128 KB, which were chained together to form a virtual buffer, which the stream abstracted. We had separate pools for larger buffers in multiples of 1 MB, up to 8 MB. This new implementation dramatically reduced our fragmentation problem, with a tradeoff. We occasionally had to copy multiple 128KB buffers into a single 1 MB buffer when someone needed a consecutive buffer, but since everything was pooled, this was worth it.

Force Full GCs in Some Circumstances

In nearly all cases, you should not force collections to happen outside of their normal schedule as determined by the GC itself. Doing so disrupts the automatic tuning the garbage collector performs and may lead to worse behavior overall. However, there are some considerations in a high-performance system that may cause you to reconsider this advice in very specific situations.

In general, it may be beneficial to force a GC to occur during a more optimal time to avoid a GC occurring during a worse time later on. Note that we are only talking about the expensive, ideally rare, full GCs. Gen 0 and gen 1 GCs can and should happen frequently to avoid building up a too-large gen 0 size.

Some situations may merit a forced collection:

1. You are using low latency GC mode. In this mode, heap size can grow and you will need to determine appropriate points to perform a full collection. See the section earlier in this chapter about low latency GC.
2. You occasionally make a large number of allocations that will live for a long time (forever, ideally). It makes sense to get these objects into gen 2 as quickly as possible. If these objects replace other objects that will now become garbage, you can just get rid of them immediately with a forced collection.
3. You are in a state where you need to compact the large object heap because of fragmentation. See the section about large object heap compaction.

Situations 1 and 2 are all about avoiding full GCs during specific times by forcing them at other times. Situation 3 is about reducing your overall heap size if you have significant fragmentation on the LOH. If your scenario does not fit into one of those categories, you should not consider this a useful option.

To perform a full collection, call the GC.Collect method with the generation of the collection you want it to perform. Optionally, you can specify a GCCollectionMode enumeration argument to tell the GC to decide for itself whether to do the collection. There are three possible values:

- Default—Currently, Forced.
- Forced—Tells the garbage collector to start the collection immediately.
- Optimized—Allows the garbage collector to decide if now is a good time to run.

```
GC.Collect(2);
// equivalent to:
GC.Collect(2, GCCollectionMode.Forced);
```

> **Story** This exact situation existed on a server that took user queries. Every few hours we needed to reload over a gigabyte of data, replacing the existing data. Since this was an expensive operation and we were already reducing the number of requests the machine was receiving, we also forced two full GCs after the reload happened. This removed the old data and ensured that everything allocated in gen 0 either got collected or made it to gen 2 where it belonged. Then, once we resumed a full query load, there would not be a huge, full GC to affect the queries.

Compact the Large Object Heap On-Demand

Even if you do pooling, it is still possible that there are allocations you cannot control and the large object heap will become fragmented over time. Starting in .NET 4.5.1, you can tell the GC to compact the LOH on the next full collection.

```
GCSettings.LargeObjectHeapCompactionMode =
    GCLargeObjectHeapCompactionMode.CompactOnce;
```

Depending on the size of the LOH, this can be a slow operation, up to multiple seconds. You may want to put your program in a state where it stops doing real work and force an immediate collection with the GC.Collect method.

This setting only affects the next full GC that happens. Once the next full collection occurs, GCSettings.LargeObjectHeapCompactionMode resets automatically to GCLargeObjectHeapCompactionMode.Default.

Because of the expense of this operation, I recommend you reduce the number of LOH allocations to as little as possible and pool those that you do make. This will significantly reduce the need for compaction. View this feature as a last resort and only if fragmentation and very large heap sizes are an issue.

Get Notified of Collections Before They Happen

If your application absolutely should not be impacted by gen 2 collections, then you can tell the GC to notify you when a full GC is approaching. This will give you a chance to stop processing temporarily, perhaps by shunting requests off the machine, or otherwise putting the application into a more favorable state.

It may seem like this notification mechanism is the answer to all GC woes, but I recommend extreme caution. You should only implement this after you have optimized as much as you can in other areas. You can only take advantage of GC notifications if all of the following statements are true:

1. A full GC is so expensive that you cannot afford to endure a single one during normal processing.
2. You are able to turn off processing for the application completely. (Perhaps other computers or processes can do the work meanwhile.)
3. You can turn off processing quickly (so you do not waste more time stopping processing than actually performing the GC).
4. Gen 2 collections happen rarely enough to make this worth it.

Gen 2 collections will happen rarely only if you have large object allocations minimized and little promotion beyond gen 0, so it will still take a fair amount of work to get to the point where you can reliably take advantage of GC notifications.

Unfortunately, because of the imprecise nature of GC triggering, you can only specify the pre-trigger time in an approximate way with a number in the range 1 - 99. With a number that is very low, you will be notified much closer to when the GC will happen, but you risk having the GC occur before you can react to it. With a number that is too high, the GC may be quite far away and you will get a notification far too frequently, which is quite inefficient. It all depends on your allocation rate and overall memory load. Note that you specify two numbers: one for the gen 2 threshold and one for the large object heap threshold. As with other features, this notification is a best effort by the garbage collector. The garbage collector never guarantees you can avoid doing a collection.

To use this mechanism, follow these general steps:

1. Call the `GC.RegisterForFullGCNotification` method with the two threshold values.

2. Poll the GC with the GC.WaitForFullGCApproach method. This can wait forever or accept a timeout value.
3. If the WaitForFullGCApproach method returns Success, put your program in a state acceptable for a full GC (e.g., turn off requests to the machine).
4. Force a full collection yourself by calling the GC.Collect method.
5. Call GC.WaitForFullGCComplete (again with an optional timeout value) to wait for the full GC to compete before continuing.
6. Turn requests back on.
7. When you no longer want to receive notifications of full GCs, call the GC.CancelFullGCNotification method.

Because this requires a polling mechanism, you will need to run a thread that can do this check periodically. Many applications already have some sort of "housekeeping" thread that performs various actions on a schedule. This may be an appropriate task, or you can create a separate dedicated thread.

Here is a full example from the GCNotification sample project demonstrating this behavior in a simple test application that allocates memory continuously. See the accompanying source code project to test this.

```
class Program
{
  static void Main(string[] args)
  {
    const int ArrSize = 1024;
    var arrays = new List<byte[]>();

    GC.RegisterForFullGCNotification(25, 25);

    // Start a separate thread to wait for GC notifications
    Task.Run(()=>WaitForGCThread(null));

    Console.WriteLine("Press any key to exit");
    while (!Console.KeyAvailable)
    {
      try
      {
        arrays.Add(new byte[ArrSize]);
      }
      catch (OutOfMemoryException)
      {
        Console.WriteLine("OutOfMemoryException!");
```

```
      arrays.Clear();
    }
  }

  GC.CancelFullGCNotification();
}

private static void WaitForGCThread(object arg)
{
  const int MaxWaitMs = 10000;
  while (true)
  {
    // There is also an overload of WaitForFullGCApproach
    // that waits indefinitely
    GCNotificationStatus status =
                   GC.WaitForFullGCApproach(MaxWaitMs);
    bool didCollect = false;
    switch (status)
    {
      case GCNotificationStatus.Succeeded:
        Console.WriteLine("GC approaching!");
        Console.WriteLine(
          "-- redirect processing to another machine -- ");
        didCollect = true;
        GC.Collect();
        break;
      case GCNotificationStatus.Canceled:
        Console.WriteLine("GC Notification was canceled");
        break;
      case GCNotificationStatus.Timeout:
        Console.WriteLine("GC notification timed out");
        break;
    }

    if (didCollect)
    {
      do
      {
        status = GC.WaitForFullGCComplete(MaxWaitMs);
        switch (status)
        {
          case GCNotificationStatus.Succeeded:
            Console.WriteLine("GC completed");
            Console.WriteLine(
            "-- accept processing on this machine again --");
            break;
          case GCNotificationStatus.Canceled:
```

```
                    Console.WriteLine("GC Notification was canceled");
                    break;
                case GCNotificationStatus.Timeout:
                    Console.WriteLine("GC completion notification timed out");
                    break;
            }
            // Looping isn't necessary, but it's useful if you want
            // to check other state before waiting again.
        } while (status == GCNotificationStatus.Timeout);
        }
      }
    }
}
```

Another possible reason is to compact the LOH heap, but you could trigger this based on memory usage instead, which may be more appropriate.

Use Weak References for Caching

Weak references are references to an object that still allow the garbage collector to clean up the object. This is in contrast to strong references, which prevent collection completely (for that object). They are mostly useful for caching expensive objects that you would like to keep around, but are willing to let go if there is enough memory pressure.

```
WeakReference weakRef = new WeakReference(myExpensiveObject);
...
// Create a strong reference to the object,
// now no longer eligible for GC
var myObject = weakRef.Target;
if (myObject != null)
{
    myObject.DoSomethingAwesome();
}
```

WeakReference has an IsAlive property, but it is only useful to determine if the object is dead, not if it is alive. If you check IsAlive and see that it is true, you are in a race with the garbage collector, which could collect the object after you check the IsAlive property. Just copy the object reference to a strong reference of your own and check it there.

A very good way to use WeakReference is part of a cache where objects can start by being held by a strong reference and after enough time of not being used, they can be demoted to being held by weak references, which may eventually disappear.

Measuring and Investigating GC Performance

In this section, you will learn many tips and techniques to investigate what is happening on the GC heap. In many cases, multiple tools can give you the same information. I will endeavor to describe the use of a few in each scenario, where applicable.

Performance Counters

.NET supplies a number of Windows performance counters, all in the .NET CLR Memory category. All of these counters except for *Allocated Bytes/sec* are updated at the end of a collection. If you notice values getting stuck, it is likely because collections are not happening very often.

- **# Bytes in all Heaps**—Sum of all heaps, except generation 0 (see the description for Gen 0 heap size).
- **# GC Handles**—Number of handles in use.
- **# Gen 0 Collections**—Cumulative number of generation 0 collections since process start. Note that this counter is incremented for generation 1 and 2 collections as well because higher generation collections always imply collections of the lower generations as well.
- **# Gen 1 Collections**—Cumulative number of gen 1 collections since process start. Note that this counter is incremented for generation 2 collections as well because a generation 2 collection implies a generation 1 collection.
- **# Gen 2 Collections**—Cumulative number of generation 2 collections since process start.
- **# Induced GC**—Number of times GC.Collect was called to explicitly start garbage collection.
- **# of Pinned Objects**—Number of pinned objects the garbage collector observes during collection.
- **# of Sink Blocks in use**—Each object has a header that can store limited information, such as a hash code, or synchronization information. If there is any contention for use of this header, a sink block is created. These blocks are also used for interop metadata. A high counter value here can indicate lock contention.
- **# Total committed Bytes**—Number of bytes the garbage collector has allocated that are actually backed by the paging file.
- **# Total reserved Bytes**—Number of bytes reserved by garbage collector, but not yet committed.
- **% Time in GC**—Percentage of time the processor has spent in the GC threads compared to the rest of the process since the last collection. This counter does not account for background GC.

- **Allocated Bytes/sec**—Number of bytes allocated on a GC heap per second. This counter is not updated continuously, but only when a garbage collection starts.
- **Finalization Survivors**—Number of finalizable objects that survived a collection because they are waiting for finalization (which only happens in generation 1 collections). Also, see the Promoted Finalization-Memory from Gen 0 counter.
- **Gen 0 heap size**—*Maximum* number of bytes that can be allocated in generation 0, not the actual number of bytes allocated.
- **Gen 0 Promoted Bytes/Sec**—The rate of promotion from generation 0 to generation 1. You want this number to be as low as possible, indicating short memory lifetimes.
- **Gen 1 heap size**—Number of bytes in generation 1, as of the last garbage collection.
- **Gen 1 Promoted Bytes/Sec**—Rate of promotion from generation 1 to generation 2. A high number here indicates memory having a very long lifetime, and good candidates for pooling.
- **Gen 2 heap size**—Number of bytes in generation 2, as of the last garbage collection.
- **Large Object Heap Size**—Number of bytes on the large object heap.
- **Promoted Finalization-Memory from Gen 0**—Total number of bytes that were promoted to generation 1 because an object somewhere in their tree is awaiting finalization. This is not just the memory from finalizable objects directly, but also the memory from any references those objects hold.
- **Promoted Memory from Gen 0**—Number of bytes promoted from generation 0 to generation 1 at the last collection.
- **Promoted Memory from Gen 1**—Number of bytes promoted from generation 1 to generation 2 at the last collection.

ETW Events

The CLR publishes numerous events about GC behavior. In most cases, you can rely on the tools to analyze these in aggregate for you, but it is still useful to understand how this information is logged in case you need to track down specific events and relate them to other events in your application. You can examine these in detail in PerfView with the Events view. Here are some of the most important:

- **GCStart**—Garbage collection has started. Fields include:
  - Count—The number of collections that have occurred since the process began.
  - Depth—Which generation is being collected.
  - Reason—Why the collection was triggered.
  - Type—Blocking, background, or blocking during background.
- **GCEnd**—Garbage collection has ended. Fields include:
  - Count, Depth—Same as for GCStart.

- **GCHeapStats**—Shows stats at the end of a garbage collection.
  - ○ There are many fields, describing all aspects of the heap such as generation sizes, promoted bytes, finalization, handles, and more.
- **GCCreateSegment**—A new segment was created. Fields include:
  - ○ Address—Address of the segment
  - ○ Size—Size of the segment
  - ○ Type—Small or large object heap
- **GCFreeSegment**—A segment was released. Just one field:
  - ○ Address—Address of the segment
- **GCAllocationTick**—Emitted every time about 100KB (cumulative) was allocated. Fields include:
  - ○ AllocationSize—Exact size of the allocation that triggered the event.
  - ○ Kind—Small or large object heap allocation.

There are other events as well, such as for finalizers and thread control during GC. You can find more information about these at http://www.writinghighperf.net/go/16.

How Long Does A Collection Take?

The GC records many events about its operation. You can use PerfView to examine these events in a very efficient way.

To see statistics on GC, start the AllocateAndRelease sample program.

Start PerfView and follow these steps:

1. Menu Collect | Collect (Alt+C).
2. Expand Advanced Options. You can optionally turn off all event categories except GC Only, but for now just leave the default selection, as GC events are included in .NET events.
3. Check No V3.X NGEN Symbols. (This will make symbol resolution faster.)
4. Click Start.
5. Wait for a few minutes while it measures the process's activity. (If collecting for more than a few minutes, you may want to turn off CPU events.)
6. Click Stop Collection.
7. Wait for the files to finish merging.
8. In the resulting view tree, double-click on the GCStats node, which will open up a new view.

9. Find the section for your process and look at the summary table, which will show you average pause time per generation, how many GCs there were, the number of bytes allocated, and much more. Here is a sample table:

GC Rollup By Generation										
All times are in msec.										
Gen	Count	Max Pause	Max Peak MB	Max Alloc MB/sec	Total Pause	Total Alloc MB	Alloc MB/ MSec GC	Survived MB/ MSec GC	Mean Pause	Induced
ALL	12651	12.3	5.5	291.128	1,495.3	25,648.2	17.2	Infinity	0.1	0
0	11780	0.7	5.4	261.359	716.6	23,816.5	0.0	Infinity	0.1	0
1	0	0.0	0.0	0.000	0.0	0.0	0.0	NaN	NaN	0
2	871	12.3	5.5	291.128	778.7	1,831.7	0.0	Infinity	0.9	0

Figure 2-1. The GCStats table for the AllocateAndRelease sample program. This shows you the number of GCs that occurred as well as interesting stats like the mean/max pause times, and allocation rates.

Where Are My Allocations Occurring?

PerfView is a good option to find out which objects are being allocated and how often.

1. With PerfView, collect either .NET or just GC Only events.
2. Once completed, open the GC Heap Alloc Stacks view and select the desired process from the process list. (For a simple example, use the AllocateAndRelease sample program) from the process list.)
3. On the By Name tab, you will see types sorted in order of total allocation size. Double-clicking a type name will take you to the Callers tab, which shows you the stacks that made the allocations.

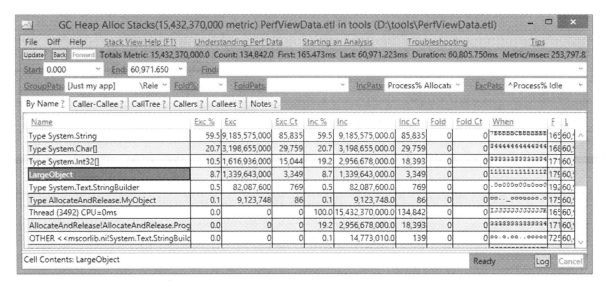

Figure 2-2. The GC Heap Alloc Stacks view shows the most common allocations in your process. The LargeObject entry is a pseudo node; double-clicking on it will reveal the actual objects allocated on the LOH.

See Chapter 1 for more information on using PerfView's interface to get the most out of the view.

Using the above information, you should be able to find the stacks for all the allocations that occur in the test program, and their relative frequency. For example, in my trace, string allocation accounts for roughly 59.5% of all memory allocations.

You can also use CLR Profiler to find this information and display it in a number of ways.

Once you have collected a trace and the Summary window opens, click on the Allocation Graph button to open up a graphical trace of object allocations and the methods responsible for them.

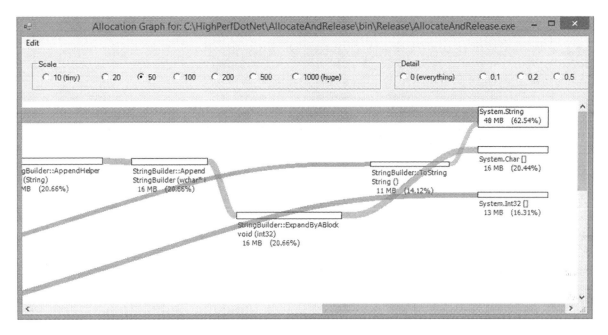

Figure 2-3. CLR Profiler's visual depiction of object allocation stacks quickly points you to objects you need to be most concerned about.

The Visual Studio profiler can also get this information for you and display it like it does CPU profile data.

The most frequently allocated objects are also the ones most likely to be triggering garbage collections. Reduce these allocations and the rate of GCs will go down.

Which Objects Are Being Allocated On The Large Object Heap?

Understanding which objects are being allocated on the large object heap is critical to ensuring a well-performing system. The very first rule discussed in this chapter states that all objects should be cleaned up in a gen 0 collection, or they need to live forever.

Large objects are only cleaned up by an expensive gen 2 GC, so it violates that rule out of the gate.

To find out which objects are on the LOH, use PerfView and follow the previously given instructions for getting a GC event trace. In the resulting GC Heap Alloc Stacks view, in the By Name tab, you will find a special node that PerfView creates called "LargeObject." Double click on this to go to the Callers view, which shows which "callers" LargeObject has. In the sample program, they are all Int32 arrays. Double-clicking on those in turn will show where the allocations occurred.

Methods that call LargeObject

Name ?	Inc % ?	Inc ?
☑LargeObject	8.8	302,824,200.0
+☑Type System.Int32[]	8.8	302,824,200.0
+☑OTHER <<clr!JIT_NewArr1>>	8.8	302,824,200.0
+☑AllocateAndRelease!AllocateAndRelease.Program.CreateArray(bool)	8.8	302,824,200.0
+☑AllocateAndRelease!AllocateAndRelease.Program.DoAnAllocation()	8.8	302,824,200.0
+☐AllocateAndRelease!AllocateAndRelease.Program.Main(class System.Strin	8.8	302,824,200.0

Figure 2-4. PerfView can show large objects and their types with the stacks that allocated them.

CLR Profiler can also show you the types of objects on the large object heap. After you get a trace, click on the View Objects by Address button, which will bring up a simple graph of the labeled heaps with color-coded objects.

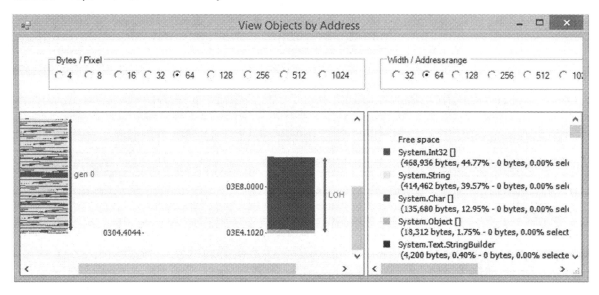

Figure 2-5. CLR Profiler can visually show you which objects are allocated on the LOH heap.

To see the allocation stack for these objects, right click on the type in the graph you want to see and select Show Who Allocated. This will bring up a window displaying a visual representation of the allocation graph, a colorful version of what PerfView will show you.

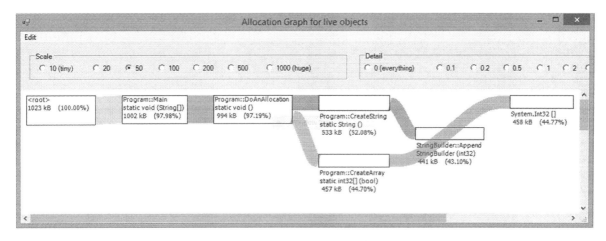

Figure 2-6. CLR Profiler shows a visual equivalent of a call stack for allocations.

What Are All The Objects On My Heap?

One option is to use PerfView to dump the entire heap and show you the relationship of object ownership. PerfView will use the stacks view to display this for you, but there is a subtle difference from other uses. The stacks you see in the GC Heap Alloc Stacks view, for example, are stacks of who allocated the memory, while the GC Heap Dump view shows you stacks of object references—that is, who currently "owns" the object.

To use this feature, in PerfView:

1. From the Memory menu, select Take Heap Snapshot. Note that this does not pause the process (unless you check the option to Freeze), but it does have a significant impact on the process's performance.
2. Highlight the desired process in the resulting dialog.
3. Click Dump GC Heap.
4. Wait until collection is finished, then close the window.
5. Open the file from the PerfView file tree (it may automatically open for you when you close the collection window).

Consider the LargeMemoryUsage sample program:

```
class Program
{
  const int ArraySize = 1000;
  static object[] staticArray = new object[ArraySize];
```

```csharp
  static void Main(string[] args)
  {
    object[] localArray = new object[ArraySize];

    Random rand = new Random();
    for (int i = 0; i < ArraySize; i++)
    {
      staticArray[i] = GetNewObject(rand.Next(0, 4));
      localArray[i] = GetNewObject(rand.Next(0, 4));
    }

    Console.WriteLine(
        "Use PerfView to examine heap now. Press any key to exit...");
    Console.ReadKey();

    // This will prevent localArray from being
    // garbage collected before you take the snapshot
    Console.WriteLine(staticArray.Length);
    Console.WriteLine(localArray.Length);
  }

  private static Base GetNewObject(int type)
  {
    Base obj = null;
    switch (type)
    {
      case 0: obj = new A(); break;
      case 1: obj = new B(); break;
      case 2: obj = new C(); break;
      case 3: obj = new D(); break;
    }
    return obj;
  }
}

class Base
{
  private byte[] memory;
  protected Base(int size) { this.memory = new byte[size]; }
}

class A : Base { public A() : base(1000) { } }
class B : Base { public B() : base(10000) { } }
class C : Base { public C() : base(100000) { } }
class D : Base { public D() : base(1000000) { } }
```

You should see a table like this:

Name	Exc % ?	Exc ?	Exc Ct ?	Inc % ?	Inc ?
LargeMemoryUsage!LargeMemoryUsage.D	88.5	462,013,000	924	88.5	462,013,000.0
LargeMemoryUsage!LargeMemoryUsage.C	10.4	54,213,010	1,084	10.4	54,213,010.0
LargeMemoryUsage!LargeMemoryUsage.B	1.0	5,242,552	1,046	1.0	5,242,552.0
LargeMemoryUsage!LargeMemoryUsage.A	0.1	484,352	946	0.1	484,352.0
[Pinned handle]	0.0	21,586	153	0.0	22,926.0
[local var]	0.0	4,032	3	49.5	258,117,400.0
[static var LargeMemoryUsage.Program.staticArray]	0.0	4,016	2	50.5	263,847,600.0

Figure 2-7. A PerfView trace of the largest objects in the heap.

It tells you immediately that D accounts for 88% of the program's memory at 462 MB with 924 objects. You can also see local variables are holding on to 258 MB of memory and the staticArray object is holding onto 263 MB of memory.

Double-clicking the entry for the D class switches to the Referred-From view, which looks like this:

Objects that refer to LargeMemoryUsage!LargeMemoryUsage.D

Name ?	Inc % ?	Inc ?	Inc Ct ?	Exc % ?	Exc ?
☑ LargeMemoryUsage!LargeMemoryUsage.D ?	88.5	462,013,000.0	924	88.5	462,013,000
+ ☐ [static var LargeMemoryUsage.Program.staticArray] ?	44.8	234,006,300.0	468	0.0	0
+ ☑ [local var] ?	43.7	228,006,800.0	456	0.0	0
+ ☑ [.NET Roots] ?	43.7	228,006,800.0	456	0.0	0
+ ☑ ROOT ?	43.7	228,006,800.0	456	0.0	0

Figure 2-8. PerfView shows stacks in a tabular format, which is easily understandable once you get used to it.

This view clearly shows that the D objects belong to the staticArray variable and a local variable (those lose their names during compilation).

Visual Studio 2013 has a new Managed Heap Analysis view that is similar in spirit to PerfView. You can access it after opening a managed memory dump.

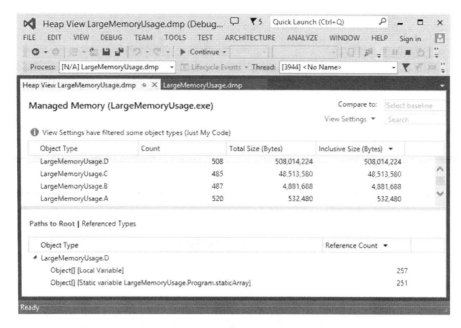

Figure 2-9. Visual Studio 2013 includes this heap analysis view, which works off of managed memory dumps.

You can also get a graphical view of the same information with CLR Profiler. While the program is running, click the Show Heap now button to capture a heap sample. It will produce a view like this:

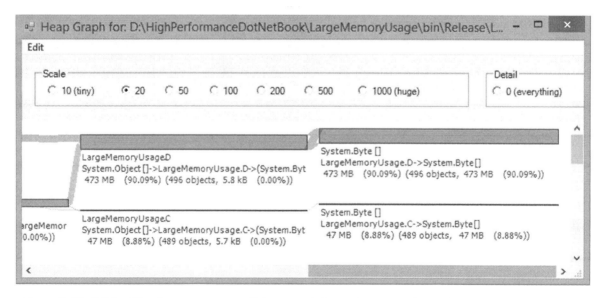

Figure 2-10. CLR Profiler shows you some of the same information as PerfView, but in a graphical format.

Why Are My Objects Not Being Garbage Collected?

To see why an object is not being collected, you need to find out what is maintaining a reference to that object. The previous section about dumping the heap will tell you what is maintaining a reference to the objects you are interested in, and thus what is preventing garbage collection.

If you are interested in a particular object, you can use Windbg. Once you have the object's address, you can use the !gcroot command:

```
0:003> !gcroot 02ed1fc0
HandleTable:
  012113ec (pinned handle)
  -> 03ed33a8 System.Object[]
  -> 02ed1fc0 System.Random

Found 1 unique roots (run '!GCRoot -all' to see all roots).
```

To get the address of an object in Windbg, you can dump all of objects on the current stack with the !dso command, or use !DumpHeap to find objects of interest on heap, as in this example:

```
0:004> !DumpHeap -type LargeMemoryUsage.C
 Address       MT    Size
021b17f0 007d3954       12
021b664c 007d3954       12
...

Statistics:
    MT   Count   TotalSize Class Name
007d3954     475        5700 LargeMemoryUsage.C
Total 475 objects
```

!gcroot is often adequate, but it may miss some cases, in particular if your object is rooted from an older generation. For this, you will need to use the !findroots command.

In order for this command to work you first need to set a breakpoint in the GC, right before a collection is about to happen, which you can do by executing:

```
!findroots –gen 0
g
```

This sets a breakpoint right before the next gen 0 GC happens. It then loses effect and you will need to run the command again to break on the following GC.

Once the code breaks, you need to find the object you are interested in and execute this command:

```
!findroots 027624fc
```

If the object is already in a higher generation than the current collection generation, you will see output like this:

```
Object 027624fc will survive this collection:
  gen(0x27624fc) = 1 > 0 = condemned generation.
```

If the object itself is in the current generation being collected, but it has roots from an older generation, you will see something like this:

```
older generations::Root:  027624fc (object)->
  023124d4(System.Collections.Generic.List`1
  [[System.Object, mscorlib]])
```

What Objects Are Being Pinned?

As covered earlier, a performance counter will tell you how many pinned objects the GC encounters during a collection, but that will not help you determine which objects are being pinned.

Use the Pinning sample project, which pins things via explicit fixed statements and by calling some Windows APIs.

Use Windbg to view pinned objects with these commands (including sample output):

```
0:010> !gchandles
  Handle Type       Object    Size    Data Type
...
003511f8 Strong     01fa5dbc    52         System.Threading.Thread
003511fc Strong     01fa1330   112         System.AppDomain
003513ec Pinned     02fa33a8  8176         System.Object[]
003513f0 Pinned     02fa2398  4096         System.Object[]
003513f4 Pinned     02fa2178   528         System.Object[]
003513f8 Pinned     01fa121c    12         System.Object
003513fc Pinned     02fa1020  4420         System.Object[]
003514fc AsyncPinned 01fa3d04    64        System.Threading.OverlappedData
```

You will usually see lots of System.Object[] objects pinned. The CLR uses these arrays internally for things like statics and other pinned objects. In the case above, you can see one AsyncPinned handle. This object is related to the FileSystemWatcher in the sample project.

Unfortunately, the debugger will not tell you why something is pinned, but often you can examine the pinned object and trace it back to the object that is responsible for it.

The following Windbg session demonstrates tracing through object references to find higher-level objects that may give a clue to the origins of the pinned object. Follow the trail of bolded references.

```
0:010> !do 01fa3d04
Name:   System.Threading.OverlappedData
MethodTable: 64535470
EEClass:     646445e0
Size:   64(0x40) bytes
File:
C:\windows\Microsoft.Net\assembly\GAC_32\mscorlib\v4.0_4.0.0.0__b77a5c56193
4e089\mscorlib.dll
Fields:
  MT    Field   Offset    Type VT   Attr   Value Name
64927254  4000700  4   System.IAsyncResult   0 instance 020a7a60
m_asyncResult
64924904  4000701  8   ...ompletionCallback   0 instance 020a7a70 m_iocb
...
0:010> !do 020a7a70
Name:   System.Threading.IOCompletionCallback
MethodTable: 64924904
EEClass:     6463d320
Size:   32(0x20) bytes
File:
C:\windows\Microsoft.Net\assembly\GAC_32\mscorlib\v4.0_4.0.0.0__b77a5c56193
4e089\mscorlib.dll
Fields:
  MT    Field   Offset    Type VT   Attr   Value Name
649326a4  400002d  4   System.Object   0 instance 01fa2bcc _target
...
0:010> !do 01fa2bcc
Name:   System.IO.FileSystemWatcher
MethodTable: 6a6b86c8
EEClass:     6a49c340
Size:   92(0x5c) bytes
File:
C:\windows\Microsoft.Net\assembly\GAC_MSIL\System\v4.0_4.0.0.0__b77a5c56193
4e089\System.dll
Fields:
  MT    Field   Offset    Type VT   Attr   Value Name
649326a4  400019a  4   System.Object   0 instance 00000000 __identity
6a699b44  40002d2  8   ...ponentModel.ISite   0 instance 00000000 site
...
```

While the debugger gives you the maximum power, it is cumbersome at best. Instead, you can use PerfView, which can simplify a lot of the drudgery.

With a PerfView trace, you will see a view called "Pinning at GC Time Stacks" that will show you stacks of the objects being pinned across the observed collections.

Methods that call NonGen2

Name ?
☑ NonGen2
+ ☑ Type System.Byte[]
I + ☑ LikelyAsyncDependentPinned
I I + ☑ GC Location
I I + ☑ Thread (6496) CPU=200ms
I I   + ☑ Process32 Pinning (7748)
I I   + ☑ ROOT

Figure 2-11. PerfView will show you information about what types of objects are pinned across a GC, as well as some information about its likely origin.

You can also approach pinning problems by looking at the free space holes created in the various heaps, which is covered in the next section.

Where Is Fragmentation Occurring?

Fragmentation occurs when there are freed blocks of memory inside segments containing used blocks of memory. Fragmentation can occur at multiple levels, inside a GC heap segment, or at the virtual memory level for the whole process.

Fragmentation in gen 0 is usually not an issue, unless you have a very severe pinning problem where you have pinned so many objects and each block of free space is too small to fulfill any new allocations. This will cause the size of the small object heap to grow and more garbage collections will occur. Fragmentation is usually more of an issue in gen 2 or the large object heap, especially if you are not using background GC. You may see fragmentation rates that seem high, perhaps even 50%, but this is not necessarily an indication of a problem. Consider the size of the overall heap and if it is acceptable and not growing over time, you probably do not need to take action.

GC heap fragmentation is more likely and easy to diagnose. Start by understanding how to do this in Windbg.

Get a list of free blocks with !DumpHeap -type Free:

```
0:010> !DumpHeap -type Free
 Address     MT    Size
02371000 008209f8      10 Free
0237100c 008209f8      10 Free
02371018 008209f8      10 Free
023a1fe8 008209f8      10 Free
023a3fdc 008209f8      22 Free
023abdb4 008209f8     574 Free
023adfc4 008209f8      46 Free
023bbd38 008209f8     698 Free
023bdfe0 008209f8      18 Free
023d19c0 008209f8    1586 Free
023d3fd8 008209f8      26 Free
023e578c 008209f8    2150 Free
...
```

For each block, figure out which heap segment it is in with !eeheap –gc

```
0:010> !eeheap -gc
Number of GC Heaps: 1
generation 0 starts at 0x02371018
generation 1 starts at 0x0237100c
generation 2 starts at 0x02371000
ephemeral segment allocation context: none
    segment        begin    allocated  size
02370000  02371000  02539ff4  0x1c8ff4(1871860)
Large object heap starts at 0x03371000
    segment        begin    allocated  size
03370000  03371000  03375398  0x4398(17304)
Total Size:        Size: 0x1cd38c (1889164) bytes.
------------------------------
GC Heap Size:  Size: 0x1cd38c (1889164) bytes.
```

Dump all of the objects in that segment, or within a narrow range around the free space.

```
0:010> !DumpHeap 0x02371000 02539ff4
 Address     MT    Size
02371000 008209f8      10 Free
0237100c 008209f8      10 Free
02371018 008209f8      10 Free
02371024 713622fc      84
02371078 71362450      84
023710cc 71362494      84
02371120 713624d8      84
02371174 7136251c      84
023711c8 7136251c      84
```

```
0237121c 71362554      12
...
```

This is a manual and tedious process, but it does come in handy and you should understand how to do it. You can write scripts to process the output and generate the Windbg commands for you based on previous output, but CLR Profiler can show you the same information in a graphical, aggregated manner that may be good enough for your needs.

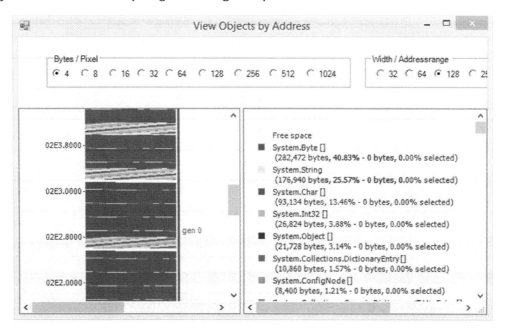

Figure 2-12. CLR Profiler can show you a visual representation of the heap that makes it possible to see what types of objects are next to free space blocks. In this image, the free space blocks are bordered by blocks of System.Byte[] and an assortment of other types.

You may also get virtual memory fragmentation, which can cause the unmanaged allocations to fail because they cannot find a range large enough to satisfy the memory request. This can include allocating a new GC heap segment, which means your managed memory allocations can also fail.

Virtual memory fragmentation is far more likely in 32-bit processes, where you are limited to just two gigabytes of address space for your program by default. The biggest symptom of this is an OutOfMemoryException. The easiest way to fix this is to convert your application to a 64-bit process and reap the 128-terabyte address space. If you cannot do this, your only choice is to become far more efficient in both unmanaged and managed memory allocations. You need to ensure that the heaps can be compacted, and you may need to implement significant pooling.

Use VMMap (part of SysInternals' suite of utilities) to get a visual representation of your process. It will divide the heap into managed, native, and free regions. Selecting the Free portion will show you all segments currently marked as free. If the maximum size is smaller than your requested memory allocation, you will get an `OutOfMemoryException`.

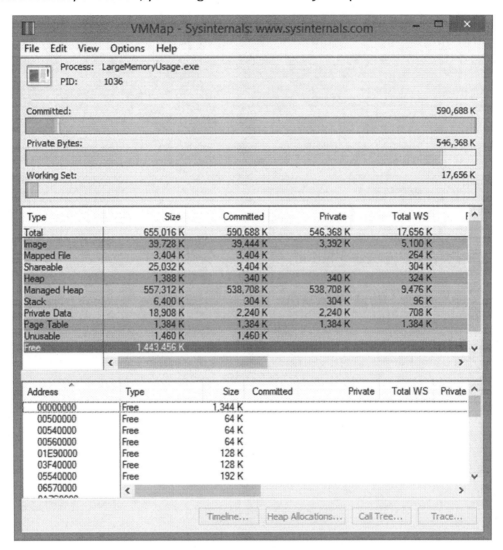

Figure 2-13. VMMap shows you a wealth of memory-related information, including the size of all the free blocks in the address range. In this case, the largest bloc is over 1.3 GB in size—plenty!

VMMap also has a fragmentation view that can show where these blocks fit in the overall process space.

Figure 2-14. VMMap's fragmentation view shows free space in the context of other segments.

You can also retrieve this information in Windbg:

```
!address -summary
```

This command produces this output:

```
...
-- Largest Region by Usage -- Base Address -- Region Size --
Free                26770000    49320000 (1.144 Gb)
...
```

You can retrieve information about specific blocks with the command:

```
!address -f:Free
```

This produces output similar to:

```
BaseAddr EndAddr+1 RgnSize  Type State  Protect       Usage
------------------------------------------------------------
     0   150000   150000    MEM_FREE  PAGE_NOACCESS Free
```

What Generation Is An Object In?

To find the current generation of a specific object, use Windbg. Once you obtain the address of the object of interest (say from !DumpStackObjects or !DumpHeap), use the !gcwhere command:

```
0:003> !gcwhere 02ed1fc0
Address   Gen Heap segment  begin   allocated size
02ed1fc0  1    0  02ed0000 02ed1000 02fe5d4c  0x14(20)
```

You can also retrieve this information from code by using the GC.GetGeneration method and passing it the object in question.

Which Objects Survive Gen 0?

The easiest way to see this is with CLR Profiler. Once you collect a trace, click on the Timeline button in the results summary dialog window. This will bring up a timeline of allocations, color-coded by type. The vertical axis is memory address. GC events are marked so you can see which objects disappear or stick around.

In the following screenshot, you can see a trace of the AllocateAndRelease sample program:

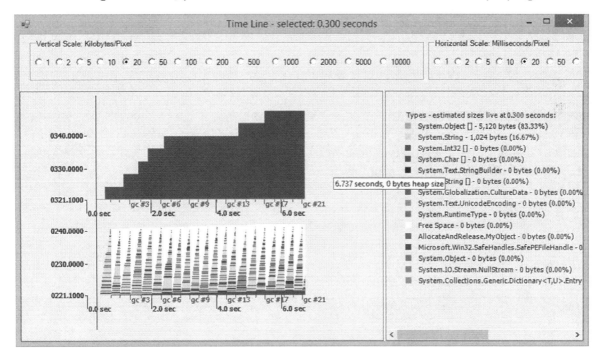

Figure 2-15. CLR Profiler's timeline view makes it easy to see which objects survive garbage collections.

Each GC is marked (gen 0 GCs are marked in red). In the bottom portion of the graph, you can see that many types of objects are being cleaned up on each GC, causing a familiar saw-tooth pattern. There is a slowly growing area of dark green, `System.Char[]`, that is surviving these GCs and being promoted to gen 1. At the top of the graph you see a growing region of `System.Int32[]` allocations. This is the large object heap region, and since there have not been any gen 2 GCs yet, these have not been cleaned up yet.

While CLR Profiler is great for getting an overall picture and it can be your first step in diagnosing these types of problems, sometimes you will just need to get extremely detailed information, perhaps on specific objects. Or perhaps CLR Profiler does not work on your process because of its size or some other limiting factor. In this case, you can use Windbg to see precisely which objects are still around after a GC. With a little bit of scripting work you could even automate this analysis to give you an aggregate picture.

After you have attached Windbg to the process and loaded SOS, execute these commands:

```
!FindRoots –gen 0
g
```

This will set a breakpoint right before the next gen 0 collection begins. Once it breaks, you can send whatever commands you want to dump the objects on the heap. You can simply do:

```
!DumpHeap
```

This will dump every object on the heap, which may be excessive. Optionally, you can add the –stat parameter to limit output to a summary of the found objects (their counts, sizes, and types). However, if you want to limit your analysis to just gen 0, the !DumpHeap command allows you to specify an address range. This begs the question: How do you find the address range for the gen 0 heap? There is another SOS command that will give this to you. Recall the description of memory segments from the top of the chapter. A basic segment is laid out like this:

Gen 2	Gen 1	Gen 0

Note than Gen 0 is at the end of the segment, and its end is the segment's end. Refer back to the beginning of this chapter for more information.

To get a list of heaps and segments, you can use the eeheap –gc command:

```
0:003> !eeheap -gc
Number of GC Heaps: 1
generation 0 starts at 0x02ef0400
generation 1 starts at 0x02ed100c
generation 2 starts at 0x02ed1000
ephemeral segment allocation context: none
     segment   begin   allocated   size
02ed0000  02ed1000  02fe5d4c  0x114d4c(1133900)
Large object heap starts at 0x03ed1000
     segment   begin     allocated   size
03ed0000  03ed1000  041e2898  0x311898(3217560)
Total Size:        Size: 0x4265e4 (4351460) bytes.
------------------------------
GC Heap Size:   Size: 0x4265e4 (4351460) bytes.
```

This command will give you a printout of each generation and each segment. The segment that contains gen 0 and gen 1 is called the ephemeral segment. !eeheap tells you the start of gen 0. To get the end of it, you merely need to find the segment that contains the start address. Each segment contains a number of addresses and the length. In the example above, the ephemeral segment starts at 02ed0000 and ends at 02fe5d4c. Therefore, the range of gen 0 on this heap is 02ef0400 - 02fe5d4c.

Now that you know this, you can put some limits on the DumpHeap command and print only the objects in gen 0:

```
!DumpHeap 02ef0400 02fe5d4c
```

Once you have done that, you will want to compare what happens as soon as the GC is complete. This is a little trickier. You will need to set a breakpoint on an internal CLR method. This method is called when the CLR is ready to resume managed code. If you are using workstation GC, call:

```
bp clr!WKS::GCHeap::RestartEE
```

For server GC:

```
bp clr!SVR::GCHeap::RestartEE
```

Once you have set the breakpoints, continue execution (F5 or the 'g' command). Once the GC is complete, the program will break again and you can repeat the !eeheap –gc and !DumpHeap commands.

Now you have two sets of outputs and you can compare them to see what changed and which objects are remaining after a GC. By using the other commands and techniques in this section, you can see who maintains a reference to that object.

> **Note** If you use server GC, then remember there will be multiple heaps. To do this kind of analysis, you will need to repeat the commands for each heap. The !eeheap command will print information for every heap in the process.

Who is Calling GC.Collect Explicitly?

In Windbg, set a managed breakpoint on the GC class's Collect method:

```
!bpmd mscorlib.dll System.GC.Collect
```

Continue executing. Once the breakpoint is hit, to see the stack trace of who called the explicit collection, do:

```
!DumpStack
```

What Weak References Are In My Process?

Because weak references are a type of GC handle, you can use the !gchandles command in Windbg to find them:

```
0:003> !gchandles
PDB symbol for clr.dll not loaded
  Handle Type        Object  Size  Data Type
006b12f4 WeakShort   022a3c8c  100    System.Diagnostics.Tracing...
006b12fc WeakShort   022a3afc  52   System.Threading.Thread
006b10f8 WeakLong    022a3ddc  32   Microsoft.Win32.UnsafeNati...
006b11d0 Strong      022a3460  48   System.Object[]
...

Handles:
  Strong Handles:       11
  Pinned Handles:       5
  Weak Long Handles:    1
  Weak Short Handles:    2
```

The difference between Weak Long and Weak Short is mostly unimportant for this discussion, but Weak Long handles track whether a finalized object has been resurrected. Resurrection can occur when an object has been finalized, and rather than letting the GC clean it up, you decide to reuse it. This can be relevant for pooling scenarios. However, it is possible to do pooling without finalization, and given the complexities of resurrection, just avoid this in favor of deterministic methods.

Summary

You need to understand garbage collection in-depth to truly optimize your applications. Choose the right configuration settings for your application, such as server GC if your application is the only one running on the machine. Ensure that object lifetime is short, allocation rates are low, and that any objects that must live longer than the average GC frequency are pooled or otherwise kept alive in gen 2 forever.

Avoid pinning and finalizers if possible. Any LOH allocations should be pooled and kept around forever to avoid full GCs. Reduce LOH fragmentation by keeping objects a uniform size and occasionally compacting the heap on-demand. Consider GC notifications to avoid having full collections impact application processing at inopportune times.

The garbage collector is a deterministic component and you can control its operation by closely managing your object allocation rate and lifetime. You are not giving up control by adopting .NET's garbage collector, but it does require a little more subtlety and analysis.

3 JIT Compilation

.NET code is distributed as assemblies of Microsoft Intermediate Language (MSIL, or just IL for short). This language is somewhat assembly-like, but simpler. If you wish to learn more about IL or other CLR standards, see the extensive documentation Microsoft provides at http://www.writinghighperf.net/go/17.

When your managed program executes, it loads the CLR which will start executing some wrapper code. This is all assembly code. The first time a managed method is called from your assembly, it actually runs a stub that executes the Just-in-Time (JIT) compiler which will convert the IL for that method to the hardware's assembly instructions. This process is called just-in-time compilation ("JITting"). The stub is replaced and the next time that method is called, the assembly instructions are called directly. This means, the first time any method is called, there is always a performance hit. In most cases, this hit is small and can be ignored. Every time after that, the code executes directly and incurs no overhead.

This process can be summarized in the following diagram:

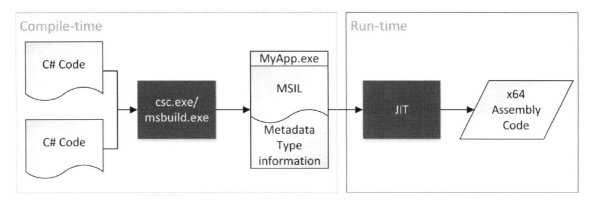

Figure 3-1. Compilation and JITting flow.

While all code in a method will be converted to assembly instructions when JITted, some pieces may be placed into "cold" code sections of memory, separate from the method's normal execution path. These rarely executed paths will thus not push out other code from the "warm" sections, allowing for better overall performance as the commonly executed code is kept in memory, but the cold pages may be paged out. For this reason, rarely used things like error and exception-handling paths can be expensive.

In most cases, a method will only need to be JITted once. The exception is when the method has generic type arguments. In this case, the JIT may be called for each invocation with a different type parameter.

You need to be concerned about JIT costs if this first-time warm-up cost is important to your application or its users. Most applications only care about steady-state performance, but if you must have extremely high-availability, JIT can be an issue that you will need to optimize for. This chapter will tell you how.

Benefits of JIT Compilation

Code that is just-in-time compiled has some significant advantages over compiled unmanaged code.

1. Good Locality of Reference—Code that is used together will often be in the same page of memory, preventing expensive page faults.
2. Reduced Memory Usage—It only compiles those methods that are actually used.
3. Cross-assembly Inlining—Methods from other DLLs, including the .NET Framework, can be inlined into your own application, which can be a significant savings.

There is also a benefit of hardware-specific optimizations, but in practice there are only a few actual optimizations for specific platforms. However, it is becoming increasingly possible to target multiple platforms with the same code, and it is likely we will see more aggressive platform-specific optimizations in the future.

Most code optimizations in .NET do not take place in the language compiler (the transformation from C#/VB.NET to IL). Rather, they occur on-the-fly in the JIT compiler.

Costs of JIT Compilation

You can easily see the IL-to-assembly-code transformation in action. As a simple example, here is the JitCall sample program that demonstrates the code fix up that JIT does behind the scenes:

```
static void Main(string[] args)
{
  int val = A();
  int val2 = A();
  Console.WriteLine(val + val2);
}

[MethodImpl(MethodImplOptions.NoInlining)]
static int A()
{
  return 42;
}
```

To see what happens, first get the disassembly of Main. Getting to this point is a little bit of a trick.

1. Launch Windbg.
2. File | Open Executable... (Ctrl+E).
3. Navigate to the JitCall binary. Make sure you pick the Release version of the binary or the assembly code will look quite different than what is printed here.
4. The debugger will immediately break.
5. Run the command: sxe ld clrjit. This will cause the debugger to break when clrjit.dll is loaded. This is convenient because once this is loaded you can set a breakpoint on the Main method before it is executed.
6. Run the command: g.
7. The program will execute until clrjit.dll is loaded and you see output similar to the following:

```
(1a74.2790): Unknown exception - code 04242420 (first chance)
ModLoad: 6fe50000 6fecd000
    C:\Windows\Microsoft.NET\Framework\v4.0.30319\clrjit.dll
```

8. Run the command: .loadby sos clr.
9. Run the command: !bpmd JitCall Program.Main. This sets the breakpoint at the beginning of the Main function.
10. Run the command: g.
11. Windbg will break right inside the Main method. You should see output similar to this:

```
(11b4.10f4): CLR notification exception - code e0444143 (first chance)
JITTED JitCall!JitCall.Program.Main(System.String[])
Setting breakpoint: bp 007A0050 [JitCall.Program.Main(System.String[])]
Breakpoint 0 hit
```

12. Now open the Disassembly window (Alt+7). You may also find the Registers window interesting (Alt+4).

The disassembly of `Main` looks like this:

```
push    ebp
mov     ebp,esp
push    edi
push    esi

; Call A
call    dword ptr ds:[0E537B0h] ds:002b:00e537b0=00e5c015
mov     edi,eax
call    dword ptr ds:[0E537B0h]
mov     esi,eax

call    mscorlib_ni+0x340258 (712c0258)
mov     ecx,eax
add     edi,esi
mov     edx,edi
mov     eax,dword ptr [ecx]
mov     eax,dword ptr [eax+38h]

; Call Console.WriteLine
call    dword ptr [eax+14h]
pop     esi
pop     edi
pop     ebp
ret
```

There are two calls to the same pointer. This is the function call to A. Set break points on both of these lines and start stepping through the code one instruction at a time, making sure to step into the calls. This pointer at 0E537B0h will get updated after the first call.

Stepping into the first call to A, you can see that it is little more than a `jmp` to the CLR method ThePreStub. There is no return from this method here because `ThePreStub` will do the return.

```
mov     al,3
jmp     00e5c01d
mov     al,6
jmp     00e5c01d
(00e5c01d) movzx   eax,al
shl     eax,2
add     eax,0E5379Ch
jmp     clr!ThePreStub (72102af6)
```

On the second call to A, you can see that the function address of the original pointer was updated and the code at the new location looks more like a real method. Notice the 2Ah (our decimal 42 constant value from the source) being assigned and returned via the eax register.

```
012e0090 55          push   ebp
012e0091 8bec        mov    ebp,esp
012e0093 b82a000000      mov    eax,2Ah
012e0098 5d          pop    ebp
012e0099 c3          ret
```

For most applications, this first-time, or warm-up, cost is not significant, but there are certain types of code that lend themselves to high JIT time, which we will examine in the next few sections.

As an exercise, what happens to the JITted code when you remove the NoInlining attribute from A? You should see a few compiler optimizations in action.

JIT Compiler Optimizations

The JIT compiler will perform some standard optimizations such as method inlining and array range check elimination, but there are things now that you should be aware of that can prevent the JIT compiler from optimizing your code. Some of these topics have their own treatments in Chapter 5. Note that because the JIT compiler executes during runtime, it is limited in how much time it can spend doing optimizations. Despite this, it can do many important optimizations.

One of the biggest classes of optimizations is method inlining, which puts the code from the method body into the call site, avoiding a method call in the first place. Inlining is critical for small methods which are called frequently, where the overhead of a function call is larger than the function's own code.

All of these things prevent inlining:

- Virtual methods.
- Interfaces with diverse implementations in a single call site. See Chapter 5 for a discussion of the interface dispatch problem.
- Loops.
- Exception handling.
- Recursion.
- Method bodies larger than 32 bytes of IL.

As of the time of this writing, the next version of the JIT, code-named RyuJIT, features significantly improved code generation performance as well as improved generated code quality, particularly for 64-bit code. Read more at http://www.writinghighperf.net/go/18. RyuJIT has been released as Community Technology Preview (CTP) which you can test out now.

Reducing JIT and Startup Time

The other major factor in considering the JIT compiler is the amount of time it takes to generate the code. This mostly comes down to a factor of how much code needs to be JITted.

In particular, be careful of the use of:

- LINQ
- The dynamic keyword
- Regular expressions
- Code generation

All of these have a simple fact in common: Much more code is possibly hidden from you and actually executed than is obvious from your source. All of that hidden code may require significant time to be JITted. With regular expressions and generated code in particular, there is likely to be a pattern of large, repetitive blocks of code.

While code generation is usually something you would write for your own purposes, there are some areas of the .NET Framework that will do this for you, the most common being regular expressions. Before execution, regular expressions are converted to an IL state machine in a dynamic assembly and then JITted. This takes more time up front, but saves a lot of with repeated execution. You usually want to enable this option, but you probably want to defer it until it is needed so that the extra compilation does not impact application start time. Regular expressions can also trigger some complex algorithms in the JIT that take longer than normal, most of which are improved in RyuJIT. As with everything else in the book, the only way to know for sure is to measure. See Chapter 6 for more discussion of regular expressions.

Even though code generation is implicated as a potential exacerbation of JIT challenges, as we will see in Chapter 5, code generation in a different context can get you out of some other performance issues.

LINQ's syntactic simplicity can belie the amount of code that actually runs for each query. It can also hide things like delegate creation, memory allocations, and more. Simple LINQ queries may be ok, but as in most things, you should definitely measure.

The primary issue with dynamic code is, again, the sheer amount of code that it translates to. Jump to Chapter 5 to see what dynamic code looks like under the covers.

There are other factors besides JIT, such as I/O, that can increase your warm-up costs, and it behooves you to do an accurate investigation before assuming JIT is the only issue. Each assembly has a cost in terms of disk access for reading the file, internal overhead in the CLR data structures, and type loading. You may be able to reduce some of the load time by combining many small assemblies into one large one, but type loading is likely to consume as much time as JITting.

If you do have a lot of JIT happening, you should see stacks like the following show up in CPU profiles of your application:

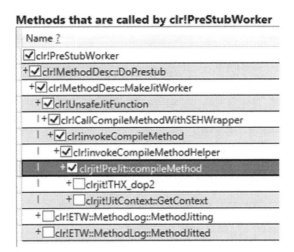

Figure 3-2. PerfView's CPU profiling will show you any JIT stubs that are being called.

Also see the Measurement section in this chapter for a demonstration of how PerfView can show you exactly which methods are being JITted and how long each one took.

Optimizing JITting with Profiling

.NET 4.5 includes an API that tells .NET to profile your application's startup and store the results on disk for future references. On subsequent startups, this profile is used to start generating the assembly code before it is executed. This happens in a separate thread. The saved profiles allow this generated code to have all the same benefits of locality as JITting. The profiles are updated automatically on each execution of your program.

To use it, simply call this at the beginning of your program:

```
ProfileOptimization.SetProfileRoot(@"C:\MyAppProfile");
ProfileOptimization.StartProfile("default");
```

Note that the profile root folder must already exist, and you can name your profiles, which is useful if your app has different modes with substantially different execution profiles.

When to Use NGEN

NGEN stands for Native Image Generator. It works by converting your IL assembly to a native image—in effect, running the JIT compiler and saving the results to a native image assembly cache. This native image should not be confused with native code in the sense of unmanaged code. Despite the fact that the image is now mostly assembly language, it is still a managed assembly because it must run under the CLR.

If your original assembly is called foo.dll, NGEN will generate a file called foo.ni.dll and put it in the native image cache. Whenever foo.dll is loaded, the CLR will inspect the cache for a matching .ni. file and verify that it matches the IL exactly. It does this using a combination of time stamps, name, and GUIDs to 100% ensure that it is the correct file to load.

In general, NGEN should be your last resort. While it has its place, it does have some disadvantages. The first is that you lose locality of reference, as all the code in an assembly is placed sequentially, regardless of how it is actually executed. In addition, you can lose certain optimizations such as cross-assembly inlining. You can get most of these optimizations back if all of the assemblies are available to NGEN at the same time.

That said, if application startup or warm-up costs are too high and the profile optimization mentioned above does not satisfy your performance requirements, then NGEN may be appropriate. Before making such a decision, remember the prime directive of performance: **Measure, Measure, Measure**! See the tips at the end of this chapter for how to measure JIT costs in your application.

NGENed applications can have an advantage in faster load time, but there are drawbacks. You must also update the native images every time there is a change—not a big deal, but an extra step for deployment. NGEN can be very slow and native images can be significantly larger than their managed counterparts. Sometimes, JIT will produce more optimized code, especially for commonly executed paths.

Most usages of generics can be successfully NGENed, but there are cases where the compiler cannot figure out the right generic types ahead of time. This code will still be JITted at runtime.

And of course, any time you rely on dynamically type loading or generation, those pieces cannot always be NGENed ahead of time.

To NGEN an assembly from the command line, execute this command:

```
D:\Book\ReflectionExe\bin\Release>ngen install ReflectionExe.exe

1> Compiling assembly D:\Book\ReflectionExe\bin\Release\ReflectionExe.exe
(CLR v4.0.30319) ...
2> Compiling assembly ReflectionInterface, Version=1.0.0.0,
Culture=neutral, PublicKeyToken=null (CLR v4.0.30319) ...
```

From the output you see that there are actually two files being processed. NGEN will automatically look in the target file's directory and NGEN any dependencies it finds. It does this by default to allow the code to make cross-assembly calls in an efficient away (such as inlining small methods). You can suppress this behavior with the /NoDependencies flag, but there may be a significant performance hit during runtime.

To remove an assembly's native image from the machine's native image cache, you can run:

```
D:\Book\ReflectionExe\bin\Release>ngen uninstall ReflectionExe.exe

Uninstalling assembly D:\Book\ReflectionExe\bin\Release\ReflectionExe.exe
```

You can verify that a native image was created by displaying the native image cache:

```
D:\Book\ReflectionExe\bin\Release>ngen display ReflectionExe

NGEN Roots:
D:\Book\ReflectionExe\bin\Release\ReflectionExe.exe
NGEN Roots that depend on "ReflectionExe":
D:\Book\ReflectionExe\bin\Release\ReflectionExe.exe
Native Images:
ReflectionExe, Version=1.0.0.0, Culture=neutral, PublicKeyToken=null
```

You can also display all cached native images by running the command ngen display.

Optimizing NGEN images

I said above that one of the things you lose with NGEN is locality of reference. Starting with .NET 4.5, you can use a tool called Managed Profile Guided Optimization (MPGO) to fix this problem to a large extent. Similar to Profile Optimization for JIT, this is a tool that you manually run to profile your application's startup (or whatever scenario you want). NGEN will then use the profile to create a native image that is better optimized for the common function chains.

MPGO is included with Visual Studio 2012 and higher. To use, run the command:

```
Mpgo.exe -scenario MyApp.exe -assemblyList *.* -OutDir c:\Optimized
```

This will cause MPGO to run on some framework assemblies and then it will execute MyApp.exe. Now the application is in training mode. You should exercise the application appropriately and then shut it down. This will cause a new, optimized assembly to be created in the C:\Optimized directory.

To take advantage of the optimized assembly, you must run NGEN on it:

```
Ngen.exe install C:\Optimized\MyApp.exe
```

This will create optimized images in the native image cache. Next time the application is run, these new images will be used.

To use the MPGO tool effectively, you will need to incorporate it into your build system so that its output is what gets shipped with your application.

The Future of Native Code Generation

On April 2, 2014, Microsoft announced the .NET Native Developer Preview. This is a technology that radically changes how the CLR works by statically linking core framework libraries into applications. It completely removes the need for JIT and uses the Visual C++ compiler optimizer to produce extremely high quality assembly code in a small footprint. In effect, we get to have our cake and eat it too—all the benefits of rapid development in .NET as well as a native image that needs no JITting at runtime!

The bad news is that this only works for Windows Store apps now, but I am hopeful that the target platform will expand to eventually include all .NET applications.

When JIT Can't Compete

The JIT is great for most applications. If there are performance problems, there are usually bigger issues than pure code generation quality or speed. However, there are some areas where the JIT has room to improve.

For example, there are some processor instructions the JIT will not use, even though they are available on the current processor. A big example is much of the category of SSE or SIMD instructions which execute a single set of instructions across multiple data sets. Most modern x64-platform processors from both Intel and AMD support these instructions, and they are critical for parallel computations required in things like gaming and scientific and mathematical computation. The current JIT compiler as of this writing (4.5.2) makes very limited use of these instructions and registers, but the good news is that RyuJIT will support more SIMD instructions with SSE2, bringing many of these advantages to the managed world.

The other major situation where the JIT compiler is not going to be quite as good as a native code compiler is with direct native memory access vs. managed array access. For one, accessing native memory directly usually means you can avoid the memory copy that will come with marshalling it to managed code. While there are ways around this with things like UnmanagedMemoryStream, which will wrap a native buffer inside a Stream, you are really just making an unsafe memory access.

If you do transfer the bytes to a managed buffer, the code that accesses the buffer will have boundary checks. In many cases, these checks can be optimized away, but it is not guaranteed. With managed buffers, you can wrap a pointer around them and do some unsafe access to get around some of these checks.

With applications that do an extreme amount of array or matrix manipulation, you will have to consider this tradeoff between performance and safety. For most applications, frankly, you will not have to care and the boundary checks are not a significant overhead.

If you find that native code really is more efficient at this kind of processing, you can try marshalling the entire data set to a native function via P/Invoke, compute the results with a highly optimized C++ DLL, and then return the results back to managed code. You will have to profile to see if the data transfer cost is worth it.

Mature C++ compilers may also be better at other types of optimizations such as inlining or optimal register usage, but this is more likely to change with RyuJIT and future versions of the JIT compiler.

Measurement

Performance Counters

The CLR publishes a number of counters in the .NET CLR Jit category, including:

- # of IL Bytes Jitted
- # of Methods Jitted
- % Time in Jit
- IL Bytes Jitted / sec

- Standard Jit Failures
- Total # of IL Bytes Jitted (exactly the same as "# of IL Bytes Jitted")

Those are all fairly self-explanatory except Standard Jit Failures. Failures can occur only if the IL is unverified or there is an internal JIT error.

Closely related to JITting, there is also a category for loading, called .NET CLR Loading. A few of them are:

- % Time Loading
- Bytes in Loader Heap
- Total Assemblies
- Total Classes Loaded

ETW Events

With ETW events, you can get extremely detailed performance information on every single method that gets JITted in your process, including the IL size, native size, and the amount of time it took to JIT.

- **MethodJittingStarted**—A method is being JIT-compiled. Fields include:
    - MethodID—Unique ID for this method.
    - ModuleID—Unique ID for the module to which this method belongs.
    - MethodILSize—Size of the method's IL.
    - MethodNameSpace—Full class name to which this method belongs.
    - MethodName—Name of the method.
    - MethodSignature—Comma-separated list of type names from the method signature.
- **MethodLoad**—A method is done JITting and has been loaded. Generic and dynamic methods do not use this version. Fields include:
    - MethodID—Unique ID for this method.
    - ModuleID—Unique ID for this module to which this method belongs.
    - MethodSize—Size of the compiled assembly code after JIT.
    - MethodStartAddress—Start address of the method.
    - MethodFlags:
        - 0x1—Dynamic method
        - 0x2—Generic method
        - 0x4—JIT-compiled (if missing, it was NGENed)
        - 0x8—Helper method
- **MethodLoadVerbose**—A generic or dynamic method has been JITted and loaded.

o   It has most of the same fields as MethodLoad and MethodJittingStarted.

What Methods and Modules Take the Longest To JIT?

In general, JIT time is directly proportional to the amount of IL instructions in a method, but this is complicated by the fact that type loading time can also be included in this time, especially the first time a module is used. Some patterns can also trigger complex algorithms in the JIT compiler, which may run longer. You can use PerfView to get very detailed information about JITting activity in your process. If you collect the standard .NET events, you will get a special view called "JITStats." Here is some of the output from running it on the PerfCountersTypingSpeed sample project:

Name	JitTime msec	Num Methods	IL Size	Native Size
PerfCountersTypingSpeed.exe	12.9	8	1,756	3,156

JitTime msec	IL Size	Native Size	Method Name
9.7	22	45	PerfCountersTypingSpeed.Program.Main()
0.3	176	313	PerfCountersTypingSpeed.Form1..ctor()
1.4	1,236	2,178	PerfCountersTypingSpeed.Form1.InitializeComponent()
0.8	107	257	PerfCountersTypingSpeed.Form1.CreateCustomCategories()
0.3	143	257	PerfCountersTypingSpeed.Form1.timer_Tick(class System.Object,class System.EventArgs)
0.1	23	27	PerfCountersTypingSpeed.Form1.OnKeyPress(class System.Object,class System.Windows.Forms.KeyPressEventArgs)
0.2	19	36	PerfCountersTypingSpeed.Form1.OnClosing(class System.ComponentModel.CancelEventArgs)
0.1	30	43	PerfCountersTypingSpeed.Form1.Dispose(bool)

The only method that takes more time to JIT than its IL size would suggest is Main, which makes sense because this is where you will pay for more loading costs.

Summary

To minimize the impact of JIT, carefully consider large amounts of generated code, whether from regular expressions, code generation, dynamic, or any other source. Use profile-guided optimization to decrease application startup time by pre-JITting the most useful code in parallel.

To encourage function inlining, avoid things like virtual methods, loops, exception handling, recursion, or large method bodies. But do not sacrifice the integrity of your application by over-optimizing in this area.

Consider using NGEN for large applications or situations where you cannot afford the JIT cost during startup. Use MPGO to optimize the native images before using NGEN.

4 Asynchronous Programming

With the ubiquity of multicore processors in today's computers, even on small devices such as cell phones, the ability to program effectively for multiple threads is a critical skill for all programmers.

There are essentially three reasons for using multiple threads:

1. You do not want to block the main thread of a UI with some background work.
2. You have so much work to do that you cannot afford to waste CPU time waiting for I/O to complete.
3. You want to use all of the processors at your disposal.

The first reason does not have as much to do with performance as it does with not annoying the end user, which is vitally important, but is not the primary focus of this book. This chapter will focus on optimizing the second and third situations, which is all about efficient use of computing resources.

Computer processors have effectively hit a wall in terms of raw clock speed. The main technique we are going to use in the foreseeable future to achieve higher computing throughput is parallelism. Taking advantage of multiple processors is critical to writing a high-performance application, particularly servers handling many simultaneous requests.

There are a few ways to execute code concurrently in .NET. For example, you can manually spin up a thread and assign it a method to run. This is fine for a relatively long-running method, but for many things, dealing with threads directly is very inefficient. If you want to execute a lot of short-running tasks, for example, the overhead of scheduling individual threads could easily outweigh the cost of actually running your code. To understand why, you need to know how threads are scheduled in Windows.

Each processor can execute only a single thread at a time. When it comes time to schedule a thread for a processor, Windows needs to do a context switch. During a context switch, Windows saves the processor's current thread's state to the operating system's internal thread object, picks from all the ready threads, transfers the thread's context information from the thread object to the processor, and then finally starts it executing. If Windows switches to a thread from a different process, even more expense is incurred as the address space is swapped out.

The thread will then execute the code for the thread quantum, which is a multiple of the clock interval (the clock interval is about 15 milliseconds on current multiprocessor systems). When the code returns from the top of its stack, enters a wait state, or the time quantum is expired, the scheduler will pick another ready thread to execute. It may be the same thread, or not, depending on the contention for the processors. A thread can enter a wait state if it blocks on I/O of any kind, or voluntarily enters this state by calling Thread.Sleep.

> **Note** Windows Server has a higher thread quantum than the desktop version of Windows, meaning it runs threads for longer periods of times before a context switch. This setting can be controlled to some extent in the Performance Options of Advanced System Settings.
>
>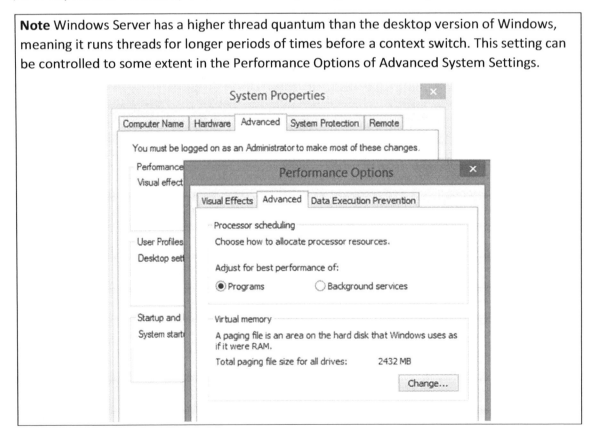

> Setting the option to "Background services" will increase the default thread quantum for the system, possibly at the expense of program responsiveness. These settings are stored in the registry, but you should not manipulate them directly.

Creating new threads is an expensive procedure. It requires allocation in the kernel, the creation of stack space, and more context switching. For these reasons, .NET manages a thread pool for each managed process. These threads are created as needed and stick around to handle future needs, avoiding the recreation cost. See http://www.writinghighperf.net/go/19 for a good discussion of how the thread pool works. The program saves on the overhead of creation and deletion and there is almost always a thread ready to handle the asynchronous tasks that come up. The thread pool handles explicit worker thread tasks that run delegates as well as I/O completions (such as what happens when the file you requested from disk is now ready) from the underlying operating system.

If your program consists of pure CPU tasks longer than the length of the thread quantum, then creating and using threads directly is acceptable, though unnecessary as we will see. However, if your code consists of many smaller tasks that are unlikely to take this long, using threads directly is inefficient because the program will spend a significant time context switching rather than executing its actual code. While you can utilize the thread pool directly, it is no longer recommended to do so and I will not cover it here. Instead, you can use Tasks for both long and short actions.

Use Tasks

.NET 4.0 introduced an abstraction of threads called the Task Parallel Library (TPL), which is the preferred way of achieving parallelism in your code. The TPL gives you a lot of control over how your code is run, allows you to determine what happens when errors occur, provides the ability to conditionally chain multiple methods in sequence, and much more.

Internally, the TPL uses the .NET thread pool, but does so more efficiently, executing multiple Tasks on the same thread sequentially before returning the thread back to the pool. It can do this via intelligent use of delegate objects. This effectively avoids the problem described previously of wasting a thread's quantum with a single small task and causing too many context switches.

TPL is a large and comprehensive set of APIs, but it is easy to get started. The basic principle is that you pass a delegate to the Task's Start method. You also optionally call ContinueWith on the Task and pass a second delegate, which is executed once the Task is complete.

You can execute Tasks with both CPU-bound computations as well as I/O. All of these first examples will show pure CPU processing. There is a section dedicated to effective I/O later in this chapter.

The following code listing from the Tasks sample project demonstrates creating a Task for each processor. When each Task completes, it schedules for execution a continuation Task that has a reference to a callback method.

```csharp
class Program
{
  static Stopwatch watch = new Stopwatch();
  static int pendingTasks;

  static void Main(string[] args)
  {
    const int MaxValue = 1000000000;

    watch.Restart();
    int numTasks = Environment.ProcessorCount;
    pendingTasks = numTasks;
    int perThreadCount = MaxValue / numTasks;
    int perThreadLeftover = MaxValue % numTasks;

    var tasks = new Task<long>[numTasks];

    for (int i = 0; i < numTasks; i++)
    {
      int start = i * perThreadCount;
      int end = (i + 1) * perThreadCount;
      if (i == numTasks - 1)
      {
        end += perThreadLeftover;
      }
      tasks[i] = Task<long>.Run(() =>
      {
        long threadSum = 0;
        for (int j = start; j <= end; j++)
        {
          threadSum += (long)Math.Sqrt(j);
        }
        return threadSum;
      });
      tasks[i].ContinueWith(OnTaskEnd);
    }
  }
}
```

```
  private static void OnTaskEnd(Task<long> task)
  {
    Console.WriteLine("Thread sum: {0}", task.Result);
    if (Interlocked.Decrement(ref pendingTasks) == 0)
    {
      watch.Stop();
      Console.WriteLine("Tasks: {0}", watch.Elapsed);
    }
  }
}
```

If your continuation Task is a fast, short piece of code, you should specify that it runs on the same thread as its owning Task. This is vitally important in an extremely multithreaded system as it can be a significant waste to spend time queuing Tasks to execute on a separate thread which may involve a context switch.

```
task.ContinueWith(OnTaskEnd,
    TaskContinuationOptions.ExecuteSynchronously);
```

If the continuation Task is called back on an I/O thread, then you might not want to use TaskContinuationOptions.ExecuteSynchronously, as this could tie up an I/O thread that you need for pulling data off the network. As always, you will need to experiment and measure the result carefully. It is often more efficient for the I/O thread to just do the quick continuation work and avoid the extra scheduling.

If do need a long-running Task, you can create it with the TaskCreationOptions.LongRunning flag with the Task.Factory.StartNew method. There is also a version of this flag for continuations:

```
var task = Task.Factory.StartNew(action,
            TaskCreationOptions.LongRunning);
task.ContinueWith(OnTaskEnd, TaskContinuationOptions.LongRunning);
```

Continuations are the real power of the TPL. You can do all sorts of complex things that are outside the scope of performance and I will mention a few of them briefly here.

You can execute multiple continuations for a single Task:

```
Task task = ...
task.ContinueWith(OnTaskEnd);
task.ContinueWith(OnTaskEnd2);
```

OnTaskEnd and OnTaskEnd2 have no relationship with each other and execute independently, in parallel.

On the other hand, you can also chain continuations:

```
Task task = ...
task.ContinueWith(OnTaskEnd).ContinueWith(OnTaskEnd2);
```

Chained continuations have serial dependency relationships with each other. When task ends, OnTaskEnd will run. Once that completes, OnTaskEnd2 will execute.

Continuations can be told to execute only when their antecedent Task ends successfully (or fails, or is canceled, etc.):

```
Task task = ...
task.ContinueWith(OnTaskEnd,
TaskContinuationOptions.OnlyOnRanToCompletion);
task.ContinueWith(OnTaskEnd, TaskContinuationOptions.NotOnFaulted);
```

You can invoke a continuation only when multiple Tasks are completed (or any one of them has):

```
Task[] tasks = ...
Task.Factory.ContinueWhenAll(tasks, OnAllTaskEnded);
Task.Factory.ContinueWhenAny(tasks, OnAnyTaskEnded);
```

To cancel a Task that is already running requires some cooperation. It is never a good idea to force-terminate a thread, and the Task Parallel Library does not allow you to access the underlying thread, let alone abort it. (If you do program directly with a Thread object, then you can call the Abort method, but this dangerous and not recommended. Just pretend this API does not exist.)

To cancel a Task, you need to pass the Task's delegate a CancellationToken object which it can then poll to determine if it needs to end processing. This example also demonstrates using a lambda expression as a Task delegate.

```
static void Main(string[] args)
{
  var tokenSource = new CancellationTokenSource();
  CancellationToken token = tokenSource.Token;

  Task task = Task.Run(() =>
  {
    while (true)
    {
      // do some work...
      if (token.IsCancellationRequested)
      {
```

```
            Console.WriteLine("Cancellation requested");
            return;
        }
        Thread.Sleep(100);
    }
}, token);

Console.WriteLine("Press any key to exit");

Console.ReadKey();

tokenSource.Cancel();

task.Wait();

Console.WriteLine("Task completed");
}
```

You can find this code in the sample TaskCancellation project.

Parallel Loops

One of the examples in the previous section demonstrates a pattern that is so common that there is an API just for parallel execution of loops.

```
long sum = 0;
Parallel.For(0, MaxValue, (i) =>
  {
     Interlocked.Add(ref sum, (long)Math.Sqrt(i));
  });
```

There is also a version for foreach for handling generic IEnumerable<T> collections.

```
var urls = new List<string>
{
  @"http://www.microsoft.com",
  @"http://www.bing.com",
  @"http://msdn.microsoft.com"
};
var results = new ConcurrentDictionary<string,string>();
var client = new System.Net.WebClient();

Parallel.ForEach(urls, url => results[url] =
     client.DownloadString(url));
```

If you want to interrupt loop processing, you can pass a `ParallelLoopState` object to the loop delegate. There are two options for stopping the loop:

- Break—Tells the loop not to execute any iterations that are sequentially greater than the current iteration. In a `Parallel.For` loop, if you call `ParallelLoopState.Break` on the ith iteration then any iterations less than i will still be allowed to run, but any iterations greater than i will be prevented from running. This also works on a `Parallel.ForEach` loop, but each item is assigned an index, and this may be arbitrary from the program's point of view. Note that it is possible for multiple loop iterations to call Break, depending on the logic you code inside the loop.
- Stop—Tells the loop not to execute any more iterations at all.

The following example uses Break to stop the loop at an arbitrary location.

```
Parallel.ForEach(urls, (url, loopState) =>
{
  if (url.Contains("bing"))
  {
    loopState.Break();
  }
  results[url] = client.DownloadString(url);
});
```

When using parallel loops, you want to ensure that the amount of work you do per iteration is significantly larger than the amount of time you spend synchronizing any shared state. It is very easy to lose all of the benefits of parallelism if your loop spends all of its time blocked on access to a variable that all the loops use. You can avoid this by having each your loops iterate on local state as much as possible.

Another problem with parallel loops is that a delegate is invoked for each iteration, which may be wasteful if the work to be done is less than the cost of a delegate or method invocation (See Chapter 5).

Both problems can be solved with the `Partitioner` class which transforms a range into a set of `Tuple` objects that describe a range to be iterated over on the original collection.

The following example demonstrates just how much synchronization can negatively affect the effectiveness of parallelism.

```
static void Main(string[] args)
{
  Stopwatch watch = new Stopwatch();
  const int MaxValue = 1000000000;
```

```
long sum = 0;

// Naive For-loop
watch.Restart();
sum = 0;
Parallel.For(0, MaxValue, (i) =>
{
  Interlocked.Add(ref sum, (long)Math.Sqrt(i));
});
watch.Stop();
Console.WriteLine("Parallel.For: {0}", watch.Elapsed);

// Partitioned For-loop
var partitioner = Partitioner.Create(0, MaxValue);
watch.Restart();
sum = 0;
Parallel.ForEach(partitioner,
  (range) =>
  {
    long partialSum = 0;
    for (int i = range.Item1; i < range.Item2; i++)
    {
      partialSum += (long)Math.Sqrt(i);
    }
    Interlocked.Add(ref sum, partialSum);
  });
watch.Stop();
Console.WriteLine("Partitioned Parallel.For: {0}", watch.Elapsed);
}
```

You can find this code in the ParallelLoops sample project. On one run on my machine, the output was this:

```
Parallel.For: 00:01:47.5650016
Partitioned Parallel.For: 00:00:00.8942916
```

The above partitioning scheme is static in that once the partitions are determined, a delegate executes each range and if one finishes early there is no attempt to repartition to get other processors working. You can create static partitions on any IEnumerable<T> collection without specifying a range, but there will be a delegate call for each item, not for a sub-range. It is possible to get around this by creating a custom Partitioner, which can be quite involved. For more information and to see some extensive examples, see the article by Stephen Toub at http://www.writinghighperf.net/go/20.

Avoid Blocking

You may notice that in some of the samples, I call `task.Wait()`. I do this for expediency in such small sample projects where I do not want the process to exit, but in real production code, you should rarely or never do this. Use continuations instead. Waiting on a `Task` is a subset of the larger problem of blocking calls.

To obtain the highest performance you must ensure that your program never wastes one resource while waiting for another. Most commonly, this takes the form of blocking the current thread while waiting for some I/O to complete. This situation will cause one of two things to happen:

1. The thread will be blocked in a waiting state, get unscheduled, and cause another thread to run. This could mean creating a new thread to handle pending work items or tasks if all current threads are in use or blocked.
2. The thread will hit a synchronization object which might spin for a few milliseconds waiting for a signal. If it does not get it in time, it will enter the same state as 1.

In both cases, it needlessly increases the size of the thread pool, and possibly also wastes CPU spinning in locks. Neither situation is desirable.

Locking and other types of direct thread synchronization are all explicit blocking calls and easy to detect. However, it is not always so obvious what other method calls may lead to blocking. They often revolve around I/O of various kinds so you need to make sure that any interactions with the network, the file system, databases, or any other high-latency service is done asynchronously. Thankfully, .NET makes it fairly easy to do that with `Task`s.

When making use of any I/O API, whether it is for network, file system, databases, or anything else, make sure that it returns a `Task`; otherwise, it is highly suspect and probably doing blocking I/O. Note that older asynchronous APIs will return an `IASyncResult` and usually start with `Begin-`. Either find an alternate API that returns a `Task` instead, or use the `Task.Factory.FromAsync` to wrap these methods inside of `Task`s to keep your own programming interface consistent.

Use Tasks for Non-Blocking I/O

.NET 4.5 added `Async` methods to the `Stream` class so that now all `Stream`-based communication can be entirely asynchronous quite easily. Here is a simple example:

```
int chunkSize = 4096;
var buffer = new byte[chunkSize];

var fileStream = new FileStream(filename, FileMode.Open);

var task = fileStream.ReadAsync(buffer, 0, buffer.Length);
task.ContinueWith((readTask) =>
  {
    int amountRead = readTask.Result;
    fileStream.Dispose();
    Console.WriteLine("Async(Simple) read {0} bytes", amountRead);
  });
```

You can no longer take advantage of the using syntax to clean up IDisposable objects such as Streams. Instead, you must pass those objects to the continuation method to make sure they are disposed along every path.

The above example is actually quite incomplete. In a real scenario, you will often have to make multiple reads to a stream to get the full contents. This can happen if the files are larger than the buffer you provide, or if you are dealing with a network stream instead of files. In that case, the bytes have not even arrived at your machine yet. To handle this situation asynchronously, you need to continue reading the stream until it tells you there is no data left.

An additional wrinkle is that now you need two levels of Tasks. The top level is for the overall read—the portion your calling program is interested in. The level below that is the Tasks for each individual chunked read.

Consider why this is so. The first asynchronous read will return a Task. If you return that up to the caller to wait or continue on, then they will continue executing after the first read is done. What you really want is for them to continue executing after all the reads are complete. This means you cannot return that first Task back to the caller. You need a fake Task that completes once all the reads are done.

To accomplish all of this, you will need to use the TaskCompletionSource<T> class, which can generate that fake Task for you to return. When your series of asynchronous reads are complete, you call the TrySetResult method on the TaskCompletionSource, which will cause it to trigger whoever is waiting or continuing on it.

The following example expands on the previous example and demonstrates the use of TaskCompletionSource:

```
private static Task<int> AsynchronousRead(string filename)
{
  int chunkSize = 4096;
  var buffer = new byte[chunkSize];
  var tcs = new TaskCompletionSource<int>();

  var fileContents = new MemoryStream();
  var fileStream = new FileStream(filename, FileMode.Open);
  fileContents.Capacity += chunkSize;

  var task = fileStream.ReadAsync(buffer, 0, buffer.Length);
  task.ContinueWith(
      readTask =>
      ContinueRead(readTask, fileStream, fileContents, buffer, tcs));

  return tcs.Task;
}

private static void ContinueRead(Task<int> task,
                  FileStream stream,
                  MemoryStream fileContents,
                  byte[] buffer,
                  TaskCompletionSource<int> tcs)
{
  if (task.IsCompleted)
  {
    int bytesRead = task.Result;
    fileContents.Write(buffer, 0, bytesRead);
    if (bytesRead > 0)
    {
      // More bytes to read, so make another async call
      var newTask = stream.ReadAsync(buffer, 0, buffer.Length);
      newTask.ContinueWith(
        readTask => ContinueRead(readTask, stream,
                    fileContents, buffer, tcs));
    }
    else
    {
      // All done, dispose of resources and
      // complete top-level task.
      tcs.TrySetResult((int)fileContents.Length);
      stream.Dispose();
      fileContents.Dispose();
    }
  }
}
```

Adapt the Asynchronous Programming Model (APM) to Tasks

Older style asynchronous methods in the .NET Framework have methods prefixed with Begin- and End-. These methods continue to work fine and can be easily wrapped inside a Task for a consistent interface, as in the following example, taken from the TaskFromAsync sample project:

```
const int TotalLength = 1024;
const int ReadSize = TotalLength / 4;

static Task<string> GetStringFromFileBetter(string path)
{
  var buffer = new byte[TotalLength];


  var stream = new FileStream(
    path,
    FileMode.Open,
    FileAccess.Read,
    FileShare.None,
    buffer.Length,
    FileOptions.DeleteOnClose | FileOptions.Asynchronous);

  var task = Task<int>.Factory.FromAsync(
    stream.BeginRead,
    stream.EndRead,
    buffer,
    0,
    ReadSize, null);

  var tcs = new TaskCompletionSource<string>();

  task.ContinueWith(readTask => OnReadBuffer(readTask,
                    stream, buffer, 0, tcs));

  return tcs.Task;
}

static void OnReadBuffer(Task<int> readTask,
            Stream stream,
            byte[] buffer,
            int offset,
            TaskCompletionSource<string> tcs)
{
  int bytesRead = readTask.Result;
  if (bytesRead > 0)
  {
```

```
    var task = Task<int>.Factory.FromAsync(
      stream.BeginRead,
      stream.EndRead,
      buffer,
      offset + bytesRead,
      Math.Min(buffer.Length - (offset + bytesRead), ReadSize),
      null);

    task.ContinueWith(
      callbackTask => OnReadBuffer(
        callbackTask,
        stream,
        buffer,
        offset + bytesRead,
        tcs));
  }

  else
  {
    tcs.TrySetResult(Encoding.UTF8.GetString(buffer, 0, offset));
  }
}
```

The FromAsync method takes as arguments the stream's BeginRead and EndRead methods as well as the target buffer to store the data. It will execute the methods and after EndRead is done, call the continuation, passing control back to your code, which in this example closes the stream and returns the converted file contents.

Use Efficient I/O

Just because you are using asynchronous programming with all I/O calls does not mean you are making the most out of the I/O you're doing. I/O devices have different capabilities, speeds, and features which means that you often need to tailor your programming to them.

In the examples above, I chose a 16KB buffer size for reading and writing to the disk. Is this a good value? Considering the size of buffers on hard disks, the speed of solid state devices, maybe not. Experimentation is required to figure out how to chunk the I/O efficiently. The smaller your buffers, the more overhead you will have. The larger your buffers, the longer you may need to wait for results to start coming in. The rules that apply to disks will not apply to network devices and vice-versa.

The most crucial thing, however, is that you also need to structure your program to take advantage of I/O. If part of your program ever blocks waiting for I/O to finish then that is time not spent crunching useful data with the CPU or at least wasting the thread pool. While waiting for I/O to complete, do as much other work as possible.

Also, note that there is a huge difference between true asynchronous I/O and performing synchronous I/O on another thread. In the former case, you have actually handed control to the operating system and hardware and no code anywhere in the system is blocked waiting for it to come back. If you do synchronous I/O on another thread, you are just blocking a thread that could be doing other work while still waiting for the operating system to get back to you. This might be acceptable in a non-performance situation (e.g., doing background I/O in a UI program instead of the main thread), but it is never recommended.

In other words, the following example is bad and defeats the purpose of asynchronous I/O:

```
Task.Run( ()=>
{
  using (var inputStream = File.OpenRead(filename))
  {
    byte[] buffer = new byte[16384];
    var input = inputStream.Read(buffer, 0, buffer.Length);
    ...
  }
});
```

For additional tips on doing effective I/O with the .NET Framework APIs specifically for disk or network access, see Chapter 6.

Async and Await

In .NET 4.5, there are two new keywords that can simplify your code in many situations: async and await. Used together, they turn your TPL code into something that looks like easy, linear, synchronous code. Under the hood, however, it is really using Tasks and continuations.

The following example comes from the AsyncAwait sample project.

```
static Regex regex = new Regex("<title>(.*)</title>",
RegexOptions.Compiled);

private static async Task<string> GetWebPageTitle(string url)
{
  System.Net.Http.HttpClient client = new System.Net.Http.HttpClient();
  Task<string> task = client.GetStringAsync(url);
```

```
    // now we need the result so await
    string contents = await task;

  Match match = regex.Match(contents);
  if (match.Success)
  {
    return match.Groups[1].Captures[0].Value;
  }
  return string.Empty;
}
```

To see where the real power of this syntax lies, consider a more complex example, where you are simultaneously reading from one file and writing to another, compressing the output along the way. It is not very difficult to use Tasks directly to accomplish this, but consider how trivial it looks when you use the async/await syntax. The following is from the CompressFiles sample project.

First, the synchronous version for comparison:

```
private static void SyncCompress(IEnumerable<string> fileList)
{
  byte[] buffer = new byte[16384];
  foreach (var file in fileList)
  {
    using (var inputStream = File.OpenRead(file))
    using (var outputStream = File.OpenWrite(file+".compressed"))
    using (var compressStream = new GZipStream(outputStream,
                        CompressionMode.Compress))
    {
      int read = 0;
      while ((read = inputStream.Read(buffer, 0, buffer.Length)) > 0)
      {
        compressStream.Write(buffer, 0, read);
      }
    }
  }
}
```

To make this asynchronous, all we have to do is add the async and await keywords and change the Read and Write methods to ReadAsync and WriteAsync, respectively:

```
private static async Task AsyncCompress(IEnumerable<string> fileList)
{
  byte[] buffer = new byte[16384];
```

```
  foreach (var file in fileList)
  {
    using (var inputStream = File.OpenRead(file))
    using (var outputStream = File.OpenWrite(file + ".compressed"))
    using (var compressStream =
            new GZipStream(outputStream, CompressionMode.Compress))
    {
      int read = 0;
      while ((read = await inputStream.ReadAsync(buffer, 0,
                            buffer.Length)) > 0)
      {
        await compressStream.WriteAsync(buffer, 0, read);
      }
    }
  }
}
```

Your code can await any method that returns a Task<T>, as long as it is in a method marked async. With these keywords, the compiler will do the heavy lifting of transforming your code into a structure similar to the previous TPL examples. It looks like this code will get blocked waiting for the HTTP result, but do not confuse "await" for "wait"; they are similar, but deliberately just different enough. Everything before the await keyword happens in the calling thread. Everything from the await onwards is in the continuation.

Using async/await can dramatically simplify your code, but there are some Task-based situations for which they cannot be used. For example, if the completion of a Task is nondeterministic, or you must have multiple levels of Tasks and are using TaskCompletionSource, then async/await may not fit.

Story I ran into this determinism problem myself when I was implementing retry functionality on top of .NET's HTTP client functionality, which is fully Task-enabled. I started with a simple HTTP client wrapper class and I used async/await initially because it simplified the code. However, when it came time to actually implement the retry functionality, I immediately knew I was stuck because I had given up control of when the tasks completed. For my implementation, I wanted to send the retry request before the first request had actually timed out. Whichever request finished first is the one I wanted to return up to the caller. Unfortunately, async/await will not handle this nondeterministic situation of arbitrarily choosing from multiple child Tasks that you are waiting on. One way to resolve this is to use the ContinueOnAny method described earlier. Alternatively, you could use TaskCompletionSource to manually control when the top-level Task is complete.

A Note on Program Structure

There's a crucial tidbit from the previous section: all `await`s must be in methods marked `async`, which means those methods must return `Task` objects. This kind of restriction does not technically exist if you are using `Task`s directly, but the same idea applies. Using asynchronous programming is like a beneficial "virus" that infects your program at all layers. Once you let it into one part, it will of necessity move up the layers of function calls as high as it can.

Of course, using `Task`s directly, you can create the following (bad) example:

```
Task<string> task = Task<string>.Run(()=> { ... });
task.Wait();
```

But unless you are doing only trivial multithreaded work, this completely ruins the scalability of your application. Yes, you could insert some work between the task's creation and the call to `Wait`, but this is missing the point. You should almost never wait on `Task`s, unlike some of the examples here that do it for convenience. That wastes a thread that could otherwise be doing useful work. It may lead to more context switching and higher overhead from the thread pool as more threads are needed to handle the available work items.

If you carry this idea of never waiting to its logical conclusion, you will realize that it is very possible (even likely) that nearly all of your program's code will occur in a continuation of some sort. This makes intuitive sense if you think about it. A UI program does essentially nothing until a user clicks or types—it is reacting to input via an event mechanism. A server program is analogous, but instead of mouse and keyboard, the I/O is via the network or file system.

As a result, a high-performance application can easily start to feel disjointed as you split logic based on I/O (or responsiveness in a UI) boundaries. The earlier you plan for this, the better off you will be. It is critical to settle on just a few standard patterns that most or all of your program uses. For example:

- Determine where `Task` and continuation methods live. Do you use a separate method or a lambda expression? Does it depend on its size?
- If you use methods for continuations, settle on a standard prefix (e.g., OnMyTaskEnd).
- Standardize error handling. Do you have a single continuation method that handles all errors, cancellations, and normal completions? Or do you have separate methods to handle each or some of these and use `TaskContinuationOptions` to selectively execute them?
- Decide whether to use `async`/`await` or `Task`s directly.
- If you have to call old style Begin.../End... asynchronous methods, wrap them in `Task`s to standardize your handling, as described earlier.

- Do not feel like you have to use every feature of the TPL. Some features are not recommended for most situations (AttachedToParent tasks, for example). Standardize on the minimal feature set you can get away with.

Use Timers Correctly

To schedule a method to execute after a certain timespan and optionally at regular intervals thereafter, use the System.Threading.Timer object. You should not use mechanisms like Thread.Sleep that block the thread for the specified amount of time, though we will see below that it can be useful in some situations.

The following example demonstrates how to use a timer by specifying a callback method and passing in two timeout values. The first value is the time until the timer fires for the first time and the second value is how often to repeat it thereafter. You can specify Timeout.Infinite (which has value -1) for either value. This example fires the timer only once, after 15 milliseconds.

```
private System.Threading.Timer timer;

public void Start()
{
   this.timer = new Timer(TimerCallback, null, 15, Timeout.Infinite);
}

private void TimerCallback(object state)
{
   // Do your work
}
```

Do not create an excessive number of timers. All Timers are serviced from a single thread in the thread pool. A huge number of Timers will cause delays in executing their callbacks. When the time comes due, the timer thread will schedule a work item to the thread pool, and it will be picked up by the next available thread. If you have a large number of tasks, queued work items, or high CPU usage, this means your Timers will not be accurate. In fact, they are guaranteed to never be more accurate than the operating system's timer tick count, which is set to 15.625 milliseconds by default. This is the same value that determines thread quantum lengths. Setting a timeout value less than that will not get you the results you need. If you need more precision than 15 milliseconds, you have a few options:

1. Reduce the operating system's timer tick resolution. This can result in higher CPU usage and severely impact battery life, but may be justified in some situations. Note that

changing this could have far reaching impacts like more context switches, higher system overhead, and worse performance in other areas.

2. Spin in a loop, using a high-resolution timer (See Chapter 6) to measure elapsed time. This also uses more CPU and power, but is more localized.

3. Call Thread.Sleep. This will block the thread, and is generally accurate in my testing, but there is no guarantee this will always work. On a highly loaded system, it is possible the thread could be context switched out and you will not get it back until after your desired interval.

When you use a Timer, be aware of a classic race condition. Consider the code:

```
private System.Threading.Timer timer;

public void Start()
{
   this.timer = new Timer(TimerCallback, null, 15, Timeout.Infinite);
}

private void TimerCallback(object state)
{
   // Do your work
   this.timer.Dispose();
}
```

This code sets up a Timer to execute a callback in 15 milliseconds. The callback just disposes the timer object once it is done with it. This code is also likely to throw a NullReferenceException in TimerCallback. The reason is that it is very possible for the callback to execute before the Timer object is assigned to the this.timer field in the Start method. Thankfully, it is quite easy to fix:

```
this.timer = new Timer(TimerCallback, null, Timeout.Infinite,
                       Timeout.Infinite);
this.timer.Change(15, Timeout.Infinite);
```

Ensure Good Startup Thread Pool Size

Just because you are not programming directly against the thread pool does not mean you do not need to understand how it works. In particular, you may need to give the thread pool some hints for how it should allocate threads and keep them ready.

The thread pool tunes itself over time, but at startup it has no history and will start in a default state. If your software is extremely asynchronous and uses a lot of CPU, then it may be hit with a steep startup cost as it waits for more threads to be created and become available. To reach the steady state sooner, you can tweak the startup parameters to maintain a minimum number of threads ready upon startup.

```
const int MinWorkerThreads = 25;
const int MinIoThreads = 25;
ThreadPool.SetMinThreads(MinWorkerThreads, MinIoThreads);
```

You do need to exercise caution here. If you are using Tasks then they will be scheduled based on the number of threads available for scheduling. If there are too many threads then the Tasks can become overscheduled, leading to less CPU efficiency, not more, as more context switching happens. The thread pool will still eventually switch to using an algorithm that can reduce the number of threads to below this number, if the work load is lighter.

You can also set a maximum with the SetMaxThreads method and this has the same risks.

To figure out how many threads you really need, leave this setting alone and analyze your app during its steady state using the ThreadPool.GetMaxThreads and ThreadPool.GetMinThreads methods, or by using performance counters to examine how many threads are in the process.

Do Not Abort Threads

Terminating threads without their cooperation is a dangerous procedure. Threads have their own clean up to do and calling Abort on them does not allow a graceful shutdown. When you kill a thread, you leave portions of the application in an undefined state. It would be better to just crash the program, but ideally, just do a clean restart.

If you are using Tasks, as you should, then this will not be an issue for you. There is no API provided to force-terminate a Task.

Do Not Change Thread Priorities

In general, it is a bad idea to change thread priorities. Windows schedules threads according to their priority. If high priority threads are always ready to run, then lower priority threads will be starved and rarely given a chance to run. By increasing a thread's priority you are saying that its work must have priority over all other work, including other processes. This notion is not a safe part of a stable system.

It is more acceptable to lower a thread's priority if it is doing something that can wait until all the normal-priority tasks have completed. One good reason to lower a thread's priority is that you have detected a runaway thread doing an infinite loop. You cannot safely terminate threads, so the only way to get that thread and processor resource back is by restarting the process. Until you can shut down and do that cleanly, lowering the runaway thread's priority is a reasonable mitigation. Note that even threads with lower priorities are still guaranteed to run after a while because Windows will increase their dynamic priority the longer it goes without executing. The exception is Idle priority (THREAD_PRIORITY_IDLE), which the operating system will only ever schedule if literally nothing else can run.

You may find a legitimate reason to increase thread priority, such as reacting to rare situations that require faster responses, but this should be used with care. Windows schedules threads agnostic of the process they belong to, so a high-priority thread from your process will run at the expense not only of your other threads, but all the other threads from other applications running on your system.

If you are using the thread pool, then any thread priority changes are reset every time the thread reenters the pool. If you are using Tasks and still manipulating the underlying thread, then keep in mind that the same thread can run multiple tasks before being placed back in the pool.

Thread Synchronization and Locks

As soon as you start talking about multiple threads, the question of synchronization among those threads is going to appear. Synchronization is the practice of ensuring that only a single thread can access some shared state, such as a class's field. Thread synchronization is usually accomplished with synchronization objects such as Monitor, Semaphore, ManualResetEvent, and others. In aggregate, these are sometimes referred to informally as locks, and the process of synchronizing in a specific thread as locking.

One of the fundamental truth of locks is: locking *never* improves performance. At best, it can be neutral, with a well-implemented synchronization primitive and no contention. A lock explicitly stops other threads from doing productive work, wasting CPU, increasing context switching time, and more. We tolerate this because the one thing more critical than raw performance is correctness. It does not matter how fast you calculate a wrong result!

Before attacking the problem of which locking apparatus to use, first consider some more fundamental principles.

Do I Need To Care About Performance At All?

Validate that you actually need to care about performance in the first place. This goes back to the principles discussed in the first chapter. Not all code is equal in your application. Not all of it should be optimized to the nth degree. Typically, you start at the "inner loop"—the code that is most commonly executed or is most performance critical—and work outwards until the cost outweighs the benefit. There are many other areas in your code that are much less critical, performance-wise. In these situations, if you need a lock, take a lock and don't worry about it.

Now, you do have to be careful here. If your non-critical piece of code is executing on a thread pool thread, and you block it for a significant amount of time, the thread pool could start injecting more threads to keep up with other requests. If a couple of threads do this once in a while, it's no big deal. However, if you have lots of threads doing things like this, then it could become a problem because it wastes resources that should be going to real work. If you are running a program that processes a heavy, constant workload, then even parts of your program that are not performance-sensitive can negatively affect the system by context switching or perturbing the thread pool if you are not careful. As in all things, you must measure.

Do I Need A Lock At All?

The most performant locking mechanism is one that is not there. If you can completely remove your need for thread synchronization, than you are in the best place as far as performance goes. This is the ideal, but it might not be easy. It usually means you have to ensure there is no writable shared state—each request through your application can be handled without regard to another request or any centralized volatile (read/write) data.

Be careful, though. It is easy to go overboard in the refactoring and make your code a spaghetti mess that no one (including you) can understand. Unless performance is really that critical and cannot be obtained any other way, you should not carry it that far. Make it asynchronous and independent, but make it clear.

If multiple threads are just reading from a variable (and there is no chance at all of any thread writing to it), then no synchronization is necessary. All threads can have unrestricted access. This is automatically the case for immutable objects like strings or immutable value types, but can be the case for any type of object if you ensure its immutability while multiple threads are reading it.

If you do have multiple threads writing to some shared variable, see if you can remove the need for synchronized access by converting usage to a local variable. If you can create a temporary copy to act on, no synchronization is necessary. This is especially important for repeated synchronized access. You will need to convert repeated access to a shared variable to repeated access of a local variable followed by a single shared access, as in the following simple example of multiple threads adding items to a shared collection.

```
object syncObj = new object();
var masterList = new List<long>();
const int NumTasks = 8;
Task[] tasks = new Task[NumTasks];

for (int i = 0; i < NumTasks; i++)
{
  tasks[i] = Task.Run(()=>
  {
    for (int j = 0; j < 5000000; j++)
    {
      lock (syncObj)
      {
        masterList.Add(j);
      }
    }
  });
}
Task.WaitAll(tasks);
```

This can be converted to the following:

```
object syncObj = new object();
var masterList = new List<long>();
const int NumTasks = 8;
Task[] tasks = new Task[NumTasks];

for (int i = 0; i < NumTasks; i++)
{
  tasks[i] = Task.Run(()=>
  {
    var localList = new List<long>();
    for (int j = 0; j < 5000000; j++)
    {
      localList.Add(j);
    }
    lock (syncObj)
    {
      masterList.AddRange(localList);
    }
  });
}
Task.WaitAll(tasks);
```

On my machine, the second code fragment takes less than half of the time as the first.

Synchronization Preference Order

If you decide you do need some sort of synchronization, then understand that not all of them have equal performance or behavior characteristics. If performance is not critical, just use lock for simplicity and clarity. Using anything other than a lock should require some intense measurement to justify the additional complexity. In general, consider synchronization mechanisms in this order:

1. No synchronization at all
2. Simple Interlocked methods
3. lock/Monitor class
4. Asynchronous locks (see later in this chapter)
5. Everything else

These are roughly in order of performance impact, but specific circumstances may dictate or preclude the use of some of them. For example, combining multiple Interlocked methods is not likely to outperform a single lock statement.

Memory Models

Before discussing the details of thread synchronization, we must take a short detour into the world of memory models. The memory model is the set of the rules in a system (hardware or software) that govern how read and write operations can be reordered by the compiler or by the processor across multiple threads. You cannot actually change anything about the model, but understanding it is critical to having correct code in all situations.

A memory model is described as "strong" if it has an absolute restriction on reordering, which prevents the compiler and hardware from doing many optimizations. A "weak" model allows the compiler and processor much more freedom to reorder read and write instructions in order to get potentially better performance. Most platforms fall somewhere between absolutely strong and weak.

The ECMA standard (see http://www.writinghighperf.net/go/17) defines the minimum set of rules that the CLR must follow. It defines a very weak memory model, but a given implementation of the CLR may actually have a stronger model in place on top of it.

A specific processor architecture may also enforce a stronger memory model. For example, the x86/x64 architecture has a relatively strong memory model which will automatically prevent certain kinds of instruction reordering, but allows others. On the other hand, the ARM architecture has a relatively weak memory model. It is the JIT compiler's responsibility to ensure that not only are machine instructions emitted in the proper order, but that special instructions are used to ensure that the processor itself doesn't reorder instructions in a way to violate the CLR's memory model.

The practical difference between x86/x64 and ARM architectures has significant impact on your code, particularly if you have bugs in thread synchronization. Because the JIT compiler under ARM is more free to reorder reads and writes than it is under x86/x64, certain classes of synchronization bugs can go completely undetected on x86/x64 and only become apparent when ported to ARM.

In some cases, the CLR will help cover these differences for compatibility's sake, but it is good practice to ensure that the code is correct for the weakest memory model in use. The biggest requirement here is the correct use of volatile on state that is shared between threads. The volatile keyword is a signal to the JIT compiler that ordering matters for this variable. On x86/x64 it will enforce instruction ordering rules, but on ARM there will also be extra instructions emitted to enforce the correct semantics in the hardware. If you neglect volatile, the ECMA standard allows these instructions to be completely reordered and bugs could surface.

Other ways to ensure proper ordering of shared state is to use Interlocked or keep all accesses inside a full lock.

All of these methods of synchronization create what is called a memory barrier. Any reads that occur before that place in code may not be reordered after the barrier and any writes may not be reordered to be before the barrier. In this way, updates to variables are seen by all CPUs.

Use volatile When Necessary

Consider the following classic example of an incorrect double-checked locking implementation that attempts to efficiently protect against multiple threads calling DoCompletionWork. It tries to avoid potentially expensive contentious calls to lock in the common case that there is no need to call DoCompletionWork.

```
private bool isComplete = false;
private object syncObj= new object();

// Incorrect implementation!
private void Complete()
{
  if (!isComplete)
  {
    lock (syncObj)
    {
```

```
      if (!isComplete)
      {
        DoCompletionWork();
        isComplete = true;
      }
    }
  }
}
```

While the `lock` statement will effectively protect its inner block, the outer check of `isComplete` is simultaneously accessed by multiple threads with no protection. Unfortunately, updates to this variable may be out of order due to compiler optimizations allowed under the memory model, leading to multiple threads seeing a `false` value even after another thread has set it to `true`. It is actually worse than that, though: It is possible that `isComplete` could be set to true before `DoCompletionWork()` completes, which means the program could be in an invalid state if other threads are checking and acting on the value of `isComplete`. Why not always use a lock around any access to `isComplete`? You could do that, but this leads to higher contention and is a more expensive solution than is strictly necessary.

To fix this, you need to instruct the compiler to ensure that accesses to this variable are done in the right order. You do this with the `volatile` keyword. The only change you need is:

```
private volatile bool isComplete = false;
```

To be clear, `volatile` is for program correctness, not performance. In most cases it does not noticeably help or hurt performance. If you can use it, it is better than using a `lock` in any high-contention scenario, which is why the double-checked locking pattern is useful.

Double-checked locking is often used for the singleton pattern when you want the first thread that uses the value to initialize it. This pattern is encapsulated in .NET by using the Lazy<T> class, which internally uses the double-checked locking pattern. You should prefer to use Lazy<T> rather than implement your own pattern. See Chapter 6 for more information about using Lazy<T>.

Use Interlocked Methods

Consider this code with a lock that is guaranteeing that only a single thread can execute the `Complete` method:

```
private bool isComplete = false;
private object completeLock = new object();

private void Complete()
```

```
{
  lock(completeLock)
  {
    if (isComplete)
    {
      return;
    }
    isComplete = true;
  }
  ...
}
```

You need two fields and a few lines of code to determine if you should even enter the method, which seems wasteful. Instead, use a simple call to the `Interlocked.Increment` method:

```
private int isComplete = 0;

private void Complete()
{
  if (Interlocked.Increment(ref isComplete) == 1)
  {
    ...
  }
}
```

Or consider a slightly different situation where `Complete` may be called multiple times, but you want only to enter it based on some internal state, and then enter it only once.

```
enum State { Executing, Done };
private int state = (int)State.Executing;

private void Complete()
{
  if (Interlocked.CompareAndExchange (ref state, (int)State.Done,
            (int)State.Executing) == (int)State.Executing)
  {
    ...
  }
}
```

The first time `Complete` executes, it will compare the `state` variable against `State.Executing` and if they are equal replace `state` with the value `State.Done`. The next thread that executes this code will compare state against `State.Executing`, which will not be true, and `CompareAndExchange` will return State.Done, failing the `if` statement.

`Interlocked` methods translate into a single processor instruction and are atomic. They are perfect for this kind of simple synchronization. There are a number of `Interlocked` methods you can use for simple synchronization, all of which perform the operation atomically:

- `Add`—Adds two integers, replacing the first one with the sum and returning the sum.
- `CompareAndExchange`—Accepts values A, B, and C. Compares values A and C, and, if equal, replaces A with B, and returns original value. See the LockFreeStack example below.
- `Increment`—Adds one to the value and returns the new value.
- `Decrement`—Subtracts one from the value and returns the new value.
- `Exchange`—Sets a variable to a specified value and returns the original value.

All of these methods have multiple overloads for various data types.

`Interlocked` operations are memory barriers, thus they are not as fast as a simple write in a non-contention scenario.

As simple as they are, `Interlocked` methods can implement more powerful concepts such as lock-free data structures. But a word of caution: Be very careful when implementing your own data structures like this. The seductive words "lock-free" can be misleading. They are really a synonym for "repeat the operation until correct." Once you start having multiple calls to `Interlocked` methods, it is possible to be less efficient than just calling `lock` in the first place. It can also be very difficult to get it right or performant. Implementing data structure like this is great for education, but in real code your default choice should always be to use the built-in .NET collections. If you do implement your own thread-safe collection, take great pains to ensure that it is not only 100% functionally correct, but that it performs better than the existing .NET choices. If you use `Interlocked` methods, ensure that they provide more benefit than a simple `lock`.

As an example (from the accompanying source in the LockFreeStack project), here is a simple implementation of a stack that uses `Interlocked` methods to maintain thread safety without using any of the heavier locking mechanisms.

```
class LockFreeStack<T>
{
  private class Node
  {
    public T Value;
    public Node Next;
  }

  private Node head;
```

```csharp
public void Push(T value)
{
  var newNode = new Node() { Value = value };

  while (true)
  {
    newNode.Next = this.head;
    if (Interlocked.CompareExchange(ref this.head, newNode,
                      newNode.Next)
      == newNode.Next)
    {
      return;
    }
  }
}

public T Pop()
{
  while (true)
  {
    Node node = this.head;
    if (node == null)
    {
      return default(T);
    }
    if (Interlocked.CompareExchange(ref this.head, node.Next, node)
      == node)
    {
      return node.Value;
    }
  }
}
```

This code fragment demonstrates a common pattern with implementing data structures or more complex logic using Interlocked methods: looping. Often, the code will loop, continually testing the results of the operation until it succeeds. In most scenarios, only a handful of iterations will be performed.

While Interlocked methods are simple and relatively fast, you will often need to protect more substantial areas of code and they will fall short (or at least be unwieldy and complex).

Use Monitor (lock)

The simplest way to protect any code region is with the Monitor object, which in C# has a keyword equivalent.

This code:

```
object obj = new object();
bool taken = false;
try
{
  Monitor.Enter(obj, ref taken);
}
finally
{
  if (taken)
  {
    Monitor.Exit(obj);
  }
}
```

is equivalent to this:

```
object obj = new object();

lock(obj)
{
...
}
```

The taken parameter is set to true if no exceptions occurred. This is guaranteed so that you can correctly call Exit.

In general, you should prefer using Monitor/lock versus other more complicated locking mechanisms until proven otherwise. Monitor is a hybrid lock in that it first tries to spin in a loop for a while before it enters a wait state and gives up the thread. This makes it ideal for places where you anticipate little or short-lived contention.

Monitor also has a more flexible API that can be useful if you have optional work to do if you cannot acquire the lock immediately.

```
object obj = new object();
bool taken = false;
try
{
  Monitor.TryEnter(obj, ref taken);
```

```
    if (taken)
    {
        // do work that needs the lock
    }
    else
    {
        // do something else
    }
}
finally
{
    if (taken)
    {
        Monitor.Exit(obj);
    }
}
```

In this case, TryEnter returns immediately, regardless of whether it got the lock. You can test the taken variable to know what to do. There are also overloads that accepts a timeout value.

Which Object To Lock On?

The Monitor class takes a synchronization object as its argument. You can pass any object into this method, but care should be taken in selecting which object to use. If you pass in a publically visible object, there is a possibility that another piece of code could also use it as a synchronization object, even if the synchronization is not needed between those two sections of code. If you pass in a complex object, you run the risk of functionality in that class taking a lock on itself. Both of these situations can lead to poor performance or worse: deadlocks.

To avoid this, it is almost always wise to allocate a plain, private object specifically for your locking purposes, as in the examples above.

On the other hand, I have seen situations where explicit synchronization objects can lead to problems, particularly when there were an enormous number of objects and the overhead of an extra field in the class was burdensome. In this case, you can find some other safe object that can serve as a synchronization object, or better, refactor your code to not need the lock in the first place.

There are some classes of objects you should never use as a sync object for Monitor. These include any MarshalByRefObject (a proxy object that will not protect the underlying resource), strings (which are interned and shared unpredictably), or value type (which will be boxed every time you lock on it, prohibiting any synchronization from happening at all).

Asynchronous Locks

Starting in .NET 4.5, there is some interesting functionality that may expand to other types in the future. The SemaphoreSlim class has a WaitAsync method that returns a Task. Instead of blocking on a wait, you can schedule a continuation on the Task that will execute once the semaphore permits it to run. There is no entry into kernel mode and no blocking. When the lock is no longer contended, the continuation will be scheduled like a normal Task on the thread pool. Usage is the same as for any other Tasks.

To see how it works, consider first an example using the standard, blocking wait mechanisms. This sample code (from the WaitAsync project in the sample code) is rather silly, but demonstrates how the threads hand off control via the semaphore.

```
class Program
{
  const int Size = 256;
  static int[] array = new int[Size];
  static int length = 0;
  static SemaphoreSlim semaphore = new SemaphoreSlim(1);

  static void Main(string[] args)
  {
    var writerTask = Task.Run((Action)WriterFunc);
    var readerTask = Task.Run((Action)ReaderFunc);

    Console.WriteLine("Press any key to exit");
    Console.ReadKey();
  }

  static void WriterFunc()
  {
    while (true)
    {
      semaphore.Wait();
      Console.WriteLine("Writer: Obtain");
      for (int i = length; i < array.Length; i++)
      {
        array[i] = i * 2;
      }
      Console.WriteLine("Writer: Release");
      semaphore.Release();
    }
  }

  static void ReaderFunc()
```

```
  {
    while (true)
    {
      semaphore.Wait();
      Console.WriteLine("Reader: Obtain");
      for (int i = length; i >= 0; i--)
      {
        array[i] = 0;
      }
      length = 0;
      Console.WriteLine("Reader: Release");
      semaphore.Release();
    }
  }
}
```

Each thread loops indefinitely while waiting for the other thread to finish its loop operation. When the Wait method is called, that thread will block until the semaphore is released. In a high-throughput program, that blocking is extremely wasteful and can reduce processing capacity and increase the size of the thread pool. If the block lasts long enough, a kernel transition may occur, which is yet more wasted time.

To use WaitAsync, replace the reader/writer threads with these implementations:

```
static void WriterFuncAsync()
{
  semaphore.WaitAsync().ContinueWith(_ =>
  {
    Console.WriteLine("Writer: Obtain");
    for (int i = length; i < array.Length; i++)
    {
      array[i] = i * 2;
    }
    Console.WriteLine("Writer: Release");
    semaphore.Release();
  }).ContinueWith(_=>WriterFuncAsync());
}

static void ReaderFuncAsync()
{
  semaphore.WaitAsync().ContinueWith(_ =>
  {
    Console.WriteLine("Reader: Obtain");
    for (int i = length; i >= 0; i--)
    {
      array[i] = 0;
```

```
    }
    length = 0;
    Console.WriteLine("Reader: Release");
    semaphore.Release();
  }).ContinueWith(_=>ReaderFuncAsync());
}
```

Note that the loop was removed in lieu of a chain of continuations that will call back into these methods. It is logically recursive, but not actually so because each continuation starts the stack fresh with a new Task.

No blocking occurs with WaitAsync, but this is not free functionality. There is still overhead from increased Task scheduling and function calls. If your program schedules a lot of Tasks, the increased scheduling pressure may offset the gains from avoiding the blocking call. If your locks are extremely short-lived (they just spin and never enter kernel mode) or rare, then it may be better to just block for the few microseconds it takes to get through the lock. On the other hand, if you need to execute a relative long-running task under a lock, this may be the better choice because the overhead of a new Task is less than the time you will block the processor otherwise. You will need to carefully measure and experiment.

If this pattern is interesting to you, see Steven Toub's series of articles of asynchronous coordination primitives at http://www.writinghighperf.net/go/21 which covers a few additional types and patterns.

Other Locking Mechanisms

There are many locking mechanisms you can use, but you should prefer to stick with as few as you can get away with. As in many things, but especially multithreading, the simpler the better.

If you know that a lock is extremely short-lived (tens of cycles) and want to guarantee that it never enters a wait state, then you can use a SpinLock. It will just spin a loop until the contention is done. In most cases, Monitor, which spins first, then enters a wait if necessary, is a better default choice.

```
private SpinLock spinLock = new SpinLock();

private void DoWork()
{
  bool taken = false;
  try
  {
    spinLock.Enter(ref taken);
  }
  finally
```

```
{
  if (taken)
  {
    spinLock.Exit();
  }
}
}
```

In general, avoid other locking mechanisms if you can. They are usually not nearly as performant as the simple `Monitor`. Objects like `ReaderWriterLockSlim`, `Semaphore`, `Mutex`, or other custom synchronization objects definitely have their place, but they are often complex and error-prone.

Completely avoid `ReaderWriterLock`—it is deprecated and should never be used for any reason.

If there is a `*Slim` version of a synchronization object, prefer it to the non-`Slim` version. The `*Slim` versions are all hybrid locks which means they implement some form of spinning before they enter a kernel transition, which is much slower. `*Slim` locks are much better when the contention is expected to be low and brief.

For example, there is both a `ManualResetEvent` class and a `ManualResetEventSlim` class, and there is an `AutoResetEvent` class, but there is no `AutoResetEventSlim` class. However, you can use `SemaphoreSlim` with the `initialCount` parameter set to one for the same effect.

Concurrent Collections

There are a handful of collections provided with .NET that allow concurrent access from multiple threads safely. They are all in the `System.Collections.Concurrent` namespace and include:

- `ConcurrentBag<T>`—unordered collection
- `ConcurrentDictionary<TKey, TValue>`—key/value pairs
- `ConcurrentQueue<T>`—first-in/first-out queue
- `ConcurrentStack<T>`—last-in/first-out stack

Most of these are implemented internally using `Interlocked` or `Monitor` synchronization primitives and I encourage you to examine their implementations using an IL reflection tool.

They are convenient, but you need to be careful—every single access to the collection involves synchronization. Often, that is overkill and could harm your performance if there is a lot of contention. If you have necessarily "chatty" read/write access patterns to the collection, this low-level synchronization may make sense.

This section will cover a few alternatives to concurrent collections that may simplify your locking requirements. See Chapter 6 for a discussion of collections in general, including those listed here, particularly for a description of the APIs unique to these collections, which can be tricky to get right.

Lock at A Higher Level

If you find yourself updating or reading many values at once, you should probably use a non-concurrent collection and handle the locking yourself at a higher level (or find a way to not need synchronization at all—see the next section for one idea).

The granularity of your synchronization mechanism has an enormous impact on overall efficiency. In many cases, making batch updates under a single lock is better than taking a lock for every single small update. In my own informal testing, I found that inserting an item into a `ConcurrentDictionary` is about 2x slower than with a standard `Dictionary`.

You will have to measure and judge the tradeoff in your application.

Also note that sometimes you need to lock at a higher level to ensure that application-specific constraints are honored. Consider the classic example of bank transfer between two accounts. The balance of both accounts must be changed individually of course, but the transaction only makes sense when considered together. Database transactions are a related concept. A single row insertion by itself may be atomic, but to guarantee integrity of your operations, you may need to utilize transactions to ensure higher-level atomicity.

Replace an Entire Collection

If your data is mostly read-only then you can safely use a non-concurrent collection when accessing it. When it is time to update the collection, you can generate a new collection object entirely and just replace the original reference once it is loaded, as in the following example:

```
private volatile Dictionary<string, MyComplexObject> data = new
  Dictionary<string, MyComplexObject>();

public Dictionary<string, MyComplexObject> Data { get { return data; } }

private void UpdateData()
{
  var newData = new Dictionary<string, MyComplexObject>();
  newData["Foo"] = new MyComplexObject();
  ...
  data = newData;
}
```

Notice the volatile keyword which ensures that data will be updated correctly for all threads.

If a consumer of this class needed to access the Data property multiple times and did not want this object swapped out from under it to a new one, it can create a local copy of the reference and use that instead of the original property.

```
private void CreateReport(DataSource source)
{
  Dictionary<string, MyComplexObject> data = source.Data;

  foreach(var kvp in data)
  {
    ...
  }
}
```

This is not foolproof, and it does make your code a little more complex. You also need to balance this replacement against the cost of incurring a full garbage collection when the new collection is allocated. As long the reload is a rare occurrence and you can handle the occasional full GC, this may be the right pattern for many scenarios. See Chapter 2 for more information on avoiding full GCs.

Copy Your Resource Per-Thread

If you have a resource that is lightweight, not thread-safe, and is used a lot on multiple threads, consider marking it [ThreadStatic]. A classic example is the Random class in .Net, which is not thread-safe.

This example comes from the MultiThreadRand sample project:

```
[ThreadStatic]
static Random safeRand;

static void Main(string[] args)
{
  int[] results = new int[100];

  Parallel.For(0, 5000,
    i =>
    {
      // thread statics are not initialized
      if (safeRand == null) safeRand = new Random();
      var randomNumber = safeRand.Next(100);
      Interlocked.Increment(ref results[randomNumber]);
    });
}
```

You should always assume that statics marked as [ThreadStatic] are not initialized at the time of first use—.NET will only initialize the first one. The rest will have default values (usually null).

Measurement

One of the most difficult types of debugging to do is any issue relating to multiple threads. Spending the effort to get the code right in the first place pays huge dividends later as a lack of time spent debugging.

On the other hand, finding sources of contention in .NET is trivially easy and there are some nice advanced tools out there that can help with some general multithreading analysis.

Performance Counters

In the Process category exists the Thread Count counter.

In the Synchronization category, you can find the following counters:

- Spinlock Acquires/sec
- Spinlock Contentions/sec
- Spinlock Spins/sec

Under System, you can find the Context Switches/sec counter. It is difficult to know what the ideal value of this counter should be. You can find many conflicting opinions about this (I have commonly seen a value of 300 being normal, with 1,000 being too high), so I believe you should view this counter mostly in a relative sense and track how it changes over time, with large increases potentially indicating problems in your app.

.NET provides a number of counters in the .NET CLR LocksAndThreads category, including:

- **# of current logical Threads**—The number of managed threads in the process.
- **# of current physical Threads**—The number of OS threads assigned to the process to execute the managed threads, excluding those used only by the CLR.
- **Contention Rate / sec**—Important for detecting "hot" locks that you should refactor or remove.
- **Current Queue Length**—The number of threads blocked on a lock.

ETW Events

Of the following events, ContentionStart and ContentionStop are the most useful. The others may be interesting in a situation where the concurrency level is changing in unexpected ways and you need insights into how the thread pool is behaving.

- **ContentionStart**—Contention has started. For hybrid locks, this does not count the spinning phase, only when when it enters an actual blocked state. Fields include:
  - o Flags—0 for managed, 1 for native.
- **ContentionStop**—Contention has ended.
- **ThreadPoolWorkerThreadStart**—A thread pool thread has started. Fields include:
  - o ActiveWorkerThreadCount—Number of worker thread available, both those processing work and those waiting for work.
  - o RetiredWorkerThreadCount—Number of worker threads being held in reserve if more threads are needed later.
- **ThreadPoolWorkerThreadStop**—A thread pool thread has ended. Fields are same as for ThreadPoolWorkerThreadStart.
- **IOThreadCreate**—An I/O thread has been created. Fields include:
  - o Count—Number of I/O threads in pool.

See http://www.writinghighperf.net/go/22 for more information about thread-related ETW events.

Which Locks Have The Highest Contention?

During development, you can use the Visual Studio profiler to collect this data. Launch the Profile Wizard and select the concurrency option.

For collecting data on a destination machine, I find PerfView is easiest. You can use the sample program HighContention to see this. Run the program and collect .NET events using PerfView. Once the .etl file is ready to view, open the Any Stacks view and look for an entry named "Event Microsoft-Windows-DotNETRuntime/Contention/Start" and double-click it. It will open a view that looks like this:

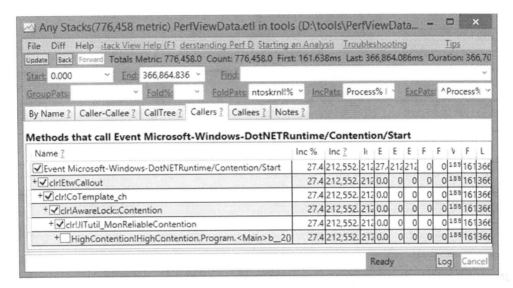

Figure 4-1. PerfView easily shows which stacks are leading to higher contention for all managed synchronization objects.

This will show you the stacks that caused lock contention. In this case, you can see that the contention comes from an anonymous method inside Main.

Where Are My Threads Blocking On I/O?

You can use PerfView to collect information about threads such as when they enter various states. This gives you more accurate information about overall wall-clock time spent in your program, if it is not using the CPU. However, be aware that turning on this option slows down your program considerably.

In PerfView's Collection dialog, check the "Thread Times" box as well as the other defaults (Kernel, .NET, and CPU events).

Once collection is done, you will see a Thread Times node in the results tree. Open that and look at the By Name tab. You should see two main categories at the top: BLOCKED_TIME and CPU_TIME. Double-click BLOCKED_TIME to see the callers for that group. Your view will look something like this:

Methods that call BLOCKED_TIME

Name
☑ BLOCKED_TIME
+ ☐ LAST_BLOCK (Last blocking operation in trace)
+ ☐ OTHER <<ntdll!_RtlUserThreadStart>>
+ ☑ OTHER <<mscorlib.ni!System.IO.TextReader+SyncTextReader.ReadLine()>>
│ + ☐ CompressFiles!CompressFiles.Program.Main(class System.String[])

Figure 4-2. A PerfView stack of blocked time, caused by a call to the TextReader.ReadLine *method.*

This shows some blocked time in TextReader.ReadLine which is being called from the Main method.

Visualizing Tasks and Threads with Visual Studio

Visual Studio ships with a tool called the Concurrency Visualizer. This tool captures the same type of events that PerfView does, but shows them in a graphical form so that you can see exactly what all the Tasks and threads do in your application. It can tell you when Tasks start and stop, whether a thread is blocked, doing CPU work, or waiting on I/O and a lot more.

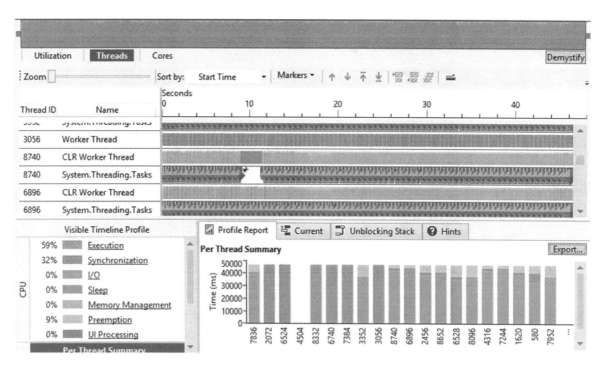

Figure 4-3. Visual Studio's Thread Times view combines threads, tasks, CPU time, blocked time, interrupts, and more into a single correlated timeline.

It is important to note that capturing this type of information can significantly degrade the application's performance, as an event will be recorded every time a thread changes state, which is extremely frequent.

Summary

Use multiple threads when you need to avoid blocking the UI thread, parallelize work on multiple CPUs, or avoid wasting CPU capacity by blocking threads waiting for I/O to complete. Use Tasks instead of pure threads. Do not wait on Tasks, but schedule a continuation to be executed when the Task is complete. Simplify Task syntax with async and await.

Never block on I/O. Always use asynchronous APIs when reading from or writing to Streams. Use continuations to schedule a callback for when the I/O completes.

Try to avoid locking if at all possible, even if you need to significantly restructure your code. When needed, use the simplest locking possible. For simple state changes, use Interlocked methods. For short or rarely contended sections, use lock/Monitor and use a private field as the synchronization object. If you have a highly contended critical section that lasts more than a few milliseconds, consider using the asynchronous locking pattern like SemaphoreSlim.

5 General Coding and Class Design

This chapter covers general coding and type design principles not covered elsewhere in this book. .NET contains features for many scenarios and while many of them are at worst performance-neutral, some are decidedly harmful to good performance. Others are neither good nor bad, just different, and you must decide what the right approach in a given situation is.

If I were to summarize a single principle that will show up throughout this chapter and the next, it is:

In-depth performance optimization will often defy code abstractions.

This means that when trying to achieve extremely good performance, you will need to understand and possibly rely on the implementation details at all layers. Many of those are described in this chapter.

Class vs. Struct

Instances of a class are always allocated on the heap and accessed via a pointer dereference. Passing them around is cheap because it is just a copy of the pointer (4 or 8 bytes). However, an object also has some fixed overhead: 12 bytes for 32-bit processes and 24 bytes for 64-bit processes. This overhead includes the pointer to the method table and a couple of other internal identification fields.

A struct has no overhead at all and its memory usage is a sum of the size of all its fields. If a struct is declared as a local variable in a method, then the struct is allocated on the stack. If the struct is declared as part of a class, then the struct's memory will be part of that class's memory layout (and thus exist on the heap). When you pass a struct to a method it is copied byte for byte. Because it is not on the heap, allocating a struct will never cause a garbage collection.

There is thus a tradeoff here. You can find various pieces of advice about the maximum recommended size of a struct, but I would not get caught up on the exact number. In most cases you will want to keep struct sizes very small, especially if they are passed around, but you can also pass structs by reference so the size may not be an important issue to you. The only way to know for sure whether it benefits you is to consider your usage pattern and do your own profiling.

There is a huge difference in efficiency in some cases. While the overhead of an object might not seem like very much, consider an array of objects and compare it to an array of structs. Assume the data structure contains 16 bytes of data, the array length is 1,000,000, and this is a 32-bit system.

For an array of objects the total space usage is:

$$12 \text{ bytes array overhead } +$$
$$(4 \text{ byte pointer size} \times 1{,}000{,}000) +$$
$$((12 \text{ bytes overhead} + 16 \text{ bytes data}) \times 1{,}000{,}000)$$
$$= 32 \text{ MB}$$

For an array of structs, the results are dramatically different:

$$12 \text{ bytes array overhead } +$$
$$(16 \text{ bytes data} \times 1{,}000{,}000)$$
$$= 16 \text{ MB}$$

With a 64-bit process, the object array takes over 48 MB while the struct array still requires only 16 MB.

As you can see, in an array of structs, the same size of data takes less amount of memory. With the overhead of objects, you are also inviting a higher rate of garbage collections just from the added memory pressure.

Aside from space, there is also the matter of CPU efficiency. CPUs have multiple levels of caches. Those closest to the processor are very small, but extremely fast and optimized for sequential access.

An array of structs has many sequential values in memory. Accessing an item in the struct array is very simple. Once the correct entry is found, the right value is there already. This can mean a huge difference in access times when iterating over a large array. If the value is already in the CPU's cache, it can be accessed an order of magnitude faster than if it were in RAM.

To access an item in the object array requires an access into the array's memory, then a dereference of that pointer to the item elsewhere in the heap. Iterating over object arrays dereferences an extra pointer, jumps around in the heap, and evicts the CPU's cache more often, potentially squandering more useful data.

This lack of overhead for both CPU and memory is a prime reason to favor structs in many circumstances—it can buy you significant performance gains when used intelligently because of the improved memory locality.

Because structs are always copied by value, you can create some interesting situations for yourself if you are not careful. For example, see this buggy code which will not compile:

```
struct Point
{
  public int x;
  public int y;
}

public static void Main()
{
  List<Point> points = new List<Point>();
  points.Add(new Point() { x = 1, y = 2 });
  points[0].x = 3;
}
```

The problem is the last line, which attempts to modify the existing Point in the list. This is not possible because calling points[0] returns a copy of the original value, which is not stored anywhere permanent. The correct way to modify the Point is:

```
Point p = points[0];
p.x = 3;
points[0] = p;
```

However, it may be wise to adopt an even more stringent policy: make your structs immutable. Once created, they can never change value. This removes the above situation from even being a possibility and generally simplifies struct usage.

I mentioned earlier that structs should be kept small to avoid spending significant time copying them, but there are occasional uses for large structs. Consider an object that tracks a lot of details of some commercial process, such as a lot of time stamps.

```
class Order
{
  public DateTime ReceivedTime {get;set;}
  public DateTime AcknowledgeTime {get;set;}
  public DateTime ProcessBeginTime {get;set;}
  public DateTime WarehouseReceiveTime {get;set;}
```

157

```
    public DateTime WarehouseRunnerReceiveTime {get;set;}
    public DateTime WarehouseRunnerCompletionTime {get;set;}
    public DateTime PackingBeginTime {get;set;}
    public DateTime PackingEndTime {get;set;}
    public DateTime LabelPrintTime {get;set;}
    public DateTime CarrierNotifyTime {get;set;}
    public DateTime ProcessEndTime {get;set;}
    public DateTime EmailSentToCustomerTime {get;set;}
    public DateTime CarrerPickupTime {get;set;}

    // lots of other data ...
}
```

To simplify your code, it would be nice to segregate all of those times into their own sub-structure, still accessible via the Order class via some code like this:

```
Order order = new Order();
Order.Times.ReceivedTime = DateTime.UtcNow;
```

You could put all of them into their own class.

```
class OrderTimes
{
  public DateTime ReceivedTime {get;set;}
  public DateTime AcknowledgeTime {get;set;}
  public DateTime ProcessBeginTime {get;set;}
  public DateTime WarehouseReceiveTime {get;set;}
  public DateTime WarehouseRunnerReceiveTime {get;set;}
  public DateTime WarehouseRunnerCompletionTime {get;set;}
  public DateTime PackingBeginTime {get;set;}
  public DateTime PackingEndTime {get;set;}
  public DateTime LabelPrintTime {get;set;}
  public DateTime CarrierNotifyTime {get;set;}
  public DateTime ProcessEndTime {get;set;}
  public DateTime EmailSentToCustomerTime {get;set;}
  public DateTime CarrerPickupTime {get;set;}
}

class Order
{
  public OrderTimes Times;
}
```

However, this does introduce an additional 12 or 24-bytes of overhead for every Order object. If you need to pass the OrderTimes object as a whole to various methods, maybe this makes sense, but why not just pass the reference to the entire Order object itself? If you have thousands of Order objects being processed simultaneously, this can cause more garbage collections to be induced. It is also an extra memory dereference.

Instead, change OrderTimes to be a struct. Accessing the individual properties of the OrderTimes struct via a property on Order (e.g., order.Times.ReceivedTime) will not result in a copy of the struct (.NET optimizes that reasonable scenario). This way, the OrderTimes struct becomes essentially part of the memory layout for the Order class almost exactly like it was with no substructure and you get to have better-looking code as well.

This technique does violate the principle of immutable structs, but the trick here is to treat the fields of the OrderTimes struct just as if they were fields on the Order object. You do not need to pass around the OrderTimes struct as an entity in and of itself—it is just an organization mechanism.

Override Equals and GetHashCode for Structs

An extremely important part of using structs is overriding the Equals and GetHashCode methods. If you don't, you will get the default versions, which are not at all good for performance. To get an idea of how bad it is, use an IL viewer and look at the code for the ValueType.Equals method. It involves reflection over all the fields in the struct. There is, however, an optimization for blittable types. A blittable type is one that has the same in-memory representation in managed and unmanaged code. They are limited to the primitive numeric types (such as Int32, UInt64, for example, but not Decimal, which is not a primitive) and IntPtr/UIntPtr. If a struct is comprised of all blittable types, then the Equals implementation can do the equivalent of byte-for-byte memory compare across the whole struct. Just avoid this uncertainty and implement your own Equals method.

If you just override Equals(object other), then you are still going to have worse performance than necessary, because that method involves casting and boxing on value types. Instead, implement Equals(T other), where T is the type of your struct. This is what the IEquatable<T> interface is for, and all structs should implement it. During compilation, the compiler will prefer the more strongly typed version whenever possible. The following code snippet shows you an example.

```
struct Vector : IEquatable<Vector>
{
  public int X { get; set; }
  public int Y { get; set; }
  public int Z { get; set; }
```

```
    public int Magnitude { get; set; }

    public override bool Equals(object obj)
    {
      if (obj == null)
      {
        return false;
      }
      if (obj.GetType() != this.GetType())
      {
        return false;
      }
      return this.Equals((Vector)obj);
    }

    public bool Equals(Vector other)
    {
      return this.X == other.X
        && this.Y == other.Y
        && this.Z == other.Z
        && this.Magnitude == other.Magnitude;
    }

    public override int GetHashCode()
    {
      return X ^ Y ^ Z ^ Magnitude;
    }
}
```

If a type implements IEquatable<T> .NET's generic collections will detect its presence and use it to perform more efficient searches and sorts.

You may also want to implement the == and != operators on your value types and have them call the existing Equals(T) method.

Even if you never compare structs or put them in collections, I still encourage you to implement these methods. You will not always know how they will be used in the future and the price of the methods is only a few minutes of your time and a few bytes of IL that will never even get JITted.

It is not as important to override Equals and GetHashCode on classes because by default they only calculate equality based on their object reference. As long as that is a reasonable assumption for your objects, you can leave them as the default implementation.

Virtual Methods and Sealed Classes

Do not mark methods virtual by default, "just in case." However, if virtual methods are necessary for a coherent design in your program, you probably should not go too far out of your way to remove them.

Making methods virtual prevents certain optimizations by the JIT compiler, notably the ability to inline them. Methods can only be inlined if the compiler knows 100% which method is going to be called. Marking a method as virtual removes this certainty, though there are other factors, covered in Chapter 3, that are perhaps more likely to invalidate this optimization.

Closely related to virtual methods is the notion of sealing a class, like this:

```
public sealed class MyClass {}
```

A class marked as sealed is declaring that no other classes can derive from it. In theory, the JIT could use this information to inline more aggressively, but it does not do so currently. Regardless, you should mark classes as sealed by default and not make methods virtual unless they need to be. This way, your code will be able to take advantage of any current as well as theoretical future improvements in the JIT compiler.

If you are writing a class library that is meant to be used in a wide variety of situations, especially outside of our organization, you need to be more careful. In that case, having virtual APIs may be more important than raw performance to ensure your library is sufficiently reusable and customizable. But for code that you change often and is used only internally, go the route of better performance.

Interface Dispatch

The first time you call a method through an interface, .NET has to figure out which type and method to make the call on. It will first make a call to a stub that finds the right method to call for the appropriate object implementing that interface. Once this happens a few times, the CLR will recognize that the same concrete type is always being called and this indirect call via the stub is reduced to a stub of just a handful of assembly instructions that makes a direct call to the correct method. This group of instructions is called a monomorphic stub because it knows how to call a method for a single type. This is ideal for situations where a call site always calls interface methods on the same type every time.

The monomorphic stub can also detect when it is wrong. If, at some point the call site uses an object of a different type, then eventually the CLR will replace the stub with another monomorphic stub for the new type.

If the situation is even more complex with multiple types and less predictability (for example, you have an array of an interface type, but there are multiple concrete types in that array) then the stub will be changed to a polymorphic stub that uses a hash table to pick which method to call. The table lookup is fast, but not as fast as the monomorphic stub. Also, this hash table is severely bounded in size and if you have too many types, you might fall back to the generic type lookup code from the beginning. This can be very expensive.

If this becomes a concern for you, you have a couple of options:

1. Avoid calling these objects through the common interface
2. Pick your common base interface and replace it with an abstract base class instead

This type of problem is not common, but it can hit you if you have a huge type hierarchy, all implementing a common interface, and you call methods through that root interface. You would notice this as high CPU usage at the call site for these methods that cannot be explained by the work the methods are doing.

> **Story** During the design of a large system, we knew we were going to have potentially thousands of types that would likely all descend from a common type. We knew there would be a couple of places where we would need to access them from the base type. Because we had someone on the team who understood the issues around interface dispatch with this magnitude of problem size, we chose to use an abstract base class rather than a root interface instead.

To learn more about interface dispatch see Vance Morrison's blog entry on the subject at http://www.writinghighperf.net/go/23.

Avoid Boxing

Boxing is the process of wrapping a value type such as a primitive or struct inside an object that lives on the heap so that it can be passed to methods that require object references. Unboxing is getting the original value back out again.

Boxing costs CPU time for object allocation, copying, and casting, but, more seriously, it results in more pressure on the GC heap. If you are careless about boxing, it can lead to a significant number of allocations, all of which the GC will have to handle.

Obvious boxing happens whenever you do things like the following:

```
int x = 32;
object o = x;
```

The IL looks like this:

```
IL_0001: ldc.i4.s 32
IL_0003: stloc.0
IL_0004: ldloc.0
IL_0005: box [mscorlib]System.Int32
IL_000a: stloc.1
```

This means that it is relatively easy to find most sources of boxing in your code—just use ILDASM to convert all of your IL to text and do a search.

A very common of way of having accidental boxing is using APIs that take object or object[] as a parameter, the most obvious of which is String.Format or the old style collections which only store object references and should be avoided completely for this and other reasons (see Chapter 6).

Boxing can also occur when assigning a struct to an interface, for example:

```
interface INameable
{
  string Name { get; set; }
}

struct Foo : INameable
{
  public string Name { get; set; }
}

void TestBoxing()
{
  Foo foo = new Foo() { Name = "Bar" };
  // This boxes!
  INameable nameable = foo;
  ...
}
```

If you test this out for yourself, be aware that if you do not actually use the boxed variable then the compiler will optimize out the boxing instruction because it is never actually touched. As soon as you call a method or otherwise use the value then the boxing instruction will be present.

Another thing to be aware of when boxing occurs is the result of the following code:

```
int val = 13;
object boxedVal = val;
val = 14;
```

What is the value of boxedVal after this?

Boxing copies the value and there is no longer any relationship between the two values. In this example, val changes value to 14, but boxedVal maintains its original value of 13.

You can sometimes catch boxing happening in a CPU profile, but many boxing calls are inlined so this is not a reliable method of finding it. What will show up in a CPU profile of excessive boxing is heavy memory allocation through new.

If you do have a lot of boxing of structs and find that you cannot get rid of it, you should probably just convert the struct to a class, which may end up being cheaper overall.

Finally, note that passing a value type by reference is not boxing. Examine the IL and you will see that no boxing occurs. The address of the value type is sent to the method.

for vs. foreach

Use the MeasureIt program described in Chapter 1 to see for yourself the difference in iterating collections using for loops or foreach. Using standard for loops is significantly faster in all the cases. However, if you do your own simple test, you might notice equivalent performance depending on the scenario. In many cases, .NET will actually convert simple foreach statements into standard for loops.

Take a look at the ForEachVsFor sample project, which has this code:

```
int[] arr = new int[100];
for (int i = 0; i < arr.Length; i++)
{
   arr[i] = i;
}

int sum = 0;
foreach (int val in arr)
{
   sum += val;
}
sum = 0;
```

```
IEnumerable<int> arrEnum = arr;
foreach (int val in arrEnum)
{
  sum += val;
}
```

Once you build this, then decompile it using an IL reflection tool. You will see that the first foreach is actually compiled as a for loop. The IL looks like this:

```
// loop start (head: IL_0034)
IL_0024: ldloc.s CS$6$0000
IL_0026: ldloc.s CS$7$0001
IL_0028: ldelem.i4
IL_0029: stloc.3
IL_002a: ldloc.2
IL_002b: ldloc.3
IL_002c: add
IL_002d: stloc.2
IL_002e: ldloc.s CS$7$0001
IL_0030: ldc.i4.1
IL_0031: add
IL_0032: stloc.s CS$7$0001
IL_0034: ldloc.s CS$7$0001
IL_0036: ldloc.s CS$6$0000
IL_0038: ldlen
IL_0039: conv.i4
IL_003a: blt.s IL_0024
// end loop
```

There are a lot of stores, loads, adds, and a branch—it is all quite simple. However, once we cast the array to an IEnumerable<int> and do the same thing, it gets a lot more expensive:

```
IL_0043: callvirt instance class
[mscorlib]System.Collections.Generic.IEnumerator`1<!0> class
[mscorlib]System.Collections.Generic.IEnumerable`1<int32>::GetEnumerator()
IL_0048: stloc.s CS$5$0002
.try
{
  IL_004a: br.s IL_005a
  // loop start (head: IL_005a)
    IL_004c: ldloc.s CS$5$0002
    IL_004e: callvirt instance !0 class
[mscorlib]System.Collections.Generic.IEnumerator`1<int32>::get_Current()
    IL_0053: stloc.s val
    IL_0055: ldloc.2
    IL_0056: ldloc.s val
```

```
    IL_0058: add
    IL_0059: stloc.2

    IL_005a: ldloc.s CS$5$0002
    IL_005c: callvirt instance bool
[mscorlib]System.Collections.IEnumerator::MoveNext()
    IL_0061: brtrue.s IL_004c
  // end loop

  IL_0063: leave.s IL_0071
} // end .try
finally
{
  IL_0065: ldloc.s CS$5$0002
  IL_0067: brfalse.s IL_0070

  IL_0069: ldloc.s CS$5$0002
  IL_006b: callvirt instance void [mscorlib]System.IDisposable::Dispose()

  IL_0070: endfinally
} // end handler
```

We have 4 virtual method calls, a try-finally, and, not shown here, a memory allocation for the local enumerator variable which tracks the enumeration state. That is much more expensive than the simple for loop. It uses more CPU and more memory!

Remember, the underlying data structure is still an array—a for loop is possible—but we are obfuscating that by casting to an IEnumerable. The important lesson here is the one that was mentioned at the top of the chapter: In-depth performance optimization will often defy code abstractions. foreach is an abstraction of a loop, and IEnumerable is an abstraction of a collection. Combined, they dictate behavior that defies the simple optimizations of a for loop over an array.

Casting

In general, you should avoid casting wherever possible. Casting often indicates poor class design, but there are times when it is required. It is relatively common to need to convert between unsigned and signed integers between various third-party APIs, for example. Casting objects should be much rarer.

Casting objects is never free, but the costs differ dramatically depending on the relationship of the objects. Casting an object to its parent is relatively cheap. Casting a parent object to the correct child is significantly more expensive, and the costs increase with a larger hierarchy. Casting to an interface is more expensive than casting to a concrete type.

What you absolutely must avoid is an invalid cast. This will cause an `InvalidCastException` exception to be thrown, which will dwarf the cost of the actual cast by many orders of magnitude.

See The CastingPerf sample project in the accompanying source code which benchmarks a number of different types of casts. It produces this output on my computer in one test run:

```
JIT (ignore): 1.00x
No cast: 1.00x
Up cast (1 gen): 1.00x
Up cast (2 gens): 1.00x
Up cast (3 gens): 1.00x
Down cast (1 gen): 1.25x
Down cast (2 gens): 1.37x
Down cast (3 gens): 1.37x
Interface: 2.73x
Invalid Cast: 14934.51x
as (success): 1.01x
as (failure): 2.60x
is (success): 2.00x
is (failure): 1.98x
```

The 'is' operator is a cast that tests the result and returns a Boolean value. The 'as' operator is similar to a standard cast, but returns null if the cast fails. From the results above, you can see this is much faster than throwing an exception.

Never have this pattern, which performs two casts:

```
if (a is Foo)
{
   Foo f = (Foo)a;
}
```

Instead, use 'as' to cast and cache the result, then test the return value:

```
Foo f = a as Foo;
if (f != null)
{
   ...
}
```

If you have to test against multiple types, then put the most common type first.

> **Note** One annoying cast that I see regularly is when using `MemoryStream.Length`, which is a `long`. Most APIs that use it are using the reference to the underlying buffer (retrieved from the `MemoryStream.GetBuffer` method), an offset, and a length, which is often an `int`, thus making a downcast from `long` necessary. Casts like these can be common and unavoidable.

P/Invoke

P/Invoke is used to make calls from managed code into native methods. It involves some fixed overhead plus the cost of marshalling the arguments. Marshalling is the process of converting types from one format to another.

You can see a simple benchmark of P/Invoke cost vs. a normal managed function call cost with the MeasureIt program mentioned in Chapter 1. On my computer, a P/Invoke call takes about 6-10 times the amount of time it takes to call an empty static method. You do not want to call a P/Invoked method in a tight loop if you have a managed equivalent, and you definitely want to avoid making multiple transitions between native and managed code. However, a single P/Invoke calls is not so expensive as to prohibit it in all cases.

There are a few ways to minimize the cost of making P/Invoke calls:

1. First, avoid having a "chatty" interface. Make a single call that can work on a lot of data, where the time spent processing the data is significantly more than the fixed overhead of the P/Invoke call.
2. Use blittable types as much as possible. Recall from the discussion about structs that blittable types are those that have the same binary value in managed and native code, mostly numeric and pointer types. These are the most efficient arguments to pass because the marshalling process is basically a memory copy.
3. Avoid calling ANSI versions of Windows APIs. For example, the `CreateProcess` function is actually a macro that resolves to one of two real functions, `CreateProcessA` for ANSI strings, and `CreateProcessW` for Unicode strings. Which version you get is determined by the compilation settings for the native code. You want to ensure that you are always calling the Unicode versions of APIs because all .NET strings are already Unicode, and having a mismatch here will cause an expensive, possibly lossy, conversion to occur.
4. Don't pin unnecessarily. Primitives are never pinned anyway and the marshalling layer will automatically pin strings and arrays of primitives. If you do need to pin something else, keep the object pinned for as short a duration as possible to. See Chapter 2 for a discussion of how pinning can negatively impact garbage collection. With pinning, you will have to balance this need for a short duration with the first recommendation of

avoiding chatty interfaces. In all cases, you want the native code to return as fast as possible.

5. If you need to transfer a large amount of data to native code, consider pinning the buffer and having the native code operate on it directly. It does pin the buffer in memory, but if the function is fast enough this may be more efficient than a large copy operation. If you can ensure that the buffer is in gen 2 or the large object heap, then pinning is much less of an issues because the GC is unlikely to need to move the object anyway.

Finally, you can reduce some of the cost of P/Invoke by disabling some security checks on the P/Invoke method declarations.

```
[DllImport("kernel32.dll", SetLastError=true)]
[System.Security.SuppressUnmanagedCodeSecurity]
static extern bool GetThreadTimes(IntPtr hThread, out long lpCreationTime,
out long lpExitTime, out long lpKernelTime, out long lpUserTime);
```

This attribute declares that the method can run with full trust. This will cause you to receive some Code Analysis (FxCop) warnings because it is disabling a large part of .NET's security model. However, if your application runs only trusted code, you sanitize the inputs, and you prevent public APIs from calling the P/Invoke methods, then it can gain you some performance, as demonstrated in this MeasureIt output:

Name	Mean
PInvoke: 10 FullTrustCall() (10 call average) [count=1000 scale=10.0]	6.945
PInvoke: PartialTrustCall() (10 call average) [count=1000 scale=10.0]	17.778

The method running with full trust can execute about 2.5 times faster.

Delegates

There are two costs associated with use of delegates: construction and invocation. Invocation, thankfully, is comparable to a normal method call in nearly all circumstances, but delegates are objects and constructing them can be quite expensive. You want to pay this cost only once and cache the result. Consider the following code:

```
private delegate int MathOp(int x, int y);
private static int Add(int x, int y) { return x + y; }
private static int DoOperation(MathOp op, int x, int y) { return op(x, y);}
```

Which of the following loops is faster?

Option 1:

```
for (int i = 0; i < 10; i++)
{
  DoOperation(Add, 1, 2);
}
```

Option 2:

```
MathOp op = Add;
for (int i = 0; i < 10; i++)
{
  DoOperation(op, 1, 2);
}
```

It looks like Option 2 is only aliasing the Add function with a local delegate variable, but this actually involves a memory allocation! It becomes clear if you look at the IL for the respective loops:Option 1:

```
// loop start (head: IL_0020)
IL_0004: ldnull
IL_0005: ldftn int32 DelegateConstruction.Program::Add(int32, int32)
IL_000b: newobj instance void
DelegateConstruction.Program/MathOp::.ctor(object, native int)
IL_0010: ldc.i4.1
IL_0011: ldc.i4.2
IL_0012: call int32 DelegateConstruction.Program::
            DoOperation(class DelegateConstruction.Program/MathOp,
                int32, int32)
...
```

While Option 2 has the same memory allocation, but it is outside of the loop:

```
L_0025: ldnull
IL_0026: ldftn int32 DelegateConstruction.Program::Add(int32, int32)
IL_002c: newobj instance void
DelegateConstruction.Program/MathOp::.ctor(object, native int)
...
// loop start (head: IL_0047)
IL_0036: ldloc.1
IL_0037: ldc.i4.1
IL_0038: ldc.i4.2
IL_0039: call int32 DelegateConstruction.Program::DoOperation(class
DelegateConstruction.Program/MathOp, int32, int32)
...
```

These examples can be found in the DelegateConstruction sample project.

Exceptions

In .NET, putting a try block around code is cheap, but exceptions are very expensive to throw. This is largely because of the rich state that .NET exceptions contain. Exceptions must be reserved for truly exceptional situations, when raw performance ceases to be important.

To see the devastating effects on performance that throwing exceptions can have, see the ExceptionCost sample project. Its output should be similar to the following:

```
Empty Method: 1x
Exception (depth = 1): 8525.1x
Exception (depth = 2): 8889.1x
Exception (depth = 3): 8953.2x
Exception (depth = 4): 9261.9x
Exception (depth = 5): 11025.2x
Exception (depth = 6): 12732.8x
Exception (depth = 7): 10853.4x
Exception (depth = 8): 10337.8x
Exception (depth = 9): 11216.2x
Exception (depth = 10): 10983.8x
Exception (catchlist, depth = 1): 9021.9x
Exception (catchlist, depth = 2): 9475.9x
Exception (catchlist, depth = 3): 9406.7x
Exception (catchlist, depth = 4): 9680.5x
Exception (catchlist, depth = 5): 9884.9x
Exception (catchlist, depth = 6): 10114.6x
Exception (catchlist, depth = 7): 10530.2x
Exception (catchlist, depth = 8): 10557.0x
Exception (catchlist, depth = 9): 11444.0x
Exception (catchlist, depth = 10): 11256.9x
```

This demonstrates three simple facts:

1. A method that throws an exception is thousands of time slower than a simple empty method.
2. The deeper the stack for the thrown exception, the slower it gets (though it is already so slow, it doesn't matter).
3. Having multiple catch statements has a slight but significant effect as the right one needs to be found.

On the flip side, while catching exceptions may be cheap, accessing the StackTrace property on an Exception object can be very expensive as it reconstructs the stack from pointers and translates it into readable text. In a high-performance application, you may want to make logging of these stack traces optional through configuration and use it only when needed.

To reiterate: exceptions should be truly exceptional. Using them as a matter of course can destroy your performance.

Dynamic

It should probably go without saying, but to make it explicit: any code using the dynamic keyword, or the Dynamic Language Runtime (DLR) is not going to be highly optimized. Performance tuning is often about stripping away abstractions, but using the DLR is adding one huge abstraction layer. It has its place, certainly, but a fast system is not one of them.

When you use dynamic, what looks like straightforward code is anything but. Take a simple, admittedly contrived example:

```
static void Main(string[] args)
{
    int a = 13;
    int b = 14;

    int c = a + b;

    Console.WriteLine(c);
}
```

The IL for this is equally straightforward:

```
.method private hidebysig static
    void Main (
        string[] args
    ) cil managed
{
    // Method begins at RVA 0x2050
    // Code size 17 (0x11)
    .maxstack 2
    .entrypoint
    .locals init (
        [0] int32 a,
        [1] int32 b,
        [2] int32 c
```

```
    )
    IL_0000: ldc.i4.s 13
    IL_0002: stloc.0
    IL_0003: ldc.i4.s 14
    IL_0005: stloc.1
    IL_0006: ldloc.0
    IL_0007: ldloc.1
    IL_0008: add
    IL_0009: stloc.2
    IL_000a: ldloc.2
    IL_000b: call void [mscorlib]System.Console::WriteLine(int32)
    IL_0010: ret
} // end of method Program::Main
```

Now let's just make those ints dynamic:

```
static void Main(string[] args)
{
  dynamic a = 13;
  dynamic b = 14;

  dynamic c = a + b;

  Console.WriteLine(c);
}
```

For the sake of space, I am actually going to *not* show the IL here, but this is what it looks like when you convert it back to C#:

```
private static void Main(string[] args)
{
  object a = 13;
  object b = 14;
  if (Program.<Main>o__SiteContainer0.<>p__Site1 == null)
  {
    Program.<Main>o__SiteContainer0.<>p__Site1 =
      CallSite<Func<CallSite, object, object, object>>.
      Create(Binder.BinaryOperation(CSharpBinderFlags.None,
                  ExpressionType.Add,
                  typeof(Program),
                  new CSharpArgumentInfo[]
    {
      CSharpArgumentInfo.Create(CSharpArgumentInfoFlags.None, null),
      CSharpArgumentInfo.Create(CSharpArgumentInfoFlags.None, null)
    }));
  }
```

173

```
object c = Program.<Main>o__SiteContainer0.
    <>p__Site1.Target(Program.<Main>o__SiteContainer0.<>p__Site1, a, b);
if (Program.<Main>o__SiteContainer0.<>p__Site2 == null)
{
  Program.<Main>o__SiteContainer0.<>p__Site2 =
    CallSite<Action<CallSite, Type, object>>.
    Create(Binder.InvokeMember(CSharpBinderFlags.ResultDiscarded,
                "WriteLine",
                null,
                typeof(Program),
                new CSharpArgumentInfo[]
  {
    CSharpArgumentInfo.Create(
      CSharpArgumentInfoFlags.UseCompileTimeType |
      CSharpArgumentInfoFlags.IsStaticType,
      null),
    CSharpArgumentInfo.Create(CSharpArgumentInfoFlags.None, null)
  }));
}
Program.<Main>o__SiteContainer0.<>p__Site2.Target(
  Program.<Main>o__SiteContainer0.<>p__Site2, typeof(Console), c);
}
```

Even the call to WriteLine isn't straightforward. From simple, straightforward code, it has gone to a mishmash of memory allocations, delegates, dynamic method invocation, and these objects called CallSites.

The JITting statistics are predictable:

Version	JIT Time	IL Size	Native Size
int	0.5ms	17 bytes	25 bytes
dynamic	10.9ms	209 bytes	389 bytes

I do not mean to dump too much on the DLR. It is a perfectly fine framework for rapid development and scripting. It opens up great possibilities for interfacing between dynamic languages and .NET. If you are interested in what it offers, read a good overview at http://www.writinghighperf.net/go/24.

Code Generation

If you find yourself doing anything with dynamically loaded types (e.g., an extension or plugin model), then you need to carefully measure your performance when interacting with those types. Ideally, you can interact with those types via a common interface and avoid most of the issues with dynamically loaded code. This approach is described in Chapter 6 when discussing reflection. If that approach is not possible, use this section to get around the performance problems of invoking dynamically loaded code.

The .NET Framework supports dynamic type allocation with the `Activator.CreateInstance` method, and dynamic method invocation with `MethodInfo.Invoke`. Here is an example using these methods:

```
Assembly assembly = Assembly.Load("Extension.dll");
Type type = assembly.GetType("DynamicLoadExtension.Extension");
object instance = Activator.CreateInstance(type);

MethodInfo methodInfo = type.GetMethod("DoWork");
bool result = (bool)methodInfo.Invoke(instance, new object[] { argument });
```

If you do this only occasionally, then it is not a big deal, but if you need to allocate a lot of dynamically loaded objects or invoke many dynamic function calls, these functions could become a severe bottleneck. Not only does `Activator.CreateInstance` use significant CPU, but it can cause unnecessary allocations, which put extra pressure on the garbage collector. There is also potential boxing that will occur if you use value types in either the function's parameters or return value (as the example above does).

If possible, try to hide these invocations behind an interface known both to the extension and the execution program, as described in Chapter 6. If that does not work, code generation may be an appropriate option.

Thankfully, generating code to accomplish the same thing is quite easy. To figure out what code to generate, use a template as an example to generate the IL for you to mimic. For an example, see the DynamicLoadExtension and DynamicLoadExecutor sample projects. DynamicLoadExecutor loads the extension dynamically and then executes the DoWork method. The DynamicLoadExecutor project ensures that DynamicLoadExtension.dll is in the right place with a post-build step and a solution build dependency configuration rather than project-level dependencies to ensure that code is indeed dynamically loaded and executed.

Let's start with creating a new extension object. To create a template, first understand what you need to accomplish. You need a method with no parameters that returns an instance of the type we need. Your program will not know about the `Extension` type, so it will just return it as an object. That method looks like this:

```
object CreateNewExtensionTemplate()
{
    return new DynamicLoadExtension.Extension();
}
```

Take a peek at the IL and it will look like this:

```
IL_0000: newobj instance void
         [DynamicLoadExtension]DynamicLoadExtension.Extension::.ctor()
IL_0005: ret
```

Armed with that knowledge, you can create a `System.Reflection.Emit.DynamicMethod`, programmatically add some IL instructions to it, and assign it to a delegate which you can then reuse to generate new `Extension` objects at will.

```
private static T GenerateNewObjDelegate<T>(Type type)
    where T:class
{
    // Create a new, parameterless (specified
    // by Type.EmptyTypes) dynamic method.
    var dynamicMethod = new DynamicMethod("Ctor_" + type.FullName, type,
Type.EmptyTypes, true);
    var ilGenerator = dynamicMethod.GetILGenerator();

    // Look up the constructor info for the type we want to create
    var ctorInfo = type.GetConstructor(Type.EmptyTypes);
    if (ctorInfo != null)
    {
        ilGenerator.Emit(OpCodes.Newobj, ctorInfo);
        ilGenerator.Emit(OpCodes.Ret);

        object del = dynamicMethod.CreateDelegate(typeof(T));
        return (T)del;
    }
    return null;
}
```

You will notice that the emitted IL corresponds exactly to our template method.

To use this, you need to load the extension assembly, retrieve the appropriate type, and pass it the generator function.

```
Type type = assembly.GetType("DynamicLoadExtension.Extension");
Func<object> creationDel = GenerateNewObjDelegate<Func<object>>(type);
object extensionObj = creationDel();
```

Once the delegate is constructed you can cache it for reuse (perhaps keyed by the Type object, or whatever scheme is appropriate for your application).

You can use the exact same trick to generate the call to the DoWork method. It is only a little more complicated due to a cast and the method arguments. IL is a stack-based language so arguments to functions must be pushed on to the stack in the correct order before a function call. The first argument for an instance method call must be the method's hidden this parameter that the object is operating on. Note that just because IL uses a stack exclusively, it does not have anything to do with how the JIT compiler will transform these function calls to assembly code, which often uses processor registers to hold function arguments.

As with object creation, first create a template method to use as a basis for the IL. Since we will have to call this method with just an object parameter (that is all we will have in our program), the function parameters specify the extension as just an object. This means we will have to cast it to the right type before calling DoWork. In the template, we have hard-coded type information, but in the generator we can get the type information programmatically.

```
static bool CallMethodTemplate(object extensionObj, string argument)
{
  var extension = (DynamicLoadExtension.Extension)extensionObj;
  return extension.DoWork(argument);
}
```

The resulting IL for this template looks like:

```
.locals init (
  [0] class [DynamicLoadExtension]DynamicLoadExtension.Extension extension
)

IL_0000: ldarg.0
IL_0001: castclass [DynamicLoadExtension]DynamicLoadExtension.Extension
IL_0006: stloc.0
IL_0007: ldloc.0
IL_0008: ldarg.1
IL_0009: callvirt instance bool
[DynamicLoadExtension]DynamicLoadExtension.Extension::DoWork(string)
IL_000e: ret
```

Notice there is a local variable declared. This holds the result of the cast. We will see later that it can be optimized away. This IL leads to a straightforward translation into a DynamicMethod:

```
private static T GenerateMethodCallDelegate<T>(
  MethodInfo methodInfo,
  Type extensionType,
```

```
     Type returnType,
     Type[] parameterTypes) where T : class
{
    var dynamicMethod = new DynamicMethod("Invoke_" + methodInfo.Name,
                returnType, parameterTypes, true);
    var ilGenerator = dynamicMethod.GetILGenerator();

    ilGenerator.DeclareLocal(extensionType);
    // object's this parameter
    ilGenerator.Emit(OpCodes.Ldarg_0);
    // cast it to the correct type
    ilGenerator.Emit(OpCodes.Castclass, extensionType);
    // actual method argument
    ilGenerator.Emit(OpCodes.Stloc_0);
    ilGenerator.Emit(OpCodes.Ldloc_0);
    ilGenerator.Emit(OpCodes.Ldarg_1);
    ilGenerator.EmitCall(OpCodes.Callvirt, methodInfo, null);
    ilGenerator.Emit(OpCodes.Ret);

    object del = dynamicMethod.CreateDelegate(typeof(T));
    return (T)del;
}
```

To generate the dynamic method, we need the MethodInfo, looked up from the extension's Type object. We also need the Type of the return object and the Types of all the parameters to the method, including the implicit this parameter (which is the same as extensionType).

This method works perfectly, but look closely at what it is doing and recall the stack-based nature of IL instructions. Here's how this method works:

1. Declare local variable
2. Push arg0 (the this pointer) onto the stack (LdArg_0)
3. Cast arg0 to the right type and push result onto the stack
4. Pop the top of the stack and store it in the local variable (Stloc_0)
5. Push the local variable onto the stack (Ldloc_0)
6. Push arg1 (the string argument) onto the stack
7. Call the DoWork method (Callvirt)
8. Return

There is some glaring redundancy in there, specifically with the local variable. We have the casted object on the stack, we pop it off then push it right back on. We could optimize this IL by just removing everything having to do with the local variable. It is possible that the JIT compiler would optimize this away for us anyway, but doing the optimization does not hurt, and could help if we have hundreds or thousands dynamic methods, all of which will need to be JITted.

The other optimization is to recognize that the `Callvirt` opcode can be changed to a simpler `Call` opcode because we know there is no virtual method here. Now our IL looks like this:

```
var ilGenerator = dynamicMethod.GetILGenerator();

// object's this parameter
ilGenerator.Emit(OpCodes.Ldarg_0);
// cast it to the correct type
ilGenerator.Emit(OpCodes.Castclass, extensionType);
// actual method argument
ilGenerator.Emit(OpCodes.Ldarg_1);
ilGenerator.EmitCall(OpCodes.Call, methodInfo, null);
ilGenerator.Emit(OpCodes.Ret);
```

To use our delegate, we just need to call it like this:

```
Func<object, string, bool> doWorkDel =
  GenerateMethodCallDelegate<
    Func<object, string, bool>>(
    methodInfo, type, typeof(bool),
    new Type[]
      { typeof(object), typeof(string) });

bool result = doWorkDel(extension, argument);
```

So how is performance with our generated code? Here is one test run:

```
==CREATE INSTANCE==
Direct ctor: 1.0x
Activator.CreateInstance: 14.6x
Codegen: 3.0x

==METHOD INVOKE==
Direct method: 1.0x
MethodInfo.Invoke: 17.5x
Codegen: 1.3x
```

Using direct method calls as a baseline, you can see that the reflection methods are much worse. Our generated code does not quite bring it back, but it is close. These numbers are for a function call that does not actually do anything, so they represent pure overhead of the function call, which is not a very realistic situation. If I add some minimal work (string parsing and a square root calculation), the numbers change a little:

```
==CREATE INSTANCE==
Direct ctor: 1.0x
Activator.CreateInstance: 9.3x
```

```
Codegen: 2.0x

==METHOD INVOKE==
Direct method: 1.0x
MethodInfo.Invoke: 3.0x
Codegen: 1.0x
```

In the end, this demonstrates that if you rely on `Activator.CreateInstance` or `MethodInfo.Invoke`, you can significantly benefit from some code generation.

> **Story** I have worked on one project where these techniques reduced the CPU overhead of invoking dynamically loaded code from over 10% to something more like 0.1%.

You can use code generation for other things as well. If your application does a lot of string interpretation or has a state machine of any kind, this is a good candidate for code generation. .NET itself does this with regular expressions (See Chapter 6) and XML serialization.

Preprocessing

If part of your application is doing something that is absolutely critical to performance, make sure it is not doing anything extraneous, or wasting time processing things that could be done beforehand. If data needs to be transformed before it is useful during runtime, make sure that as much of that transformation happens beforehand, even in an offline process if possible.

In other words, if something *can* be preprocessed, then it *must* be preprocessed. It can take some creativity and out-of-the-box thinking to figure out what processing can be moved offline, but the effort is often worth it. From a performance perspective, it is a form of 100% optimization by removing the code completely.

Measurement

Each of the topics in this chapter requires a different approach to performance, using the tools you already know from earlier chapters. CPU profiles will reveal expensive `Equals` methods, poor loop iteration, bad interop marshalling performance, and other inefficient areas.

Memory traces will show you boxing as `object` allocations and a general .NET event trace will show you where exceptions are being thrown, even if they are being caught and handled.

ETW Events

ExceptionThrown—An exception has been thrown. It does not matter if this exception is handled or not. Fields include:

- Exception Type—Type of the exception.
- Exception Message—Message property from the exception object.
- EIPCodeThrow—Instruction pointer of throw site.
- ExceptionHR—HRESULT of exception.
- ExceptionFlags
    - 0x01—Has inner exception
    - 0x02 – Is nested exception
    - 0x04 – Is rethrown exception
    - 0x08 – Is a corrupted state exception.
    - 0x10 – Is a CLS compliant exception.

See http://www.writinghighperf.net/go/25 for more information.

Finding Boxing Instructions

There is a specific IL instruction called box, which makes it fairly easy to discover in your code base. To find it in a single method or class, just use one of the many IL decompilers available (my tool of choice is ILSpy) and select the IL view.

If you want to detect boxing in an entire assembly it is easier to use ILDASM with its flexible command-line options.

ILDASM.exe ships with the Windows SDK. On my computer it is located in C:\Program Files (x86)\Microsoft SDKs\Windows\v8.0A\bin\NETFX 4.0 Tools\. You can get the Windows SDK from http://www.writinghighperf.net/go/26.

```
ildasm.exe /out=output.txt Boxing.exe
```

Take a look at the Boxing sample project, which demonstrates a few different ways boxing can occur. If you run ILDASM on Boxing.exe, you should see output similar to the following:

```
.method private hidebysig static void  Main(string[] args) cil managed
{
.entrypoint
// Code size       98 (0x62)
.maxstack  3
.locals init ([0] int32 val,
    [1] object boxedVal,
```

```
      [2] valuetype Boxing.Program/Foo foo,
      [3] class Boxing.Program/INameable nameable,
      [4] int32 result,
      [5] valuetype Boxing.Program/Foo '<>g__initLocal0')
IL_0000:  ldc.i4.s    13
IL_0002:  stloc.0
IL_0003:  ldloc.0
IL_0004:  box      [mscorlib]System.Int32
IL_0009:  stloc.1
IL_000a:  ldc.i4.s    14
IL_000c:  stloc.0
IL_000d:  ldstr    "val: {0}, boxedVal:{1}"
IL_0012:  ldloc.0
IL_0013:  box      [mscorlib]System.Int32
IL_0018:  ldloc.1
IL_0019:  call     string [mscorlib]System.String::Format(string,
                             object,
                             object)
IL_001e:  pop
IL_001f:  ldstr    "Number of processes on machine: {0}"
IL_0024:  call     class [System]System.Diagnostics.Process[]
[System]System.Diagnostics.Process::GetProcesses()
IL_0029:  ldlen
IL_002a:  conv.i4
IL_002b:  box      [mscorlib]System.Int32
IL_0030:  call     string [mscorlib]System.String::Format(string,
                             object)
IL_0035:  pop
IL_0036:  ldloca.s    '<>g__initLocal0'
IL_0038:  initobj  Boxing.Program/Foo
IL_003e:  ldloca.s    '<>g__initLocal0'
IL_0040:  ldstr    "Bar"
IL_0045:  call     instance void Boxing.Program/Foo::set_Name(string)
IL_004a:  ldloc.s  '<>g__initLocal0'
IL_004c:  stloc.2
IL_004d:  ldloc.2
IL_004e:  box      Boxing.Program/Foo
IL_0053:  stloc.3
IL_0054:  ldloc.3
IL_0055:  call     void Boxing.Program::UseItem(class
Boxing.Program/INameable)
IL_005a:  ldloca.s    result
IL_005c:  call     void Boxing.Program::GetIntByRef(int32&)
IL_0061:  ret
} // end of method Program::Main
```

You can also discover boxing indirectly via PerfView. With a CPU trace, you can find excessive calling of the JIT_new function.

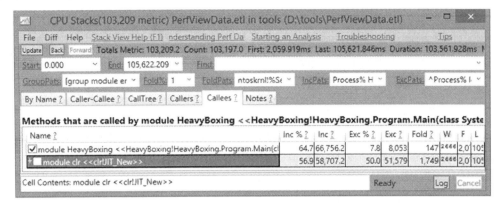

Figure 5-1. Boxing will show up in a CPU trace under the JIT_New method, which is the standard memory allocation method.

It is a little more obvious if you look at a memory allocation trace because you know that value types and primitives should not require a memory allocation at all:

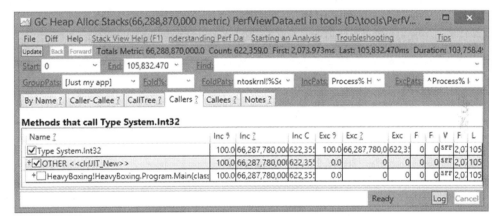

Figure 5-2. You can see in this trace that the Int32 is being allocated via new, which should not feel right.

Discovering First-Chance Exceptions

PerfView can easily show you which exceptions are being thrown, regardless of whether they are caught or not.

1. In PerfView, collect .NET events. The default settings are ok, but CPU is not necessary, so uncheck it if you need to profile for more than a few minutes.
2. When collection is complete, double-click on the "Exception Stacks" node.

3. Select the desired process from the list.
4. The Name view will show a list of the top exceptions. The CallTree view will show the stack for the currently selected exception.

By Name ?	Caller-Callee ?	CallTree ?	Callers ?	Callees ?	Notes ?		
Name					Inc %	Inc	Inc Ct
☑ROOT					100.0	15,767.0	15,767
+☑Process32 ExceptionCost.vshost (4640)					100.0	15,767.0	15,767
+☑Thread (4828) CPU=0ms					100.0	15,767.0	15,767
+☑OTHER <<ntdll!?>>					100.0	15,767.0	15,767
+☑ExceptionCost!ExceptionCost.Program.Main(class System.!					100.0	15,767.0	15,767
+☑ExceptionCost!ExceptionCost.Program.ExceptionMethod					100.0	15,767.0	15,767
+☑ExceptionCost!ExceptionCost.Program.ExceptionMetho					87.3	13,766.0	13,766
I+☑OTHER <<clr!IL_Throw>>					87.3	13,766.0	13,766
I +☑Throw(System.InvalidOperationException) Operation					87.3	13,766.0	13,766

Figure 5-3. PerfView makes finding where exceptions are coming from trivially easy.

Summary

Remember that in-depth performance optimizations will defy code abstractions. You need to understand how your code will be translated to IL, assembly code, and hardware operations. Take time to understand each of these layers.

Use a struct instead of a class when the data is relatively small, you want minimal overhead, or you are going to use them in arrays and want optimal memory locality. Consider making structs immutable and always implement Equals, GetHashCode, and IEquatable<T> on them. Avoid boxing of value types and primitives by guarding against assignment to object references.

Keep iteration fast by not casting collections to IEnumerable. Avoid casting in general, whenever possible, especially instances that could result in an InvalidCastException.

Minimize the number of P/Invoke calls by sending as much data per call as possible. Keep memory pinned as briefly as possible.

If you need to make heavy use of Activator.CreateInstance or MethodInfo.Invoke, consider code generation instead.

6 Using the .NET Framework

The previous chapter discussed general .NET coding techniques and pitfalls, especially those related to language features. In this chapter, we discuss some of the issues you must consider when using the enormous library of code that ships with .NET. I cannot possibly discuss all of the various subsystems and classes that are part of the .NET Framework, but the purpose of this chapter is to give you the tools you need to do your own investigations into performance, and to be aware of common patterns that you may need to avoid.

The .NET Framework was written with an extremely broad audience in mind (all developers everywhere, really), and is meant to be a general-purpose framework, providing stable, correct, robust code that can handle many situations. As such, it does not emphasize raw performance, and you will find many things you will need to work around in the inner loops of your codebase.

To get around weaknesses in the .NET Framework, you may need to use some ingenuity. Some possible approaches are:

- Use an alternate API with less cost
- Redesign your application to not call the API as often
- Re-implement some APIs in a more performant manner
- Do an interop into a native API to accomplish the same thing (assuming the marshalling cost is less)

Understand Every API you call

The guiding principle of this chapter is this:

You must understand the code executing behind every API call you make.

To say you have control of your performance is to assert that you know the code that executes in every critical path of your code. You should not have an opaque 3rd-party library at the center of your inner loop—that is ceding control.

You will not always have access to the source of every method you call down to the assembly level (you *do* always have access to the assembly level!), but there is usually good documentation for all Windows APIs. With .NET, you can use one of the many IL viewing tools out there to see what the Framework is doing. (This ease of inspection does not extend to the CLR itself, which is written largely in native code.)

Get used to examining Framework code for anything you are not familiar with. The more that performance is important to you, the more you need to question the implementation of APIs you do not own. Just remember to keep your pickiness proportionate to the need for speed.

What follows in this chapter is a discussion of a few general areas you should be concerned with as well as some specific, common classes every program will use.

Multiple APIs for the Same Thing

You will occasionally run into a situation where you can choose among many APIs for accomplishing the same thing. A good example is XML parsing. There are at least 9 different ways to parse XML in .NET:

- `XmlTextReader`
- `XmlValidatingReader`
- `XDocument`
- `XmlDocument`
- `XPathNavigator`
- `XPathDocument`
- `LINQ-to-XML`
- `DataContractSerializer`
- `XmlSerializer`

Which one you use depends on factors such as ease of use, productivity, suitability for the task, and performance. `XmlTextReader` is very fast, but it is forward-only and does no validation. `XmlDocument` is very convenient because it has a full object model loaded, but it is among the slowest options.

It is as true for XML parsing as it for other API choices: not all options will be equal, performance-wise. Some will be faster, but use more memory. Some will use very little memory, but may not allow certain operations. You will have to determine which features you need and measure the performance to determine which API provides the right balance of functionality vs. performance. You should prototype the options and profile them running on sample data.

Collections

.NET provides over 21 built-in collection types, including concurrent and generic versions of many popular data structures. Most programs will only need to use a combination of these and you should rarely need to create your own.

Some collections still exist in the .NET Framework only for backward compatibility reasons and should never be used by new code. These include:

- `ArrayList`
- `Hashtable`
- `Queue`
- `SortedList`
- `Stack`
- `ListDictionary`
- `HybridDictionary`

The reasons these should be avoided are casting and boxing. These collections store references to `Object` instances in them so you will always need to cast down to your actual object type.

The boxing problem is even more pernicious. Suppose you want to have an `ArrayList` of `Int32` value types. Each value will be individually boxed and stored on the heap. Instead of iterating through a contiguous array of memory to access each integer, each array reference will require a pointer dereference, heap access (likely hurting locality), and then an unboxing operation to get at the inner value. This is horrible. Use a non-resizable array or one of the generic collection classes instead.

In the early versions of .NET there were some string-specific collections that are now obsolete because of the power of generics. Examples include `NameValueCollection`, `OrderedDictionary`, `StringCollection`, and `StringDictionary`. They do not necessarily have performance problems per se, but there is no need to even consider them unless you are using an existing API that requires them.

The simplest, and likely the most-used, collection is the humble `Array`. Arrays are ideal because they are compact, using a single contiguous block, which improves processor cache locality when accessing multiple elements. Accessing them is in constant time and copying them is fast. Resizing them, however, will mean allocating a new array and copying the old values into the new object. Many of the more complicated data structures are built on top of arrays.

Choosing which collections to use depends on many factors, including: semantic meaning in the APIs (push/pop, enqueue/dequeue, Add/Remove, etc.), underlying storage mechanism and cache locality, speed of various operations on the collection such as Add and Remove, and whether you need to synchronize access to the collection. All of these factors can greatly influence the performance of your program.

Generic Collections

The generic collection classes are

- `Dictionary<TKey, TValue>`
- `HashSet<T>`
- `LinkedList<T>`
- `List<T>`
- `Queue<T>`
- `SortedDictionary<TKey, TValue>`
- `SortedList<TKey, TValue>`
- `SortedSet<T>`
- `Stack<T>`

These deprecate all of the non-generic versions and should always be preferred. They incur no boxing or casting costs and will have better memory locality for the most part (especially for the List-style structures that are implemented using arrays).

Within this set, though, there can be very large performance differences. For example, Dictionary, SortedDictionary, and SortedList all store key-value relationships, but have very different insertion and lookup characteristics.

- Dictionary is implemented as a hash table and has O(1) insertion and retrieval times. See Appendix B for a discussion of Big O notation if you are not familiar with this.
- SortedDictionary is implemented as a binary search tree and has O(log n) insertion and retrieval times.
- SortedList is implemented as a sorted array. It has O(log n) retrieval times, but can have O(n) insertion times in the worst case. If you insert random elements it will need to resize frequently and move the existing elements. It is ideal if you insert all of the elements in order, and then use it for fast lookups.

Of the three, SortedList has the smallest memory requirements because it uses arrays. The other two will have much more random memory access, but can guarantee better insertion times on average. Which one of these you use depends greatly on your application's requirements.

The difference between HashSet and SortedSet is similar to the difference between Dictionary and SortedDictionary.

- HashSet uses a hash table and has O(1) insertion and removal operations.
- SortedSet uses a binary search tree and has O(log n) insertion and removal operations.

List, Stack, and Queue all use arrays internally and thus have good locality of reference for efficient operations on many values, however when adding a lot of values, they will resize these internal arrays as needed. To avoid wasteful resizing and the CPU and GC overhead it causes, if you know the size beforehand, you should always pre-allocate the needed space by passing a capacity value via the constructor or changing the collection's Capacity property. List has O(1) insertion, but O(n) removal and searching. Stack and Queue can only add or remove from one end of the collection so have O(1) time in all operations.

LinkedList has O(1) insertion and removal characteristics, but it should be avoided for primitive types because it will allocate a new LinkedListNode object for every item you add, which can be wasteful overhead.

Concurrent Collections

See Chapter 4 for a discussion of concurrency in general, which must inform your use of the concurrent collection classes.

They are all located in the System.Collections.Concurrent namespace and are all defined for use with generics:

- ConcurrentBag<T> (A bag is similar to a set, but it allows duplicates)
- ConcurrentDictionary<TKey, TValue>
- ConccurentQueue<T>
- ConcurrentStack<T>

Most of these are implemented internally using Interlocked or Monitor synchronization primitives. You can and should examine their implementations using an IL reflection tool.

Pay attention to the APIs for insertion and removal of items from these collections. They all have Try methods which can fail to accomplish the operation in the case another thread beat them to it and there is now a conflict. For example, ConcurrentStack has a TryPop method which returns a Boolean value indicating whether it was able to pop a value. If another thread pops the last value, the current thread's TryPop will return false.

ConcurrentDictionary has a few methods which deserve special attention. You can call TryAdd to add a key and value to the dictionary, or TryUpdate to update an existing value.

Often, you will not care whether it is already in the collection and want to add or update it—it does not matter. For this, there is the AddOrUpdate method which does exactly that, but rather than having you provide the new value directly, you instead need to pass two delegates: one for add and one for update. If the key does not exist, the first delegate will be called with the key and you will need to return a value. If the key does exist, the second delegate is called with the key and existing value and you need to return a new value (which could just be the existing value).

In either case, the AddOrUpdate method will return to you the new value—but it is important to realize that this new value may not be the value from the current thread's AddOrUpdate call! These methods are *thread safe, but not atomic*. It is possible another thread calls this method with the same key and the first thread will return the value from the second thread.

There is also an overload of the method that does not have a delegate for the add case (you just pass in a value).

A simple example will be helpful:

```
dict.AddOrUpdate(
    // Key I'm trying to add
    0,
    // Delegate to call when adding--return string value based on the key
    key => key.ToString(),
    // Delegate to call when already present -- update existing value
    (key, existingValue) => existingValue);

dict.AddOrUpdate(
    // Key I'm trying to add
    0,
    // Value to add if new
    "0",
    // Delegate to call when already present--update existing value
    (key, existingValue) => existingValue);
```

The reason for having these delegates rather than just passing in the value is that in many cases generating the value for a given key is a very expensive operation and you do not want two threads to do it simultaneously. The delegate gives you a chance to just use the existing value instead of regenerating a new copy. However, note that there is no guarantee that the delegates are called only once. Also, if you need to provide synchronization around the value creation or update, you need to add that synchronization in the delegates themselves—the collection will not do it for you.

Related to AddOrUpdate is the GetOrAdd method which has almost identical behavior.

```
string val1 = dict.GetOrAdd(
  // The key to retrieve
  0,
  // A delegate to generate the value if not present
  k => k.ToString());

string val2 = dict.GetOrAdd(
  // The key to retrieve
  0,
  // The value to add if not present
  "0");
```

The lesson here is to be careful when using concurrent collections. They have special requirements and behaviors in order to guarantee safety and efficiency, and you need to understand exactly how they are used in the context of your program to use them correctly and effectively.

Other Collections

There are a handful of other specialized collections that ship with .NET, but most of them are string-specific or store Objects so can safely be ignored. Notable exceptions are BitArray and BitVector32.

BitArray represents an array of bit values. You can set individual bits and perform Boolean logic on the array as a whole. If you need only 32 bits of data, though, use BitVector32 which is faster and has less overhead because it is a struct (it is little more than wrapper around an Int32).

Creating Your Own Collection Types

I have rarely had the need to create my own collection types from scratch, but the need does occasionally arise. If the built-in types do not have the right semantics for you, then definitely create your own as an appropriate abstraction. When doing so, follow these general guidelines:

1. Implement the standard collection interfaces wherever they make sense (IEnumerable<T>, ICollection<T>, IList<T>, IDictionary<TKey, TValue>).
2. Consider how the collection will be used when deciding how to store the data internally.
3. Pay attention to things like locality-of-reference and favor arrays if sequential access is common.
4. Do you need to add synchronization into the collection itself? Or perhaps create a concurrent version of the collection?

5. Understand the run-time complexity of the add, insert, update, find, and remove algorithms. See Appendix A for a discussion of Big O complexity.
6. Implement APIs that make semantic sense, e.g. Pop for stacks, Dequeue for queues.

Strings

In .NET, strings are immutable. Once created, they exist forever in that state until garbage collected. This means that any modification of a string results in creation of a new string. Fast, efficient programs generally do not modify strings in any way. Think about it: strings represent textual data, which is largely for human consumption. Unless your program is specifically for displaying or processing text, strings should be treated like opaque data blobs as much as possible. If you have the choice, always prefer non-string representations of data.

String Comparisons

As with so many things in performance optimization, the best string comparison is the one that does not happen at all. If you can get away with it, use enums, or some other numeric data for decision-making. If you must use strings, keep them short and use the simplest alphabet possible.

There are many ways to compare strings: by pure byte value, using the current culture, with case insensitivity, etc. You should use the simplest way possible. For example:

```
String.Compare(a, b, StringComparison.OrdinalIgnoreCase);
```

is faster than

```
String.Compare(a, b, StringComparison.Ordinal);
```

which is faster than

```
String.Compare(a, b, StringComparison.CurrentCulture);
```

If you are processing computer-generated strings, such as configuration settings or some other tightly coupled interface, then ordinal comparisons with case sensitivity are all you need.

All string comparisons should use method overloads that includes an explicit StringComparison enumeration. Omitting this should be considered an error.

Finally, `String.Equals` is a special case of `String.Compare` and should be used when you do not care about sort order. It is not actually faster in many cases, but it conveys the intent of your code better.

ToLower, ToUpper

Avoid calling methods like `ToLower` and `ToUpper`, especially if you are doing this for string comparison purposes. Instead, use one of the `IgnoreCase` options for the `String.Compare` method.

There is a bit of a tradeoff, but not much of one. On the one hand, doing a case-sensitive string comparison is faster, but this still does not justify the use of `ToUpper` or `ToLower`, which are guaranteed to process every character, where a comparison might not need to. It also creates a new string, allocating memory and putting more pressure on the garbage collector.

Just avoid this.

Concatenation

For simple concatenation of a known (at compile time) quantity of strings, just use the '+' operator or the `String.Concat` method. This is usually more efficient than using a `StringBuilder`.

```
string result = a + b + c + d + e + f;
```

Do not consider `StringBuilder` until the number of strings is variable and likely larger than a few dozen. The compiler will optimize simple string concatenation in a way to lessen the memory overhead.

String Formatting

`String.Format` is an expensive method. Do not use it unless necessary. Avoid it for simple situations like this:

```
string message = String.Format("The file {0} was {1} successfully.",
    filename, operation);
```

Instead, just do some simple concatenation:

```
string message = "The file " + filename + " was " + operation + "
    successfully";
```

Reserve use of `String.Format` for cases where performance does not matter or the format specification is more complex (like specifying how many decimals to use for a `double` value).

ToString

Be wary of calling `ToString` for many classes. If you are lucky, it will return a string that already exists. Other classes will cache the string once generated. For example, the `IPAddress` class caches its string, but it has an extremely expensive string generation process that involves `StringBuilder`, formatting, and boxing. Other types may create a new string every time you call it. This can be very wasteful for the CPU and also impact the frequency of garbage collections.

When designing your own classes, consider the scenarios your class's `ToString` method will be called in. If it is called often, ensure that you are generating the string as rarely as possible. If it is only a debug helper, then it likely does not matter what it does.

Avoid String Parsing

If you can, reserve string parsing for offline processing or for during startup only. String processing is often CPU-intensive, repetitive, and memory-heavy—all things to avoid.

Avoid APIs that Throw Exceptions under Normal Circumstances

Exceptions are expensive, as you saw in Chapter 5. As such, they should be reserved for truly exceptional circumstances. Unfortunately, there are some common APIs which defy this basic assumption.

Most basic data types have a `Parse` method, which will throw a `FormatException` when the input string is in an unrecognized format. For example, `Int32.Parse`, `DateTime.Parse`, etc. Unless your program should exit completely when a parsing error occurs, avoid these methods in favor of `TryParse`, which will return a `bool` if parsing fails.

Another example is the `System.Net.HttpWebRequest` class, which will throw an exception if it receives a non-200 response from a server. This bizarre behavior is thankfully corrected in the `System.Net.Http.HttpClient` class in .NET 4.5.

Avoid APIs That Allocate From the Large Object Heap

The only way you can do this is by profiling heap allocations using PerfView, which will show the stacks allocating memory like this. Just be aware that there are some .NET APIs that will do this. For example, calling the Process.GetProcesses method will guarantee an allocation on the large object heap. You can avoid this by caching its results, calling it less frequently, or retrieving the information you need via interop directly into the Win32 API.

Use Lazy Initialization

If your program uses a large or expensive-to-create object that is rarely used, or may not be used at all during a given invocation of the program, you can use the Lazy<T> class to wrap a lazy initializer around it. As soon as the Value property is accessed, the real object will be initialized according to the constructor you used to create the Lazy<T> object.

If your object has a default constructor, you can use the simplest version of Lazy<T>:

```
var lazyObject = new Lazy<MyExpensiveObject>();
...
if (needRealObject)
{
  MyExpensiveObject realObject = lazyObject.Value;
  ...
}
```

If construction is more complex, you can pass a Func<T> to the constructor.

```
var myObject = new Lazy<MyExpensiveObject>(() =>
Factory.CreateObject("A"));
...
MyExpensiveObject realObject = myObject.Value
```

Factory.CreateObject is just a dummy method that produces MyExpensiveObject.

If myObject.Value is accessed from multiple threads, it is very possible that each thread will want to initialize the object. By default, Lazy<T> is completely thread safe and only a single thread will be allowed to execute the creation delegate and set the Value property. You can modify this with a LazyThreadSafetyMode enumeration. This enumeration has three values:

- None—No thread safety. If important, you must ensure that the Lazy<T> object is accessed via a single thread in this case.

- ExecutionAndPublication—Only a single thread is allowed to execute the creation delegate and set the Value property.
- PublicationOnly—Multiple threads can execute the creation delegate, but only a single one will initialize the Value property.

You should use Lazy<T> in place of your own singleton and double-checked locking pattern implementations.

If you have a large number of objects and Lazy<T> is too much overhead to use, you can use the static EnsureInitialized method on the LazyInitializer class. This uses Interlocked methods to ensure that the object reference is only assigned to once, but it does not ensure that the creation delegate is called only once. Unlike Lazy<T>, you must call the EnsureInitialized method yourself.

```
static MyObject[] objects = new MyObject[1024];


static void EnsureInitialized(int index)
{
  LazyInitializer.EnsureInitialized(ref objects[index],
      () => ExpensiveCreationMethod(index));
}
```

The Surprisingly High Cost of Enum

You probably do not expect methods that operate on Enums, a fundamentally integer type, to be very expensive. Unfortunately, because of the requirements of type safety, simple operations are more expensive than you realize.

Take the Enum.HasFlag method, for example. You likely imagine the implementation to be something like the following:

```
public static bool HasFlag(Enum value, Enum flag)
{
  return (value & flag) != 0;
}
```

Unfortunately, what you actually get is something similar to:

```
// C# code generated by ILSpy
public bool HasFlag(Enum flag)
{
  if (flag == null)
```

```
  {
    throw new ArgumentNullException("flag");
  }
  if (!base.GetType().IsEquivalentTo(flag.GetType()))
  {
    throw new ArgumentException("Enum types do not match",
        new object[]
      {
        flag.GetType(),
        base.GetType()
        }));
  }
  return this.InternalHasFlag(flag);
}
```

This is a good example of the side effects of using a general purpose framework. If you control your entire code base, then you can do better, performance-wise. If you find you need to do a HasFlag test a lot, then do the check yourself:

```
[Flags]
enum Options
{
  Read = 0x01,
  Write = 0x02,
  Delete = 0x04
}

...

private static bool HasFlag(Options option, Options flag)
{
  return (option & flag) != 0;
}
```

Enum.ToString is also quite expensive for enums that have the [Flags] attribute. One option is to cache all of the ToString calls for that Enum type in a simple Dictionary. Or you can avoid writing these strings at all and get much better performance just using the actual numeric value and convert to strings offline.

For a fun exercise, see how much code is invoked when you call Enum.IsDefined. Again, the existing implementation is perfectly fine if raw performance does not matter, but you will be horrified if you find out it is a real bottleneck for you!

Story I found out about the performance problems of Enum the hard way, after a release. During a regular CPU profile I noticed that a significant portion of CPU, over 3%, was going to just Enum.HasFlag and Enum.ToString. Excising all calls to HasFlag and using a Dictionary for the cached strings reduced the overhead to negligible amounts.

Tracking Time

Time means two things:

- Absolute time of day
- Time span (how long something took)

For absolute times, .NET supplies the versatile DateTime structure. However, calling DateTime.Now is a fairly expensive operation because it has to consider time zone information. Consider calling DateTime.UtcNow instead, which is more streamlined.

Even calling DateTime.UtcNow might be too expensive for you if you need to track a lot of time stamps. If that is the case, get the time once and then track offsets instead, rebuilding the absolute time offline, using the time span measuring techniques showed next.

To measure time intervals, .NET provides the TimeSpan struct. If you subtract two DateTime structs you will get a TimeSpan struct. However, if you need to measure very small time spans with minimal overhead, you must use the system's performance counter, via System.Diagnostics.Stopwatch, instead, which will return to you a 64-bit number measuring the number of clock ticks since the CPU received power. To calculate the real time difference you take two measurements of the clock tick, subtract them, and divide by the system's clock tick count frequency. Note that this frequency is not necessarily related to the CPU's frequency. Most modern processors change their CPU frequency often, but the tick frequency will not be affected.

You can use the Stopwatch class like this:

```
var stopwatch = Stopwatch.StartNew();
...do work...
stopwatch.Stop();
TimeSpan elapsed = stopwatch.Elapsed;
long elapsedTicks = stopwatch.ElapsedTicks;
```

There are also static methods to get a time stamp and the clock frequency, which may be more convenient if you are tracking a lot of time stamps and want to avoid the overhead of creating a new Stopwatch object for every interval.

```
long receiveTime = Stopwatch.GetTimestamp();
long parseTime = Stopwatch.GetTimestamp();
```

```
long startTime = Stopwatch.GetTimestamp();
long endTime = Stopwatch.GetTimestamp();

double totalTimeSeconds = (endTime - receiveTime) /
    Stopwatch.Frequency;
```

Finally, please remember that values received from the `Stopwatch.GetTimestamp` method are only valid in the current executing session and only for calculating relative time differences.

Combining the two types of time, you can see how to calculate offsets from a base `DateTime` object to get new absolute times:

```
DateTime start = DateTime.Now;
long startTime = Stopwatch.GetTimestamp();
long endTime = Stopwatch.GetTimestamp();

double diffSeconds = (endTime - startTime) / Stopwatch.Frequency;
DateTime end = start.AddSeconds(diffSeconds);
```

Regular Expressions

Regular expressions are not fast. The costs include:

- Assembly generation—With some options, an in-memory assembly is generated on the fly when you create a Regex object. This helps with the runtime performance, but is expensive to create the first time.
- JIT costs can be high—The code generated from a regular expression can be very long and have patterns that give the jitter fits. Thankfully, the most recent changes to the CLR have gone a long way to fix this, especially for 64-bit processes. See http://www.writinghighperf.net/go/27 for more information.
- Evaluation time can be long—This depends on the input text and the pattern to match. It is quite easy to write regular expressions that perform poorly and optimizing them in and of themselves is a whole topic unto itself.

There are a few things you can do to improve Regex performance:

- Ensure you are up-to-date with .NET and patches.
- Create a Regex instance variable rather than using the static methods.
- Create the Regex object with the `RegexOptions.Compiled` flag.
- Do not recreate Regex objects over and over again. Create one, save it, and reuse it to match on new input strings.

LINQ

The biggest danger with Language Integrated Query (LINQ) is that it has the potential to hide code from you—code for which you cannot be accountable because it is not present in your source file!

LINQ is phenomenally convenient at times, and many LINQ queries are perfectly performant, but it can make heavy use of delegates, interfaces, and temporary object allocation if you go crazy with temporary dynamic objects, joins, or complex where clauses.

You can often achieve some significant speedup in time by using Parallel LINQ, but keep in mind this is not actually reducing the amount of work to be done; it is just spreading it across multiple processors. For a mostly single-threaded application that just wants to use reduce the time it takes to execute a LINQ query, this may be perfectly acceptable. On the other hand, if you are writing a server that is already using all of the cores to perform processing, then spreading LINQ across those same processors will not help the big picture and may even hurt it. In this case, it may be better to do without LINQ at all and find something more efficient.

If you suspect that you have some unaccounted-for complexity, run PerfView and look at the JITStats view to see the IL sizes and JIT times for methods that involve LINQ. Also look at the CPU usage of those methods once JITted.

Reading Files

There are a number of convenience methods on the File class such as Open, OpenRead, OpenText, and OpenWrite. These are fine if performance is not critical.

If you are doing a lot of disk I/O, then you need to pay attention to the type of disk access you are doing, whether it is random, sequential, or if you need to ensure that the write has been physically written to the platter before notifying the application of I/O completion. For this level of detail, you will need to use the FileStream class and a constructor overload that accepts the FileOptions enumeration. You can logically OR multiple flags together, but not all combinations are valid. None of these options are required, but they can provide hints to the operating system or file system on how to optimize file access.

```
using (var stream = new FileStream(
            @"C:\foo.txt",
            FileMode.Open,
            FileAccess.Read,
            FileShare.Read,
            16384 /* Buffer Size*/,
```

```
                FileOptions.SequentialScan | FileOptions.Encrypted))
{
...
}
```

The options available to you are:

- Asynchronous—Indicates that you will be doing asynchronous reading or writing to the file. This is not required to actually perform asynchronous reads and writes, but if you do not specify it then, while your threads will not be blocked, the underlying I/O is performed synchronously without I/O completion ports. There are also overrides of the FileStream constructor that will take a Boolean parameter to specify asynchronous access.
- DeleteOnClose—Causes the OS to delete the file when the last handle to the file is closed. Use this for temporary files.
- Encrypted—Causes the file to be encrypted using the current account's credentials.
- RandomAccess—Gives a hint to the file system to optimize caching for random access.
- SequentialAccess—Gives a hint to the file system that the file is going to be read sequentially from beginning to end.
- WriteThrough—Ignore caching and go directly to the disk. This generally makes I/O slower. The flag will be obeyed by the file system's cache, but many storage devices also have onboard caches, and they are free to ignore this flag and report a successful completion before it is written to permanent storage.

Random access is bad for any device, such as a hard disk or tape, that needs to seek to the required position. Sequential access should be preferred for performance reasons.

Optimize HTTP Settings and Network Communication

If your application makes outbound HTTP calls, there are a number of settings you can change to optimize network transmission. You should exercise caution in changing these, however, as their effectiveness greatly depends on your network topology and the servers on the other end of the connection. You also need to take into account whether the target endpoints are in a data center you control, or are somewhere on the Internet. You will need to measure carefully to see if these settings benefit you or not.

To change these by default for all endpoints, modify these static properties on the ServicePointManager class:

- `DefaultConnectionLimit`—The number of connections per end point. Setting this higher may increase overall throughput if the network links and both endpoints can handle it.
- `Expect100Continue`—When a client initiates a POST or PUT command it normally waits for a 100-Continue signal from the server before proceeding to send the data. This allows the server to reject the request before the data is sent, saving bandwidth. If you control both endpoints and this situation does not apply to you, turn this off to improve latency.
- `ReceiveBufferSize`—The size of the buffer used for receiving requests. The default is 8 KB. You can use a larger buffer if you regularly get large requests.
- `SupportsPipelining`—Allows multiple requests to be sent without waiting for a response between each one. However, the responses are sent back in order. See RFC 2616 (the HTTP/1.1 standard) at http://www.writinghighperf.net/go/28 for more information.
- `UseNagleAlgorithm`—Nagling, described in RFC 896 at http://www.writinghighperf.net/go/29 is a way to reduce the overhead of packets on a network by combining many small packets into a single larger packet. This can be beneficial by reducing overall network transmission overhead, but it can also cause packets to be delayed. On modern networks, this value should usually be off. You can experiment with turning this off and see if there is a reduction in response times.

All of these settings can also be applied independently to individual `ServicePoint` objects, which can be useful if you want to customize settings by endpoint, perhaps to differentiate between local datacenter endpoints and those on the Internet. In addition to the above, the `ServicePoint` class also lets you control some additional parameters:

- `ConnectionLeaseTimeout`—Specifies the maximum time in milliseconds that an active connection will be kept alive. Set this to -1 to keep connections alive forever. This setting is useful for load balancing, where you will want to periodically force connections to close so they connect to other machines. Setting this value to 0 will cause the connection to close after every request. This is not recommended because making a new HTTP connection is fairly expensive.
- `MaxIdleTime`—Specifies the maximum time in milliseconds that a connection can remain open but idle. Set this to `Timeout.Infinite` to keep connections open indefinitely, regardless of whether they are active or not.
- `ConnectionLimit`—Specifies the maximum number of connections this endpoint can have.

You can also force an individual HTTP request to close its current connection (after the response has been sent back) by setting the KeepAlive header to false.

> **Story** Ensure that what you are transmitting is optimally encoded. While profiling an internal system, we noticed an extremely high memory allocation rate and CPU usage for a particular component. With some investigation, we realized that it was receiving an HTTP response, transforming the received bytes into a base64-encoded string, decoding that string into a binary blob, and then finally deserializing that blob back into a strongly typed object. It was wasting bandwidth by needlessly encoding a binary blob as a string, and wasting our CPU with multiple layers of encoding, and finally it was causing more time spent in GC with multiple large object allocations. The lesson is to send only what you need, as compactly as possible. Base64 is rarely, if ever, useful today, especially among internal components. Regardless of whether you are doing file or network I/O, encode the data as ideally as possible. For example, if you need to read a series of integers, do not waste CPU, memory, disk space, and network bandwidth wrapping that in XML.

Finally, another word of caution relating to the principle highlighted at the top of this chapter about the general purpose of much of the .NET Framework. The built-in HTTP client, while generally very good and perfectly acceptable for downloading Internet content, may not be suitable for all applications, particularly if your application is very sensitive to latencies at high percentiles, especially with intra-datacenter requests. If you care about 95th or 99th percentile latencies for HTTP requests, you may have to write your own HTTP client around the underlying WinHTTP APIs to get that last bit of performance. Doing this correctly takes quite a bit of expertise in both HTTP and multithreading in .NET to get right, so you need to justify the effort.

Reflection

Reflection is the process of loading a .NET assembly dynamically during runtime and manually loading, examining, or even executing the types located therein. This is not a fast process under any circumstance.

To demonstrate how reflection generally works in this scenario, here is some simple code from the ReflectionExe sample project that loads an "extension" assembly dynamically:

```
var assembly = Assembly.Load(extensionFile);

var types = assembly.GetTypes();
Type extensionType = null;
foreach (var type in types)
{
```

```
    var interfaceType = type.GetInterface("IExtension");
    if (interfaceType != null)
    {
      extensionType = type;
      break;
    }
}

object extensionObject = null;
if (extensionType != null)
{
  extensionObject = Activator.CreateInstance(extensionType);
}
```

At this point, there are two options we can follow to execute the code in our extension. To stay with pure reflection, we can retrieve the MethodInfo object for the method we want to execute and then invoke it:

```
MethodInfo executeMethod = extensionType.GetMethod("Execute");
executeMethod.Invoke(extensionObject, new object[] { 1, 2 });
```

This is painfully slow, about 100 times slower than casting the object to an interface and executing it directly:

```
IExtension extensionViaInterface = extensionObject as IExtension;
extensionViaInterface.Execute(1, 2);
```

If you can, you always want to execute your code this way rather than relying on the raw MethodInfo.Invoke technique. If a common interface is not possible, then see Chapter 5's section on generating code to execute dynamically loaded assemblies much faster than reflection.

Measurement

Many of the techniques for finding issues with .NET Framework performance are exactly the same as with your own code. When you use tools to profile CPU usage, memory allocations, exceptions, contention, and more, you will see the hotspots in the framework just like you see them in your own code.

Note that PerfView will group much of the framework together and you may need to change these view settings to get a better picture of where Framework performance is going.

Performance Counters

.NET has many categories of performance counters. Chapters 2 through 4, which cover garbage collection, JIT compilation, and asynchronous programming, all detail the performance counters for their specific topic. .NET has additional performance counters for the following categories:

- **.NET CLR Data**—Counters relating to SQL clients, connection pools, and commands
- **.NET CLR Exceptions**—Counters relating to rate of exceptions thrown
- **.NET CLR Interop**—Counters relating to calling native code from managed
- **.NET CLR Networking**—Counters relating to connections and amount of data transmitted
- **.NET CLR Remoting**—Counters relating to the number of remote calls, object allocations, channels, and more
- **.NET CLR Data Provider for SqlServer/Oracle**—Counters for various .NET database clients

Depending on your system's configuration you may see more or less than these.

Summary

As with all frameworks, you need to understand the implementation details of all the APIs you use. Do not take anything for granted.

Take care when picking collection classes. Consider API semantics, memory locality, algorithmic complexity, and space usage when choosing a collection. Completely avoid the older-style non-generic collections like ArrayList and HashTable. Use concurrent collections only when you need to synchronize most or all of the accesses.

Pay particular attention to string usage and avoid creating extra strings.

Avoid APIs that throw exceptions in normal circumstances, allocate from the large object heap, or have more expensive implementations than you expect.

When using regular expressions, make sure that you do not recreate the same Regex objects over and over again, and strongly consider compiling them with the RegexOptions.Compiled flag.

Pay attention to the type of I/O you are doing and use the appropriate flags when opening files to give the OS a chance to optimize performance for you. For network calls, disable Nagling and Expect100Continue. Only transmit the data you need and avoid unnecessary layers of encoding.

Avoid using reflection APIs to execute dynamically loaded code. Call this kind of code via common interfaces or through code generated delegates.

7 Performance Counters

Performance counters are critical for tracking the overall performance of your application over time. If you are responsible for tracking and improving the performance of your system, performance counters will help you do that. While you can (and should) use them for real-time monitoring, they can be even more valuable if you store them in a database for analysis over long periods of time. In this way, you can see how new releases, usage patterns, or other events affect the performance of your application.

You can consume performance counters in your own code for self-monitoring, archiving, or automated analysis. You can also create and register your own counters which are then available to the same monitoring approach. By correlating your program's custom counters with the system's counters for your application, you can often find the source of problems very quickly.

Performance counters are Windows-managed objects that track values over time. These values can be arbitrary numbers, counts, rates, time spans, or other types detailed later. Each counter has a category and a name associated with it. Most counters also have instances, which are specific subdivisions by logical, discrete entities. For example, the % Processor Time counter in the Processor category has instances for each process currently running. Many counters also have meta-instances like _Total or <Global> that aggregate the data across all instances.

Many components in Windows create their own performance counters and .NET is no exception. There are hundreds of counters available to you to track nearly every aspect of your program's performance. These counters are all described in the relevant chapters earlier in this book.

To track all the installed performance counters on a system, use the PerfMon.exe utility that comes with Windows, as described in Chapter 1. This current chapter discusses programmatic access to these counters, both consuming and creating your own.

Consuming Existing Counters

To consume a counter, you just need to create a new instance of the `PerformanceCounter` class and pass it the category and name you want to monitor. You can optionally supply the instance and machine name as well. Here is an example that attaches the counter object to the % Processor Time counter.

```
PerformanceCounter cpuCtr  = new PerformanceCounter("Process",
    "% Processor Time", process.ProcessName);
```

To retrieve values, you periodically call the `NextValue` method on the counter:

```
float value = cpuCtr.NextValue();
```

The API documentation recommends that you call `NextValue` no more frequently than once per second to allow the counter sufficient time to do the next read.

To see a simple project that demonstrates consuming multiple built-in and custom counters, see the accompanying PerfCountersTypingSpeed sample.

Creating a Custom Counter

To create your own custom counter, you create an instance of the `CounterCreationData` class, supplying a name and type. You add this to a collection, which is then added to a category.

```
const string CategoryName = "PerfCountersTypingSpeed";

if (!PerformanceCounterCategory.Exists(CategoryName))
{
  var counterDataCollection = new CounterCreationDataCollection();

  var wpmCounter = new CounterCreationData();
  wpmCounter.CounterType = PerformanceCounterType.RateOfCountsPerSecond32;
  wpmCounter.CounterName = "WPM";
  counterDataCollection.Add(wpmCounter);

  try
  {
    // Create the category.
    PerformanceCounterCategory.Create(
        CategoryName,
        "Demo category to show how to create and consume counters",
        PerformanceCounterCategoryType.SingleInstance,
```

```
        counterDataCollection);
    }
    catch (SecurityException )
    {
        // Handle error -- no permissions to make this change!
    }
}
```

To create a custom counter, you must have the `PerformanceCounterPermission` granted. In practice, this means that you should usually create new counters with an installation program that can run with elevated permissions. .NET provides the `PerformanceCounterInstaller` class, which can wrap multiple instances of the `CounterCreationData` class and install them for you, with support for rollback and removal.

There are many types of counters, grouped into a few categories, as detailed next. In addition, some counters have 32-bit and 64-bit sizes defined. You can use whichever one is most appropriate for the data you are recording.

Averages

These counters show the average of the last two measurements.

- `AverageCount64`—How many things are processed during an operation
- `AverageTimer32`—How long it takes to process an operation
- `CountPerTimeInterval32/64`—The average length of a queue for a resource
- `SampleCounter`—Counts the number of operations completed in a second

The `AverageCount64` and `AverageTimer32` counters need the help of a second counter, `AverageBase`, to determine how many operations were completed since the last time the counter was updated. The `AverageBase` counter must be initialized right after the counter to which it applies. The following code demonstrates how to create these two counters together:

```
var counterDataCollection = new CounterCreationDataCollection();

// Actual average counter
var bytesPerTx = new CounterCreationData();
bytesPerTx.CounterType = PerformanceCounterType.AverageCount64;
bytesPerTx.CounterName = "BytesPerTransmission";
counterDataCollection.Add(bytesPerTx);

// Base counter to help in calculations
var bytesPerTxBase = new CounterCreationData();
bytesPerTxBase.CounterType = PerformanceCounterType.AverageBase;
bytesPerTxBase.CounterName = "BytesPerTransmissionBase";
```

```
counterDataCollection.Add(bytesPerTxBase);

PerformanceCounterCategory.Create(
  "Network Statistics",
  "Network statistics demo counters",
  PerformanceCounterCategoryType.SingleInstance,
  counterDataCollection);
```

To set the values, you adjust each counter according to the number of items and the number of operations to which those items apply. In this example, it is fairly simple:

```
bytesPerTx.IncrementBy(request.Length);
bytesPerTxBase.IncrementBy(1);
```

Instantaneous

These are the simplest counters. They just reflect the most recent sample value.

- NumberOfItems32/64—Most recent value for a raw number.
- NumberOfItemsHEX32/64—Same as NumberOfItems32/64, displayed in hexadecimal format.
- RawFraction—With RawBase base counter, shows a percentage of the total. The total value is given to the base counter and the subset of that total value is assigned to this counter. An example would be percentage of a disk in use.

Deltas

Delta counters show the difference between the last two counter values.

- CounterDelta32/64—Shows the difference between the last two recorded values.
- ElapsedTime—Shows the time from when the component or process was started to now. For example, you can use this to track your application's up-time. You do not provide new values to this counter after initialization.
- RateOfCountsPerSecond32/64—Average number of operations completed per second.

Percentages

Percentage counters show the percent of a resource being used. In some cases, this percent can be greater than 100%. Consider a multiprocessor system: you could represent the CPU usage as a percentage of a single core. Each instance of the counter represents one of the cores. If multiple cores are simultaneously in use, then the percentage will be larger than 100.

- CounterTimer—Percent time a component is active in the total sample time.

- `CounterTimerInverse`—Similar to `CounterTimer`, except that it is measuring the time a component is NOT active and then subtracting that from 100%. In other words, this counter has the same meaning as `CounterTimer`, but arrives at the value in an inverse way.
- `CounterMultiTimer`—Similar to `CounterTimer`, but the active time is aggregated over all the instances, which can lead to percentages larger than 100.
- `CounterMultiTimerInverse`—Multiple instances, but derived from inactive time.
- `CounterMultiTimer100Ns`—Uses 100 nanosecond ticks instead of the system's performance counter ticks.
- `CounterMultiTimer100NsInverse`—Similar to `CounterMultiTimer100Ns`, but using the inverse logic.
- `SampleFraction`—The ratio of a subset of values to the total number of values. Uses the `SampleBase` base counter to track the total number of values.
- `Timer100Ns`—Percent time a component is active in the total sample time, measured in 100ns increments.
- `Timer100NsInverse`—Same as `Timer100Ns`, but uses the inverse logic.

All of the `CounterMulti-` counters require the use of the `CounterMultiBase`, similar to the `AverageCount64` example earlier.

When creating your own performance counters, note that you should not update them too often. A maximum of once per second is a good rule because the data will never be exposed more frequently than that. If you need to generate high-volume performance data, ETW events are a much better choice.

Summary

Performance counters are the most basic building block of performance analysis. While your program does not necessarily have to create its own, consider doing so if you have discrete operations, phases, or items that have performance impact.

Consider automated ingestion and analysis of counters via .NET APIs to provide archiving and continual feedback about system performance.

8 ETW Events

The previous chapter discussed performance counters which are excellent for tracking your application's overall performance. What performance counters cannot do is provide any information on a specific event or operation in your application. For that, you need to log data per operation. If you include time stamps then you now have the ability to track performance in your program in an extremely detailed way.

There are many logging libraries for .NET. There are some popular ones like log4net, as well as countless custom solutions. However, I strongly encourage you to use Event Tracing for Windows, which has a number of advantages:

1. It is built into the operating system
2. It is extremely fast and suitable for high-performance scenarios
3. It has automatic buffering
4. You can dynamically enable and disable consuming and producing events during runtime
5. It has a highly selective filtering mechanism
6. You can integrate events from multiple sources into one log stream for comprehensive analysis
7. All OS and .NET subsystems generate ETW events
8. Events are typed and ordinal-based instead of just strings

PerfView and many other profiling tools are nothing more than fancy ETW analyzers. For example, in Chapter 2 you saw how to use PerfView to analyze memory allocations. All of this information came from ETW events from the CLR.

In this chapter, you will explore how to define your own events and then consume them. All of the classes we introduce are in the System.Diagnostics.Tracing namespace and are available as of .NET 4.5.

You can define events that mark the start and stop of your program, the various stages of processing requests, errors that occur, or literally anything else. You have complete control of what information goes into an event.

Using ETW starts by defining things called providers. In .NET terms, this is a class with methods that define the events you want to log. These methods can accept any fundamental data type in .NET, such as strings, integers, and more.

Events are consumed by objects called listeners, which subscribe to the events they are interested in. If there are no subscribers for an event, then those events are discarded. This makes ETW very cheap on average.

Defining Events

Events are defined with a class that derives from the .NET Framework's EventSource class, as in this example:

```
using System.Diagnostics.Tracing;

namespace EtlDemo
{
  [EventSource(Name="EtlDemo")]
  internal sealed class Events : EventSource
  {
    ...
  }
}
```

The Name argument is necessary if you want listeners to find the source by name. You can also provide a GUID, but this is optional and if you do not provide one, it will be generated automatically for you from the name by a procedure specified in RFC 4122 (See http://www.writinghighperf.net/go/30). GUIDs are only necessary if you need to guarantee an unambiguous event source. If your source and listener are all in one process then you do not even need a name, and can pass the event source object directly to the listener.

After this basic definition, there are some conventions you should follow in defining your events. To illustrate them, I will define some events for a very simple test program (see the EtlDemo sample project).

```
using System.Diagnostics.Tracing;

namespace EtlDemo
```

```
{
  [EventSource(Name="EtlDemo")]
  internal sealed class Events : EventSource
  {
    public static readonly Events Write = new Events();

    public class Keywords
    {
      public const EventKeywords General = (EventKeywords)1;
      public const EventKeywords PrimeOutput = (EventKeywords)2;
    }

    internal const int ProcessingStartId = 1;
    internal const int ProcessingFinishId = 2;
    internal const int FoundPrimeId = 3;

    [Event(ProcessingStartId, Level = EventLevel.Informational,
           Keywords = Keywords.General)]
    public void ProcessingStart()
    {
      if (this.IsEnabled())
      { this.WriteEvent(ProcessingStartId); }
    }

    [Event(ProcessingFinishId, Level = EventLevel.Informational,
           Keywords = Keywords.General)]
    public void ProcessingFinish()
    {
      if (this.IsEnabled())
      {
        this.WriteEvent(ProcessingFinishId);
      }
    }

    [Event(FoundPrimeId, Level = EventLevel.Informational,
           Keywords = Keywords.PrimeOutput)]
    public void FoundPrime(long primeNumber)
    {
      if (this.IsEnabled())
      {
        this.WriteEvent(FoundPrimeId, primeNumber);
      }
    }
  }
}
```

First, notice that the first thing declared is a static reference to an instance of itself. This is common because events are usually global in nature and need to be accessed by many parts of your code. Having this "global" variable makes this a lot easier than passing a reference to the event source around to every object that needs it. I am used to using Write, but I have seen others use Log. You can name it whatever you want, but you should standardize on the same term for all your event sources for clarity.

After the declaration, there is an inner class which just defines some constant Keyword values. Keywords are optional and their values are arbitrary and completely up to you. They serve as a way of categorizing events in ways that are meaningful to your application. Listeners can filter what they want to listen for based on Keywords. Note that Keywords are treated like bit flags so you must assign values of multiples of two. This way, listeners can easily specify multiple Keywords to listen for.

Next come some constant declarations for the event identifiers. Using a constant declaration is not required, but it makes it more convenient if both the source and listener need to refer to the identifiers.

Finally, there is the list of events. These are specified with a void method that takes any number of arbitrary arguments. These methods are prefaced with an attribute that specifies the ID, the event level, and any keywords you want to apply (you can apply multiple keywords by ORing them together: Keywords = Keywords.General | Keywords.PrimeOutput).

There are five event levels:

- LogAlways—Always logged, no matter what, regardless of log level specified
- Critical—A very serious error, probably indicating your program cannot safely recover
- Error—A normal error
- Warning—Not quite an error, but someone may want to act on it
- Informational—A purely informational message; does not indicate an error
- Verbose—Should not be logged at all in most situations; useful for debugging specific problems or when running in certain modes

These levels are cumulative. Specifying a logging level implies that you will receive all events for that level and above. For example, if you specify a log level of Warning, you will also get events for Error, Critical, and LogAlways.

The event body is simple. Check to see if events are enabled (this is mostly a performance optimization). If they are, call the WriteEvent method (inherited from EventSource) with the event ID and your arguments.

> **Note** Do not try to log null values. The `EventSource` system does not know how to interpret them correctly because there is no type information. This is most common with string values. In that case, check for the null and supply a reasonable default:

```
[Event(5, Level = EventLevel.Informational, Keywords = Keywords.General)]
public void Error(string message)
{
  if (IsEnabled())
  {
    WriteEvent(5, message ?? string.Empty);
  }
}
```

To write your events, your code just needs to do something like this:

```
Events.Write.ProcessingStart();
Events.Write.FoundPrime(7);
```

Consume Custom Events in PerfView

Now that your application is producing ETW events, you can capture these events in any ETW listener utility, such as PerfView (or even Windows' built-in utility PerfMon).

To capture custom event sources in PerfView, you need to put the name, preceded by an asterisk (*), in the Additional Providers textbox in the Collect window:

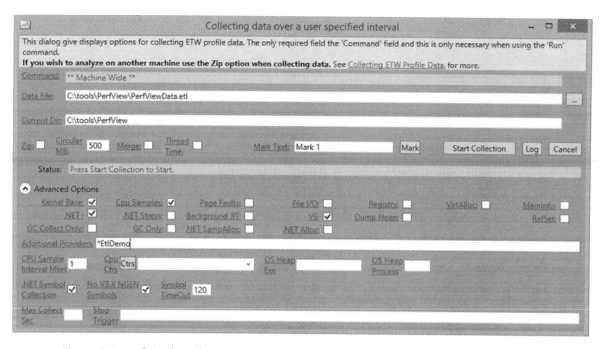

Figure 8-1. PerfView's Collect window, showing where to enter additional ETW providers.

By writing *EtlDemo, you tell PerfView to calculate the GUID automatically, as described earlier in the chapter. You can see more information by clicking on the Additional Providers title link.

Start collecting the samples, run EtlDemo, then press the Stop Collection button. Once the resulting events are recorded, open the raw Events node. You will see a list of all events captured, including these:

- EtlDemo/FoundPrime
- EtlDemo/ManifestData
- EtlDemo/ProcessingStart
- EtlDemo/ProcessingFinish

If you highlight all the events in the list and click the Update button to refresh the view, you can see a list similar to this:

EtlDemo/ProcessingStart	2,701.303	EtlDemo (8296)	ThreadID="8,556"
Microsoft-Windows-DotNETRuntime/Method/JittingStarted	2,701.345	EtlDemo (8296)	HasStack="True" ThreadID="8,556"
Microsoft-Windows-DotNETRuntime/Method/LoadVerbose	2,701.424	EtlDemo (8296)	HasStack="True" ThreadID="8,556"
Microsoft-Windows-DotNETRuntime/Method/JittingStarted	2,701.466	EtlDemo (8296)	HasStack="True" ThreadID="8,556"
Microsoft-Windows-DotNETRuntime/Method/LoadVerbose	2,701.975	EtlDemo (8296)	HasStack="True" ThreadID="8,556"
Windows Kernel/PerfInfo/SampleProf	2,702.102	EtlDemo (8296)	HasStack="True" ThreadID="8,556"
Microsoft-Windows-DotNETRuntime/Method/JittingStarted	2,702.342	EtlDemo (8296)	HasStack="True" ThreadID="8,556"
Microsoft-Windows-DotNETRuntime/Method/LoadVerbose	2,702.533	EtlDemo (8296)	HasStack="True" ThreadID="8,556"
EtlDemo/FoundPrime	2,702.564	EtlDemo (8296)	ThreadID="8,556" primeNumber="C
Microsoft-Windows-DotNETRuntime/Method/JittingStarted	2,702.596	EtlDemo (8296)	HasStack="True" ThreadID="8,556"
Windows Kernel/PerfInfo/SampleProf	2,703.167	EtlDemo (8296)	HasStack="True" ThreadID="8,556"
Microsoft-Windows-DotNETRuntime/Method/LoadVerbose	2,703.191	EtlDemo (8296)	HasStack="True" ThreadID="8,556"
EtlDemo/FoundPrime	2,704.007	EtlDemo (8296)	ThreadID="8,556" primeNumber="C

Figure 8-2. A sorted list showing Windows, .NET, and application events.

This shows you the custom events in the context of all the other captured events. You can see, for example, the JIT events that precede the FoundPrime events. This hints at the great power you can unleash with some smart ETW analysis. You can do some very detailed performance investigations in the context of your own application's scenarios. You can see a simple example of this later in the chapter.

Create a Custom ETW Event Listener

Most applications will not require you to create your own ETW listener. It is almost always sufficient to define your own events and use an application like PerfView to do the collection and analysis for you. However, you may want to create a listener if you need a custom logger or to perform real-time event analysis, for example.

In .NET, an event listener is a class that derives from the EventListener. To demonstrate multiple ways of handling the event data, I will define a base class for generic handling of listeners.

This class will need to know which events it should listen for and which level and keywords to filter by, so first define a simple structure to encapsulate that information:

```
class SourceConfig
{
  public string Name { get; set; }
  public EventLevel Level { get; set; }
  public EventKeywords Keywords { get; set; }
}
```

Then we can define our listener's constructor as taking a collection of these (one for each event source):

```
abstract class BaseListener : EventListener
{
  List<SourceConfig> configs = new List<SourceConfig>();
  protected BaseListener(
    IEnumerable<SourceConfig> sources)
  {
    this.configs.AddRange(sources);

    foreach (var source in this.configs)
    {
      var eventSource = FindEventSource(source.Name);
      if (eventSource != null)
      {
        this.EnableEvents(eventSource,
                source.Level,
                source.Keywords);
      }
    }
  }

  private static EventSource FindEventSource(string name)
  {
    foreach (var eventSource in EventSource.GetSources())
    {
      if (string.Equals(eventSource.Name, name))
      {
        return eventSource;
      }
    }
    return null;
  }
}
```

After saving the sources to its own list, it iterates over them and tries to find an existing EventSource that matches the names we want. If it finds one, it subscribes by calling the inherited method EnableEvents.

This is not enough, however. It is possible the EventSource is created after we set up our listener. For this eventuality, we can override the OnEventSourceCreated method and do essentially the same check to see if we are interested in the new EventSource.

```
protected override void OnEventSourceCreated(EventSource eventSource)
{
  base.OnEventSourceCreated(eventSource);

  foreach (var source in this.configs)
  {
    if (string.Equals(source.Name, eventSource.Name))
    {
      this.EnableEvents(eventSource, source.Level, source.Keywords);
    }
  }
}
```

The last thing we need to do is handle the OnEventWritten event which is called every time a new event is written by the sources for the current listener.

```
protected override void OnEventWritten(EventWrittenEventArgs eventData)
{
  this.WriteEvent(eventData);
}

protected abstract void WriteEvent(EventWrittenEventArgs eventData);
```

In this case, I am just deferring to an abstract method which will do the heavy lifting.

It is common practice to define multiple listener types that expose the event data in different ways. For this sample, I have defined one that writes the messages to the console and another that logs them to a file.

The ConsoleListener class looks like this:

```
class ConsoleListener : BaseListener
{
  public ConsoleListener(
    IEnumerable<SourceConfig> sources)
      :base(sources)
  {
  }

  protected override void WriteEvent(EventWrittenEventArgs eventData)
  {
    string outputString;
    switch (eventData.EventId)
    {
      case Events.ProcessingStartId:
        outputString = string.Format("ProcessingStart ({0})",
```

```
                        eventData.EventId);
        break;
      case Events.ProcessingFinishId:
        outputString = string.Format("ProcessingFinish ({0})",
                        eventData.EventId);
        break;
      case Events.FoundPrimeId:
        outputString = string.Format("FoundPrime ({0}): {1}",
                        eventData.EventId,
                        (long)eventData.Payload[0]);
        break;
      default:
        throw new InvalidOperationException("Unknown event");
    }
    Console.WriteLine(outputString);
  }
}
```

The EventId property is how you determine which event you are looking at. It is not as easy to get the name of the event, unfortunately, but it is possible with some upfront work, as you will see later. The Payload property provides you an array of the values that were passed into the original event method.

The FileListener is only slightly more complicated:

```
class FileListener : BaseListener
{
  private StreamWriter writer;

  public FileListener(IEnumerable<SourceConfig> sources, string outputFile)
    :base(sources)
  {
    writer = new StreamWriter(outputFile);
  }

  protected override void WriteEvent(EventWrittenEventArgs eventData)
  {
    StringBuilder output = new StringBuilder();
    DateTime time = DateTime.Now;
    output.AppendFormat("{0:yyyy-MM-dd-HH:mm:ss.fff} - {1} - ",
            time, eventData.Level);
    switch (eventData.EventId)
    {
      case Events.ProcessingStartId:
        output.Append("ProcessingStart");
        break;
```

```
      case Events.ProcessingFinishId:
        output.Append("ProcessingFinish");
        break;
      case Events.FoundPrimeId:
        output.AppendFormat("FoundPrime - {0:N0}",
                eventData.Payload[0]);
        break;
      default:
        throw new InvalidOperationException("Unknown event");
    }
    this.writer.WriteLine(output.ToString());
  }

  public override void Dispose()
  {
    this.writer.Close();

    base.Dispose();
  }
}
```

This code snippet from EtlDemo demonstrates how to use both listeners and have them listen to different keywords and levels:

```
var consoleListener = new ConsoleListener(
  new SourceConfig[]
  {
    new SourceConfig(){
        Name = "EtlDemo",
        Level = EventLevel.Informational,
        Keywords = Events.Keywords.General}
  });

var fileListener = new FileListener(
  new SourceConfig[]
  {
    new SourceConfig(){
        Name = "EtlDemo",
        Level = EventLevel.Verbose,
        Keywords = Events.Keywords.PrimeOutput}
  },
  "PrimeOutput.txt");

long start = 1000000;
long end = start + 10000;

Events.Write.ProcessingStart();
```

```
for (long i = start; i < end; i++)
{
  if (IsPrime(i))
  {
    Events.Write.FoundPrime(i);
  }
}

Events.Write.ProcessingFinish();
consoleListener.Dispose();
fileListener.Dispose();
```

It first creates the two types of listeners and subscribes them to a different set of events. Then it logs some events and exercises the program.

The console output has just this:

```
ProcessingStart (1)
ProcessingFinish (2)
```

While the output file contains lines like this:

```
2014-03-08-15:21:31.424 - Informational - FoundPrime - 1,000,003
2014-03-08-15:21:31.425 - Informational - FoundPrime - 1,000,033
2014-03-08-15:21:31.425 - Informational - FoundPrime - 1,000,037
```

Get Detailed EventSource Data

If you were paying attention in the previous couple of sections you will have noticed something interesting: our own event listener did not know the name of the event it was receiving, but PerfView somehow did. This is possible because every EventSource has a manifest associated with it. A manifest is just an XML description of the event source. Thankfully, .NET makes it easy to generate this manifest from an EventSource class.

```
string xml =
    EventSource.GenerateManifest(typeof(Events), string.Empty);
```

Here is the manifest for our own events defined previously:

```
<instrumentationManifest
xmlns="http://schemas.microsoft.com/win/2004/08/events">
  <instrumentation xmlns:xs="http://www.w3.org/2001/XMLSchema"
xmlns:xsi="http://www.w3.org/2001/XMLSchema-instance"
xmlns:win="http://manifests.microsoft.com/win/2004/08/windows/events">
```

```xml
<events xmlns="http://schemas.microsoft.com/win/2004/08/events">
<provider name="EtlDemo" guid="{458d4a63-7cc9-5239-62c4-f8aebbe597ac}"
resourceFileName="" messageFileName="" symbol="EtlDemo">
 <tasks>
  <task name="FoundPrime" value="65531"/>
  <task name="ProcessingFinish" value="65532"/>
  <task name="ProcessingStart" value="65533"/>
 </tasks>
 <opcodes>
 </opcodes>
 <keywords>
  <keyword name="General"  message="$(string.keyword_General)" mask="0x1"/>
  <keyword name="PrimeOutput"  message="$(string.keyword_PrimeOutput)"
mask="0x2"/>
 </keywords>
 <events>
  <event value="1" version="0" level="win:Informational" keywords="General"
task="ProcessingStart"/>
  <event value="2" version="0" level="win:Informational" keywords="General"
task="ProcessingFinish"/>
  <event value="3" version="0" level="win:Informational"
keywords="PrimeOutput" task="FoundPrime" template="FoundPrimeArgs"/>
 </events>
 <templates>
  <template tid="FoundPrimeArgs">
   <data name="primeNumber" inType="win:Int64"/>
  </template>
 </templates>
</provider>
</events>
</instrumentation>
<localization>
 <resources culture="en-US">
  <stringTable>
   <string id="keyword_General" value="General"/>
   <string id="keyword_PrimeOutput" value="PrimeOutput"/>
  </stringTable>
 </resources>
</localization>
</instrumentationManifest>
```

.NET is doing some behind-the-scenes magic for you to examine the types you use and generate the resulting manifest. For a more feature-rich logging system, you can parse this XML to get the names of the events and match them to the IDs, as well as the types of all the arguments.

Custom PerfView Analysis Extension

Using the existing tools to capture and view events is all well and good, and you may never need to go beyond that, but if you want to automate in-depth performance analysis, one of the easiest ways is by analyzing ETW data and nothing makes that easier than using PerfView as an engine to drive it. By using PerfView, you can analyze the raw event stream, but the real power comes from taking advantage of its amazing grouping and folding functionality to generate filtered, relevant stacks for your application.

PerfView ships with its own sample project to get started with this and it is actually built-in to PerfView's executable itself. To generate a sample solution, type the following at a command prompt:

```
PerfView.exe CreateExtensionProject MyProjectName
```

This will generate a solution file, project file, and sample source code file, complete with some code samples to get you started. Some examples of what you could do:

- Create a report showing you which assemblies use the most CPU. There is already a generated demo command that does exactly this.
- Automate a CPU analysis to export an XML file showing you the top most expensive stacks in your program, given some kind of criteria.
- Create views with complex folding and grouping schemes that you use frequently.
- Create a view that shows memory allocations for a specific operation in your program, where the operation is defined by your own custom ETW events.

With custom extensions and PerfView's command-line mode (no GUI), you can easily create a scriptable profiling tool that gives you easy-to-analyze reports of the most interesting areas of your application.

Here's a simple example that analyzes the frequency of the FoundPrime events from the EtlDemo sample program. I first captured the events with PerfView in a normal collection, using the *EtlDemo provider.

```
public void AnalyzePrimeFindFrequency(string etlFileName)
{
  using (var etlFile = OpenETLFile(etlFileName))
  {
    var events = GetTraceEventsWithProcessFilter(etlFile);

    const int BucketSize = 10000;
    //Each entry represents BucketSize primes and how
```

```csharp
//long it took to find them
List<double> primesPerSecond = new List<double>();

int numFound = 0;
DateTime startTime = DateTime.MinValue;

foreach (TraceEvent ev in events)
{
  if (ev.ProviderName == "EtlDemo")
  {
    if (ev.EventName == "FoundPrime")
    {
      if (numFound == 0)
      {
        startTime = ev.TimeStamp;
      }

      var primeNumber = (long)ev.PayloadByName("primeNumber");
      if (++numFound == BucketSize)
      {
        var elapsed = ev.TimeStamp - startTime;
        double rate = BucketSize / elapsed.TotalSeconds;
        primesPerSecond.Add(rate);
        numFound = 0;
      }

    }
  }
}

var htmlFileName = CreateUniqueCacheFileName(
            "PrimeRateHtmlReport", ".html");
using (var htmlWriter = File.CreateText(htmlFileName))
{
  htmlWriter.WriteLine("<h1>Prime Discovery Rate</h1>");
  htmlWriter.WriteLine("<p>Buckets: {0}</p>",
          primesPerSecond.Count);
  htmlWriter.WriteLine("<p>Bucket Size: {0}</p>", BucketSize);
  htmlWriter.WriteLine("<p>");
  htmlWriter.WriteLine("<table border=\"1\">");
  for (int i = 0; i < primesPerSecond.Count; i++)
  {
    htmlWriter.WriteLine(
      "<tr><td>{0}</td><td>{1:F2}/sec</td></tr>",
      i,
      primesPerSecond[i]);
  }
```

```
    htmlWriter.WriteLine("</table>");
  }

  OpenHtmlReport(htmlFileName, "Prime Discovery Rate");
 }
}
```

You can run the extension with this command line:

```
PerfView userCommand MyProjectName.AnalyzePrimeFindFrequency
    PerfViewData.etl
```

Everything after the extension name is passed into the method as the arguments.

The output will be a window in PerfView that looks like this:

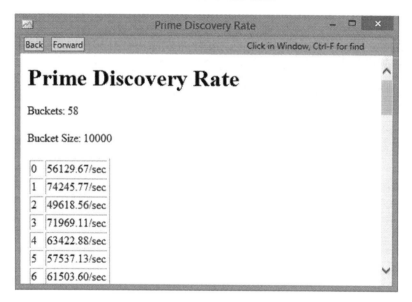

Figure 8-1. The HTML output of our custom ETW analysis.

Note that the extension capability is not an officially supported API. PerfView's internal API has had breaking changes in the past and likely will so in the future.

Summary

ETW events are the preferred method of logging discrete events in your application. They are ideal for both an application log as well as tracking detailed performance information.

In most cases, PerfView or another ETW analysis application will be able to provide all of the investigation tools you need, but if you want custom analysis, build a PerfView extension.

9 Windows Phone

.NET powers applications on Windows Phone and most of the advice presented in this book is equally applicable to mobile applications. With each release of .NET, the set of APIs common to all platforms gets larger.

That said, there are a few major and a handful of minor differences you should be aware of. All of the information in this short chapter is applicable to Windows Phone 8. As of this version, the CLR running on the devices is essentially similar to the one on the desktop or server, with some configuration differences.

Tools

The Windows Phone SDK ships with a tool that allows you to measure your application's performance along a number of metrics. The Windows Phone Application Analysis tool can run in a few different modes, depending on the type of information you need.

The most basic mode is called App Monitor and allows you to get simple feedback for user-facing issues like startup time, response time, battery usage, network usage, and high resource usage.

If you need detailed CPU or Memory profiling data, you can get that data as well.

PhoneApp1

Monitoring and profiling your application can help you diagnose performance problems and improve the quality of your application. To begin, choose one of the options below.

Monitoring (recommended)

● App Analysis (analyzes performance and quality aspects of application)

Profiling

○ Execution (evaluates application performance with advanced visual and code profiling)

▷ Advanced Settings

○ Memory (evaluates memory allocation and texture usage)

▷ Advanced Settings

Warning: The app performance observed on the emulator may not be indicative of the actual performance on the device

Start Session (App will start)

Figure 9-1. The Application Analysis tool lets you measure either general quality characteristics of your application or do a more in-depth profile of either CPU or memory.

Garbage Collection and Memory

The garbage collector is essentially the same, but the segment sizes will be smaller, reflecting the smaller memory size in general. Background GC is not supported. (Neither is server GC, but that should go without saying).

Applications are explicitly limited in the amount of memory they can use. .NET applications are limited to a maximum of 300 MB on a typical device. Background tasks are further limited to only about 20 MB of memory usage (or 11 MB for low-memory devices). Applications that exceed these limits may be immediately terminated by the operating system. These limits can vary depending on the type of application and hardware, and may change over time with future updates. See http://www.writinghighperf.net/go/31 for an up-to-date explanation.

Minimizing the static resources your program uses will go a long way to reducing the overall memory usage. Keep in mind that you can usually get away with relatively low resolution versions of most resources, such as images, sounds, documents, or other content. Use the lowest resolution you can get away with, keeping in mind that phone capabilities such as screen resolution do tend to improve over time.

The main principle to keep in mind is that you must be much more conscious of your memory usage on a mobile device. The desktop with its multiple gigabytes of RAM plus a huge page file is far more forgiving than a mobile device will be.

JIT

On a mobile device, startup speed is particularly critical. An application that is not ready to run within a short amount of time can fail quickly in the crowded app marketplace.

Before Windows Phone 8, applications were JITted on the fly the first time the program ran, just like the desktop version of the CLR. This was slow and used an excessive amount of the battery. Thankfully, Windows Phone 8 introduced cloud compilation. With this, all applications are now pre-compiled in the Windows Phone Store before being sent to the device.

This pre-compilation is not the same as NGEN. NGEN is device-specific and depends on the exact hardware and framework versions present. It would be impractical to generate every possible combination of these native image files in the Store. They could have decided that NGEN would run on the device, but this would have meant that every time there was an OS or .NET update, every single application would have to be re-NGENed, which would drastically increase the update time and could easily wipe out the battery.

Instead, cloud compilation introduces another image format, called Machine Dependent Intermediate Language, or MDIL. This language is very similar to the final assembly code that will actually execute on the mobile processor, but instead of address offsets for things like fields, there are tokens representing which field the instruction is referring to.

Once this almost-complete image is on the device, the only thing that needs to be done is replace the tokens with the actual addresses, a process called binding. You can think of this as an analogous process to linking in the world of native code compilation.

Compare the following diagram to the normal JIT flow diagram from Chapter 3:

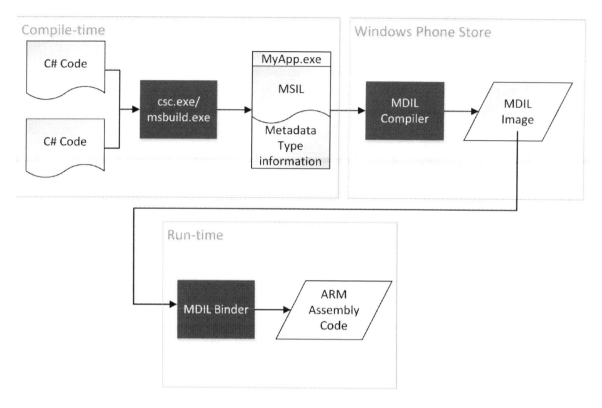

Figure 9-2. Windows Phone Application deployment process. An application passes through multiple stages of compilation before it actually executes on your device.

The benefits of this strategy are significant:

- Minimal time spent JITting
- No need to run NGEN on the phone
- No re-download of native images every time there is an OS update
- Lower battery usage
- Faster updating

Asynchronous Programming and Memory Models

You can use all of the asynchronous APIs mentioned in Chapter 4 on Windows Phone devices, but there are a few significant differences between a desktop and a mobile device that may affect your application.

I still recommend the Task APIs for general purpose asynchronous programming, but Windows Phone also has the BackgroundWorker class, which wraps thread pool worker items and adds UI-related features. It is suitable for background tasks that need to regularly notify the UI of updates to its state.

The number of processors available to you will typically be less than on a desktop or server platform. At the time of this writing, most mid- and high-end mobile devices have two to four processors.

Perhaps the most important difference is that many mobile devices, such as Windows Phone or the Surface RT devices, use ARM processors, which have a different memory model than the x86 or x64 processors that you are used to.

As described in Chapter 4, this affects you mostly if you have a bug in your thread synchronization. If you share code between the desktop version of your software and the mobile app it is possible to never see the problem on the desktop, but as soon as you port it to a device that runs on ARM, the pre-existing race conditions in your code could become apparent in the form of data corruption or random crashes. Ensure that you are correctly using volatile, Interlocked methods, and thread synchronization objects, as described in Chapter 4, and you should avoid any problems.

Other Considerations

Always keep in mind that more CPU usage translates directly into lower battery life. Use the tools mentioned in this chapter to monitor and fix any areas of high CPU usage.

Use system resources as quickly and sparingly as possible. For example, Windows Phone OS will often turn off the radio transmitter, so when you need to make network requests, batch them and send them in parallel to allow the transmitter to turn off sooner, saving battery life.

Finally, as with all UI applications, you want to avoid blocking the UI thread for any reason. Always perform long-running operations on a separate Task explicitly or by using the BackgroundWorker class. You will also need to understand the performance characteristics of XAML, which is out of scope for this book (see the bibliography at the end of the book for more resources).

Summary

Most general .NET programming advice applies to Windows Phone programming as well, but you do have to be conscious of the smaller hardware capabilities and different architecture running the code. Many types of thread synchronization bugs are far more likely to manifest on ARM hardware.

Developing mobile software forces many more constraints upon you as a developer that are not present on the desktop. Following the best practices in this book will get you quite far in dealing with these. To see what all of the certification requirements are for Windows Phone applications, see http://www.writinghighperf.net/go/37/.

10 Code Safety

There is a well-worn adage in software engineering that you should first make your code correct, then make it fast. Most of this book has focused strictly on performance, but this chapter is a little bit of an aside into some important topics that, while not strictly related to performance, may help you in your pursuit of high-performance, scalable applications. By undertaking some good practices to ensure the stability and reliability of your code, you free yourself to make more drastic changes for performance's sake. When problems do occur, you will more easily narrow down the location of the issue.

Understand the Underlying OS, APIs, and Hardware

Heavy performance optimization is going to defy any abstractions you want to impose on your software. As mentioned numerous times in this book, you must understand the APIs you call in order to make intelligent decisions about how to use them, or whether to use them at all.

That is not enough, however. Take threading, for example. While various versions of the .NET Framework have added abstraction on top of threads that make asynchronous programming easier, taking advantage of this fully will require you to understand how these features interact with the underlying OS threads and its scheduling algorithm. The same is true for debugging memory problems. The GC heap is remarkably simple to inspect, but if you have a huge process that loads thousands of types from hundreds of assemblies, you may run into problems outside of the pure managed world, which will require you to understand a process's full memory layout.

Finally, the hardware is just as important. In the chapter on JIT, I mentioned things like locality of reference—putting bits of code and data that are used together physically near each other in memory so that they can be efficiently included in a processor's cache. If you are lucky, your code will target a single hardware platform. If not, then you need to understand how it executes code differently. You may have different memory limits or different caches sizes, or even more substantial differences such as completely different memory models.

Restrict API Usage in Certain Areas of Your Code

There is no reason why you should allow all components to use the full breadth of every Framework and system API. For example, if you have a strict Task-based processing model, then centralize that functionality and prohibit any other components from accessing anything in the System.Threading namespace.

These kinds of rules are particularly important for systems with an extension model. You usually want the platform executing all the hard, dangerous code, while the extensions do simple actions in their respective domain.

An excellent tool for enforcing these rules is FxCop, which is a free static code analysis tool that ships with Visual Studio. It comes with standard rules in categories such as Performance, Globalization, Security, and more, but you can add a library of your own rules. Many of the performance rules we discuss in this book can be represented as FxCop rules, for example:

- Prohibiting use of "dangerous" namespaces
- Banning use of Regex, especially if used improperly
- Banning types or APIs that typically cause LOH allocations
- Banning APIs that have better alternatives such as TryParse in lieu of Parse
- Finding instances of double-casting
- Finding instances of boxing

Before you start writing rules, keep in mind that FxCop can only analyze IL and metadata. It has no knowledge of C# or any other high-level language. Because of this, you will not be able to enforce static checks that rely on specific language patterns. Writing your own FxCop rules is easy, but there is little to no official documentation, and you will find yourself relying on analyzing the IL of your programs and making extensive use of IntelliSense to poke through the FxCop API. The more you understand IL, the more complicated rules you can develop.

You will first need to install the FxCop SDK, which is trickier than it should be. If you have Visual Studio Professional or better, then it has been included and rebranded Code Analysis in the IDE, but it is still FxCop underneath. On my machine, the relevant files are located in C:\Program Files (x86)\Microsoft Visual Studio 11.0\Team Tools\Static Analysis Tools\FxCop.

If you cannot get access to the right version of Visual Studio, there are still a few options. The easiest way is from CodePlex at http://www.writinghighperf.net/go/32. If that project has disappeared by the time you read this, then try the Windows 7.1 SDK, which appears to have a broken web installer now, but you can get the ISO image at http://www.writinghighperf.net/go/33 and extract the installer from \Setup\WinSDKNetFxTools\cab1.cab. There is a file inside that archive that begins with the name WinSDK_FxCopSetup.exe. Extract that file and rename it to FxCopSetup.exe and you are on your way.

In the source code accompanying this book you will find projects related to FxCop. These are in their own solution file to avoid breaking the build for rest of the sample projects. FxCopRules contains the rules that will be loaded by the FxCop engine and run against some target assembly. FxCopViolator contains a class with a number of violations that the rules will test against. Follow along with these projects as I explain the various components.

Before you can build the rules, you may need to edit to the FxCopRules.csproj file to point to the correct SDK path. The current values are:

```xml
<PropertyGroup>
  <FxCopSdkDir>C:\Program Files (x86)\Microsoft Fxcop 10.0</FxCopSdkDir>
</PropertyGroup>
<ItemGroup>
  <Reference Include="$(FxCopSdkDir)\FxCopSdk.dll" />
  <Reference Include="$(FxCopSdkDir)\Microsoft.CCi.dll" />
</ItemGroup>
```

Update the FxCopSdkDir value to point to the FxCop installation directory, or wherever you have placed the appropriate DLLs.

Next, you will need to create a Rules.xml file that contains the metadata for each rule. Our first rule will look like this:

```xml
<?xml version="1.0" encoding="utf-8" ?>
<Rules FriendlyName="Custom Rules">
  <Rule TypeName="DisallowStaticFieldsRule"
    Category="Custom.Arbitrary"
    CheckId="HP100">
  <Name>Static fields are not allowed</Name>
  <Description>Static fields are not allowed because they lead to problems
with thread safety.</Description>
  <Url>http://internaldocumentationsite/FxCop/HP100</Url>
  <Resolution>Make the static field '{0}' either readonly or
const.</Resolution>
  <MessageLevel Certainty="90">Error</MessageLevel>
  <FixCategories>Breaking</FixCategories>
  <Email>feedback@high-perf.net</Email>
```

```
    <Owner>Ben Watson</Owner>
    </Rule>
</Rules>
```

Note that the TypeName attribute must match the name of the rule class that we define next. This XML file must be included in the project with the Build Action set to Embedded Resource.

Each rule we define must derive from a class provided by the FxCop SDK and include some common information, such as the location of the XML rules manifest. To make this more convenient, it is a good idea to create a base class for all of your rules that provides this common functionality.

```csharp
using Microsoft.FxCop.Sdk;
using System.Reflection;

namespace FxCopRules
{
  public abstract class BaseCustomRule : BaseIntrospectionRule
  {
    // The manifest name is the default namespace plus the name
    // of the XML rules file, without the extension.
    private const string ManifestName = "FxCopRules.Rules";

    // The assembly where the rule manifest is
    // embedded (the current assembly in our case).
    private static readonly Assembly ResourceAssembly =
                    typeof(BaseCustomRule).Assembly;

    protected BaseCustomRule(string ruleName)
      :base(ruleName, ManifestName, ResourceAssembly)
    {
    }
  }
}
```

Next, define a class that derives from BaseCustomRule that will be for a specific violation you want to check. The first example will disallow all static fields, but allow const and readonly fields.

```csharp
public class DisallowStaticFieldsRule : BaseCustomRule
{
  public DisallowStaticFieldsRule()
    : base(typeof(DisallowStaticFieldsRule).Name)
  {
  }
```

```
  public override ProblemCollection Check(Member member)
  {
    var field = member as Field;
    if (field != null)
    {
      // Find all static data that isn't const or readonly
      if (field.IsStatic && !field.IsInitOnly && !field.IsLiteral)
      {
        // field.FullName is an optional argument that will be used
        // to format the Resolution string's {0} parameter.
        var resolution = this.GetResolution(field.FullName);
        var problem = new Problem(resolution, field.SourceContext);
        this.Problems.Add(problem);
      }
    }
    return this.Problems;
  }
}
```

The BaseCustomRule class provides a number of virtual Check method overrides with various types of arguments which you can override to provide your functionality (by default, these methods do nothing). IntelliSense is your friend while writing FxCop rules, and it reveals the following Check methods:

- Check(ModuleNode moduleNode)
- Check(Parameter parameter)
- Check(Resource resource)
- Check(TypeNode typeNode)
- Check(string namespaceName, TypeNodeCollection types)

You can also examine individual lines of IL code from any method. Here's a rule that prohibits string case conversion.

```
public class DisallowStringCaseConversionRule : BaseCustomRule
{
  public DisallowStringCaseConversionRule()
    : base(typeof(DisallowStringCaseConversionRule).Name)
  { }

  public override ProblemCollection Check(Member member)
  {
    var method = member as Method;
    if (method != null)
    {
      foreach (var instruction in method.Instructions)
      {
```

```
            if (instruction.OpCode == OpCode.Call
              || instruction.OpCode == OpCode.Calli
              || instruction.OpCode == OpCode.Callvirt)
            {
                var targetMethod = instruction.Value as Method;
                if (targetMethod.FullName == "System.String.ToUpper"
                  || targetMethod.FullName == "System.String.ToLower")
                {
                    var resolution = this.GetResolution(method.FullName);
                    var problem = new Problem(resolution,
                                    method.SourceContext);
                    this.Problems.Add(problem);
                }
            }
        }
    }

    return this.Problems;
}
}
```

For a final example, let's look at a different way to tell FxCop to traverse the code. In addition to the Check methods described previously, you can override dozens of Visit* methods. These are called in a recursive descent through every node in the program graph, starting at the node you pick. You override just the Visit methods you need. Here's an example that uses this to add a rule against instantiating a Thread object:

```
public class DisallowThreadCreationRule : BaseCustomRule
{
    public DisallowThreadCreationRule() :
base(typeof(DisallowThreadCreationRule).Name) { }

    public override ProblemCollection Check(Member member)
    {
        var method = member as Method;
        if (method != null)
        {
            VisitStatements(method.Body.Statements);
        }

        return base.Check(member);
    }

    public override void VisitConstruct(Construct construct)
    {
        if (construct != null)
```

```
    {
      var binding = construct.Constructor as MemberBinding;
      if (binding != null)
      {
        var instanceInitializer =
              binding.BoundMember as InstanceInitializer;
        if (instanceInitializer.DeclaringType.FullName
          == "System.Threading.Thread")
        {
          var problem = new Problem(this.GetResolution(),
                      construct.SourceContext);
          this.Problems.Add(problem);
        }
      }
    }

    base.VisitConstruct(construct);
  }
}
```

It is pretty straightforward once you learn how it works. The biggest obstacle to creating your own rules is really the lack of documentation. To learn more about custom FxCop rules, read an excellent walkthrough by Jason Kresowaty at http://www.writinghighperf.net/go/34.

Centralize and Abstract Performance-Sensitive and Difficult Code

You should keep particularly difficult or performance-sensitive code centralized for easy maintenance and to prevent the rest of the system from making performance mistakes. This is a stronger rule than the well-known DRY (Don't Repeat Yourself) principle; that is, do not have the same code in two locations—refactor it to have a single copy of the code, reusable in multiple locations.

You should also keep as much performance-sensitive in one place for easy maintenance, preferably behind APIs that the rest of your application uses. For example, if your application downloads files via HTTP, you could wrap this in an API that exposes only the parts of downloading that the rest of your program needs to know (e.g., the URL you are requesting and the downloaded content). The API manages the complexity of the HTTP call and your entire application goes through that API every time it needs to make an HTTP call. If you discover a performance problem with downloading, or need to enforce a download queue, or any other change, it is trivial to do behind the API. Remember that those APIs need to maintain the asynchronous nature of the operation.

Isolate Unmanaged or Unsafe Code

For many reasons, you should move away from unmanaged code if at all possible. As discussed in the introduction, the benefits of unmanaged code are often exaggerated, but the danger of memory corruption is all too real.

That said, if you have to keep any unmanaged code around (say, to talk to a legacy system, and it is too expensive to move the entire interface to the managed world), then isolate it well. There are many ways to do the isolation, but you absolutely want to avoid having random bits of your system call into unmanaged code all over the place. This is a recipe for chaos.

Ideally, split the unmanaged code into its own process to provide strict OS-level isolation. If that is not possible and you need the unmanaged code to be loaded into the same process, try to keep it in as few DLLs as possible and have all calls to it go through a centralized API that can enforce standard safeguards.

Treat managed code that is marked unsafe exactly like unmanaged code and isolate it to as small a scope as you can. You will also need to enable unsafe code in the project settings.

Prefer Code Clarity to Performance Until Proven Otherwise

Code readability and maintenance is more important than performance until proven otherwise. If you find you do need to make deep changes for performance reasons, do it in a way that is as transparent to the code above it as possible. Keep the level above it as clear as possible.

Once you do make the code worse to read in favor of performance, make sure you document in the code why you are doing it so that someone does not come by after you and "clean up" your elegant optimization by making it simpler.

Summary

To ensure your code is safe, you must understand the implementation details at all levels. Isolate your riskiest code, especially native or unsafe code, to specific modules to limit exposure. Ban problematic APIs and coding patterns and enforce reasonable code standards to encourage safe practices. Enforce these practices with FxCop or other static analysis build tools. Do not sacrifice code clarity or maintainability for performance unless it is particularly justified.

11 Building a Performance-Minded Team

Most interesting software products are not built by a single person. Chances are, you are part of a team trying to build some useful and well-performing software. If you are the performance guru on your team, then there are things you can do to encourage others to be so-minded as well.

Much of the advice in this chapter presupposes an organization that understands software engineering as a true engineering effort. Unfortunately, many people find themselves in less than ideal circumstances. If this is you, do not despair. Perhaps some of the advice in this chapter can help you improve the level of engineering appreciation and competence in your company.

Understand the Areas of Critical Performance

You cannot optimize everything, almost by definition. This goes back to the first principles we discussed in Chapter 1 about measurement and finding the areas of critical performance. As a team, you will need to build consensus on which areas are critical and which can be left alone.

As engineers, we all should have pride in our work and make it the best it can be, and in no area of code should we completely slack off. However, the realities of business dictate limited time and human resources in which to accomplish the necessary work. Given these realities, you should take time to understand where the critical areas of the system are (Remember **Measure, Measure, Measure**) and make sure those receive a larger portion of careful attention to detail.

Performance is not the only metric by which you need to judge code. Maintainability, scalability, security, and other important factors must also guide your decision-making. However, of the items in that list, I suspect that performance measurement and tuning will take more of your time on a continual basis.

Effective Testing

This is not a testing book, but it should go without saying that having effective tests at all levels will greatly increase your confidence in making significant changes to code. If you have unit tests with high code coverage, drastically changing a central algorithm or data structure to be much more efficient should not fill you with dread.

More to the point of this book, if performance is critical to you, then you should be tracking it with the tools and techniques mentioned in this book. Just like you have functional tests, you can have performance tests. They may be as simple as tracking how many operations a component can do in a second, to as complicated as the performance across thousands of metrics between your pre-release server farm and the production server farm.

Performance test failures should be treated as seriously as functional test failures and should be ship blockers. You will likely find that building reliable, repeatable performance tests is far more difficult than functional tests. So much of performance is intertwined with the state of machines, other software running on the machine, history of the running process, and infinitely more variables. There are two basic approaches to handling this noise that will creep in:

1. Remove noise—Have clean machines, restart them before testing, control all the processes running, control for hardware differences, and more. This approach is required if you are testing on single machines.
2. Run tests at a large scale—If it is not practical to eliminate all the noise then ignore it and run your tests on a scale that is sufficient to eliminate the significant sources of noise. This can be quite expensive, especially for larger infrastructures. You may need dozens, hundreds, even thousands of machines to get a truly statistically significant result. If you cannot scale out the hardware, you can scale out in time and rerun tests hundreds of times, but this does not account for as many variables.

Either way, you will need to engage in A/B testing, that is, comparing the performance of one build against another in as ideal a scenario as you can manage.

Performance Infrastructure and Automation

You will probably need to build some custom infrastructure, tools, and automation support to gather performance data for you, but all the tools to read the metrics are described in this book. Thankfully, nearly all useful performance tools are scriptable in some way.

There are many ways to track performance and you will have to decide the best way for your product. Some ideas include:

- PerfMon—If all of your data is represented by performance counters and runs on a single machine, this may be sufficient.
- Performance counter aggregation—If you run on multiple machines, you probably need to aggregate the counter information into a centralized database. This has the advantage of storing performance data for historical analysis.
- Benchmarks—Your application processes a standard set of data and the resulting performance metrics are compared with historical results. Benchmarks are useful, but you must be careful with their historical validity as scenarios change. Benchmarks need occasional tuning and this can lead to invalid comparison between results.
- Automated profiling—Perform random profiling of CPU and memory allocation on either test or real data.
- Alerts that fire on performance data—For example, send off an automated alert to a support team if CPU gets too high for too long, or the number of tasks queued is increasing.
- Automated analysis of ETW events—This can get you some very nitty-gritty detail that performance counters will miss.

The things you do now to build a performance infrastructure will pay huge dividends in the future as performance maintenance becomes mostly automated. Building this infrastructure is usually far more important than fixing any arbitrary actual performance problem because a good infrastructure will be able to find and surface performance problems much earlier than any manually driven process. A good infrastructure will prevent you from being surprised by bad performance at an inconvenient time.

The most important part of your infrastructure is how much human involvement is necessary. If you are like most software engineers, there is far more work than time to do it in. Relying on manual performance analysis means it will often not get done. Thus, automation is the key to an effective performance strategy. An investment upfront will save countless hours day after day. A good time-saving device can be as simple as a script that runs the tools and generates the report for you on demand, but it will likely need to scale with the size of your application. A large server application that runs in a data center will need different kinds of performance analysis than a desktop application, and a more robust performance infrastructure.

Think of what the ideal infrastructure is for your setting and start building it. Treat it as a first-class project in every way, with milestones, adequate resourcing, and design and code reviews. Iterate it in a way that makes the infrastructure usable in some way very early on and gradually add automation features over time.

Believe Only Numbers

In many teams where performance is an afterthought, performance improvements are often pursued only when problems occur that are serious enough to affect the end-user. This means there is an ad-hoc process that basically boils down to:

User: Your application is too slow!

Dev: Why?

User: I don't know! Just fix it!

Dev: <Does something to make it faster, maybe?>

You do not ever want to have this conversation. Always have the numbers available measuring whatever it is you are judged by. Have data to back up literally everything you do. People have infinitely more credibility when backed up by numbers and charts. Of course, you will want to make sure those numbers are correct before you publically rely on them!

Another aspect of numbers is ensuring that your team has official, realistic, and tangible goals. In the example above, the only "metric" was "faster." This is an unofficial, fuzzy, and mostly worthless goal to have. Make sure you have real, official performance goals and get your leadership chain to sign off on them. Have deliverables for specific metrics. Make it known that having unofficial pressure for better performance after the fact is unacceptable.

For more information about setting good performance goals, see Chapter 1.

Effective Code Reviews

No developer is perfect and having multiple sets of eyes can dramatically improve the quality of anyone's code. All code should probably go through some code review process, whether it is via a system of reviewing diffs via email, or a formal sit down with the whole team.

Recognize that not all code is equally critical to your business. While it might be tempting to say that all code should adhere to the highest standards, that might be a high bar to reach at first. You may want to consider a special category of code reviews for software that has an especially high business impact, where a mistake in functionality or performance can cost real money (or someone's job!). For example, you could require two developers to sign off before code submission, requiring one to be a senior developer or a subject matter expert. For large, complicated code reviews, put everyone into a room with their own laptops and someone projecting and have at it. The exact process depends on your organization, resources, and culture, but develop a process and go with it, modifying as necessary.

It may be helpful to have code reviews that focus on just particular aspects of the code, such as functional correctness, security, or performance. You may ask specific people to comment only on their areas of expertise.

Effective code reviewing does not equate to nitpicking. Stylistic differences should often be ignored. Sometimes even larger issues should be glossed over if it does not truly matter and there are more important things to focus on. Just because code is different than how you would write it, does not mean it is necessarily worse. Nothing is more frustrating than going into a code review expecting to dissect some tricky multi-threaded code and instead spending all the time arguing about correct comment syntax or other trivialities. Do not tolerate such wastes of time. Set the expectations for how code reviews should run and enforce it. If there are legitimate standards violations, do not ignore them, but focus on the important things first.

On the other hand, don't accept lame excuses like, "Well, I know that line is inefficient, but does that really matter in the grand scheme of things?" The proper response to this is, "Are you asking how bad you're allowed to make your code?" You do need to balance overlooking minor issues with the need to create a culture of performance so that next time, the developer does the right thing automatically.

Finally, do not buy into the notion of total code "ownership." Everyone should feel ownership for the entire product. There are no independent, competing kingdoms, and no one should be over-protective of "their" code, regardless of original authorship. Having owners for the purposes of gatekeeping and code reviews is great, but everyone should feel empowered to make improvements to any area of code. Check your ego at the door.

Education

A performance mindset requires training. This can be informal, from a team guru or books such as this one, or formal, with paid classes from a well-known lecturer in the area.

Keep in mind that even those who already know .NET programming will need to change their programming habits once they start acquiring a serious performance mentality.

Likewise, people who are well-versed in C or C++ will need to understand that the rules for achieving good performance are often completely different or backwards from what they thought in the native code world.

Change can be hard and most people resist it, so it is best to be sensitive when trying to enforce new practices. It is also always important to build leadership support for what you are trying to accomplish.

If you want to kick-start some performance discussions with your peers, here are some ideas:

1. Host brown bag lunch meetings to share what you are learning.
2. Start an internal or public blog to share your knowledge or discuss performance issues you have discovered in the products.
3. Pick a team member to be your regular performance-related reviewer.
4. Demonstrate benefits of improving performance with simple benchmarks or proof-of-concept programs.
5. Designate someone as a performance specialist who will stay on top of the performance, do code reviews, educate others about good practices, and stay on top of industry changes and the state of the art. If you are reading this, you have already volunteered for this.
6. Bring up areas of potential improvement. Tip: It's best to start with your own code first!
7. Get your organization to buy copies of this book for everyone. (Shameless plug!)

Summary

Start small when creating a performance mindset in your team. Begin with your own code and take time to understand which areas actually matter for performance. Build an attitude that performance regressions are just as serious as functional failures. Automate as much as possible to reduce the burden on the team. Judge performance metrics on hard numbers, not gut feeling or subjective perception.

Build an effective code review culture that encourages a good coding style, a focus on things that really matter, and collective code ownership.

Recognize that change is hard and you need to be sensitive. Even those familiar with .NET will likely need to change their ways. C++ and Java veterans will not necessarily be great .NET programmers right away.

Find ways to kick-start regular performance conversations and find or create experts to disseminate this information.

Appendix A—Kick-Start Your Application's Performance

This book goes through hundreds of details that may be a problem in your application, but if you are just getting started, here is a general outline of how you can proceed and analyze your own program's performance.

Define Metrics

Before starting, you need to define the types of metrics that you analyze. Is it just pure CPU usage? Memory? Speed of operations? Define these in as much detail as possible. Come up with a set of detailed goals for each metric.

Analyze CPU Usage

- Use PerfView or VS Standalone Profiler to get a CPU profile of your application doing work.
- Analyze the stacks for functions that stand out.
- Is data processing taking a long time?
  - Can you change your data structure to be in a format that requires less processing? For example, instead of parsing XML, use a simple binary serialization format.
  - Are there alternate APIs?
  - Can you parallelize the work with `Tasks` or `Parallel.For`?

Analyze Memory Usage

- Consider the right type of GC:

- Server: Your program is the only significant application on the machine and needs the lowest possible latency for GCs.
- Workstation: You have a UI or share the machine with other important process.
- Profile memory with PerfView:
  - Check results for top allocators—are they expected and acceptable?
  - Pay close attention to the Large Object allocations.
- If gen 2 GCs happen too often:
  - Are there a lot of LOH allocations? Remove or pool these objects.
  - Is object promotion high? Reduce object lifetime so that lower generation GCs can collect them. Allocate objects only when needed and null them out when no longer needed.
  - If objects are living too long, pool them.
- If gen 2 GCs take too long:
  - Consider using GC notifications to get a signal when GC is about to start. Use this opportunity to stop processing.
- If you have high number of gen 0/1 GCs:
  - Look at highest area of allocations in the profile. Find ways to reduce the need for memory allocations.
  - Minimize object lifetime.
- If gen 0/1 GCs have a high pause time:
  - Reduce allocations overall.
  - Minimize object lifetime.
  - Are objects being pinned? Remove these if possible, or reduce the scope of the pinning.
  - Reduce object complexity by removing references between objects.
- If the LOH is growing large:
  - Check for fragmentation with Windbg or CLR Profiler.
  - Compact the LOH heap periodically.
  - Check for object pools with unbounded growth.

Analyze JIT

- If your startup time is long:
  - Is it because of JIT? Loading data is a more common cause of long startup times.
  - Use PerfView to analyze which methods take a long time to JIT.
  - Use Profile Optimization to speed up JIT on application load.
  - Consider using NGEN.

- Are there methods showing up in the profile that you would expect to be inlined?
  - Look at methods for inlining blockers such as loops, exception handling, recursion or more.

Analyze Asynchronous Performance

- Use PerfView to determine if there are a high number of contentions.
  - Remove contentions by restructuring the code to need fewer locks.
  - Use Interlocked methods or hybrid locks where necessary.
- Capture Thread Time events with PerfView to see where time is being spent. Analyze these areas of the code to ensure that threads are not blocking on I/O.
  - You may have to significantly change your program to be more asynchronous at every level to avoid waiting on Tasks or I/O.
  - Ensure you are using asynchronous stream APIs.
- Does your program take a while before it starts using the thread pool efficiently? This can manifest itself as initial slowness that goes away within a few minutes.
  - Make sure the minimum thread pool size is adequate for your workload.

Appendix B—Big O Notation

Big O notation, also known as asymptotic notation, is a way of summarizing the performance of algorithms based on problem size. The problem size is usually designated n. The "Big O"-ness of an algorithm is often referred to as its complexity. The term asymptotic is used as it describes the behavior of a function as its input size approaches infinity.

As an example, consider an unsorted array that contains a value we need to search for. Because it is unsorted, we will have to search every element until we find the value we are looking for. If the array is of size n, we will need to search, worst case, n elements. We say, therefore, that this linear search algorithm has a complexity of O(n).

That is the worst case. On average, however, the algorithm will need to look at n / 2 elements, so we could be more accurate and say the algorithm is, on average, O(n / 2), but this is not actually a significant change as far as the growth factor (n) is concerned, so constants are dropped, leaving us with the same O(n) complexity.

Big O notation is expressed in terms of functions of n, where n is the problem size, which is determined by the algorithm and the data structure it operates on. For a collection, it could be the number of items in the collection; for a string search algorithm, it is the length of the respective strings.

Big O notation is concerned with how the time required to perform an algorithm grows with ever larger input sizes. With our array example, we expect that if the array were to double in length, then the time required to search the array would also double. This implies that the algorithm has linear performance characteristics.

An algorithm with complexity of $O(n^2)$ would exhibit worse than linear performance. If the input doubles, the time is quadrupled. If problem size increases by a factor of 8, then the time increases by a factor of 64, always squared. This type of algorithm exhibits quadratic complexity. A good example of this is the bubble sort algorithm (in fact, most naïve sorting algorithms have $O(n^2)$ complexity).

```
private static void BubbleSort(int[] array)
{
  bool swapped;
  do
  {
    swapped = false;
    for (int i = 1; i < array.Length; i++)
    {
      if (array[i - 1] > array[i])
      {
        int temp = array[i - 1];
        array[i - 1] = array[i];
        array[i] = temp;
        swapped = true;
      }
    }
  } while (swapped);
}
```

Any time you see nested loops, it is quite likely the algorithm is going to be quadratic or polynomial (if not worse). In bubble sort's case, the outer loop can run up to n times while the inner loop examines up to n elements on each iteration. $O(n * n) == O(n^2)$.

When analyzing your own algorithms, you may come up with a formula that contains multiple factors, as in $O(8n^2 + n + C)$ (a quadratic portion multiplied by 8, a linear portion, and a constant time portion). For the purposes of Big O notation, only the most significant factor is kept and multiplicative constants are ignored. This algorithm would be regarded as $O(n^2)$. Remember, too, that Big O notation is concerned with the growth of the time as the problem size approaches infinity. Even though $8n^2$ is 8 times larger than n^2, it is not very relevant compared to the growth of the n^2 factor, which far outstrips every other factor for large values of n. If n is small, the difference between $O(n \log n)$, $O(n^2)$, or $O(2^n)$ is trivial and uninteresting.

Many algorithms have multiple inputs and their complexity can be denoted with both variables, e.g., $O(mn)$ or $O(m+n)$. Many graph algorithms, for example, depend on the number of edges and the number of vertices.

The most common types of complexity are:

- **O(1)—Constant**—The time required does not depend on size of the input. Many hash tables have O(1) complexity.
- **O(log n)—Logarithmic**—Time increases as a fraction of the input size. Any algorithm that cuts its problems space in half on each iteration exhibits logarithmic complexity. Note that there is no specific number base for this log.

- **O(n)—Linear**—Time increases linearly with input size.
- **O(n log n)—Loglinear**—Time increases quasilinearly, that is, the time is dominated by a linear factor, but this is multiplied by a fraction of the input size.
- **O(n²)—Quadratic**—Time increases with the square of the input size.
- **O(nᶜ) —Polynomial**—C is greater than 2.
- **O(cⁿ) —Exponential**—C is greater than 1.
- **O(n!)—Factorial**—Basically, try every possibility.

Algorithmic complexity is usually described in terms of its average and worst-case performance. Best-case performance is not very interesting because, for many algorithms, luck can be involved (e.g., it does not really matter for our analysis that the best-case performance of linear search is O(1) because that means it just happened to get lucky).

The following graph shows how fast time can grow based on problem size. Note that the difference between O(1) and O(log n) is almost indistinguishable even out to relatively large problem sizes. An algorithm with O(n!) complexity is almost unusable with anything but the smallest problem sizes.

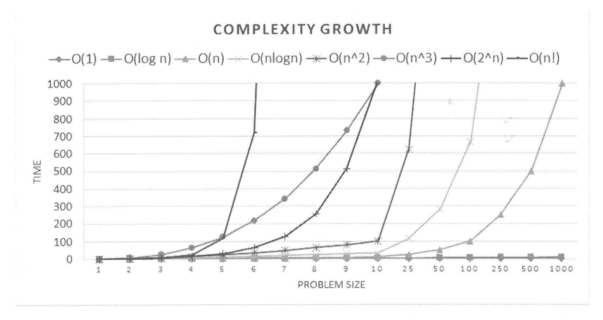

Though time is the most common dimension of complexity, space (memory usage) can also be analyzed with the same methodology.

Common Algorithms and Their Complexity

Sorting

- Quicksort—O(n log n), $O(n^2)$ worst case
- Merge sort—O(n log n)
- Heap sort—O(n log n)
- Bubble sort—$O(n^2)$
- Insertion sort—$O(n^2)$
- Selection sort—$O(n^2)$

Graphs

- Depth-first search—O(E + V) (E = Edges, V = Vertices)
- Breadth-first search—O(E + V)
- Shortest-path (using Min-heap)—O((E + V) log V)

Searching

- Unsorted array—O(n)
- Sorted array with binary search—O(log n)
- Binary search tree—O(log n)
- Hash table—O(1)

Special case

- Traveling salesman—O(n!)

Often, O(n!) is really just shorthand for "brute force, try every possibility."

Appendix C—Bibliography

Useful Books

- Hewardt, Mario and Patrick Dussud. *Advanced .NET Debugging*. Addison-Wesley Professional, November 2009.
- Richter, Jeffrey. *CLR via C#, 4th ed.* Microsoft Press, November 2012.
- Russinovich, Mark and David Solomon, Alex Ionescu. *Windows Internals, 6th ed.* Microsoft Press, March 2012.
- Rasmussen, Brian. *High-Performance Windows Store Apps*. Microsoft Press, May 2014.
- ECMA C# and CLI Standards: http://www.writinghighperf.net/go/17, Microsoft, retrieved 7 May 2014.

People and Blogs

In addition to the books mentioned above, there are a number of useful people to follow, whether they write on their own blog or articles for various publications.

- Maoni Stephens—CLR developer and GC expert. Her blog at http://blogs.msdn.com/b/maoni/ is not being updated at the moment, but there is a lot of useful information there.
- Vance Morrison—.NET Performance Architect. Blogs at http://blogs.msdn.com/b/vancem/.
- MSDN Magazine—http://msdn.microsoft.com/magazine. There are lot of great articles going into depth about CLR internals.
- .NET Framework Blog—Announcements and in-depth articles. http://blogs.msdn.com/b/dotnet/

Contact Information

Ben Watson

Email: feedback@writinghighperf.net

Website: http://www.writinghighperf.net

Blog: http://www.philosophicalgeek.com

LinkedIn: https://www.linkedin.com/in/benmwatson

Twitter: https://twitter.com/benmwatson

If you find any errors, technical, grammatical, or typographical, please let me know via email and I will correct them for future versions and credit you in the acknowledgments.

If you wish to purchase this book for your organization, please contact me for license information.

If you enjoyed this book, please leave a review at your favorite online retailer. Thank you!

Index

I

J

H

K

P

Q

R